MW01063507

ALSO BY FRED JEROME

The Einstein File

Einstein on Race and Racism
(with coauthor Rodger Taylor)

EINSTEIN ON ISRAEL AND ZIONISM

★

HIS PROVOCATIVE IDEAS ABOUT THE MIDDLE EAST

FRED JEROME

St. Martin's Press
New York

EINSTEIN ON ISRAEL AND ZIONISM. Copyright © 2009 by Fred Jerome. All rights reserved. Printed in the United States of America. For information, address St. Martin's Press, 175 Fifth Avenue, New York, N.Y. 10010.

www.stmartins.com

Library of Congress Cataloging-in-Publication Data

Jerome, Fred.
    Einstein on Israel and Zionism : his provocative ideas about the Middle East / Fred Jerome.—1st ed.
        p. cm.
    ISBN-13: 978-0-312-36228-7
    ISBN-10: 0-312-36228-5
    Includes bibliographical references and index.
    1. Einstein, Albert, 1879–1955—Political and social views.   2. Einstein, Albert, 1879–1955—Sources.   3. Zionism—Israel.   4. Jewish-Arab relations.   I. Title.

QC16.E5 J465 2009
320.54095694—dc22   2009007175

First Edition: June 2009

10   9   8   7   6   5   4   3   2   1

*Dedicated to
the memory of Rachel Corrie*

CONTENTS

TRANSLATOR'S NOTE

As it happens, as I write it is to the day two years since Fred Jerome first contacted me to ask me whether I wanted to participate in his new book project concerning Einstein on Israel and Palestine by translating several Einstein texts from the German original into English. Since Albert Einstein, next to the British philosopher-scientist Bertrand Russell, had been one of the heroes of my youth, I didn't hesitate to accept the offer.

In the following nine months, I translated a couple dozen texts by Einstein for Fred. In doing so, I once more had the feeling of privilege that struck me when I first read Einstein some thirty-five years ago, the privilege of encountering the clarity, evenhandedness, rigor, and humanity of a truly great mind. At the time, that feeling mostly related to Einstein's writings in the realm of popular science and general pacifism, whereas the writings I translated for the present book concern a specific issue in contemporary politics. Even so, and this was amazing, for me the spirit of Einstein's statements, writings, and utterances remained the same across a time gap of several decades and a shift from the scientific-philosophical to the political.

Much more important than these personal memories, however, is the fact that as I write, the Palestinian people are probably at the absolute nadir of their history and are once more being forced to undergo an unprecedented Calvary, with more than two hundred Palestinians killed today, allegedly in response to Palestinian rocket attacks on Israel where no one was killed and no one was injured but which, according to the TV stations in my home country, Germany, forced the Israeli population of the border region to live "in a state of permanent fear." On December 27, 2008, this is the state of affairs in Israel/Palestine: No physical victims on the side of the Israelis, but since they are afraid, their leaders are entitled to inflict on "the enemy" whatever carnage they deem appropriate. It is the classical colonial relation.

In the course of the last few years, each time observers were tempted to think the Palestinians' fortunes couldn't possibly sink any lower, they were proved wrong in the next couple of weeks or months. Since the breakdown of the 1993 Oslo Peace Accords in September 2000, nearly four thousand Palestinians were killed by Israeli bullets, mortars, and bombs; countless others have perished due to the permanent state of siege Israel has subjected the West Bank to since its reoccupation of the area in 2002 and to the complete encirclement of the Gaza Strip made nominally independent in 2005, which Israel has now turned into the largest ghetto in human history. In the Gaza Strip, blocked by Israel from receiving the most basic human necessities, children daily die from malnutrition. Sick patients and pregnant women daily die or suffer irremediable damage for lack of treatment. The elderly collapse on a daily basis since the conditions of life have become too hard for them to stand. Israel is responsible for all this, but is not being taken to task for it.

Worst of all, this is not taking place in one of the remoter areas of this world such as the Congo, where the horrors are so bad that, understandably, few journalists dare to tread there. On the contrary, it happens while the whole world is watching, and is doing nothing. It's an abominable spectacle that degrades us all.

What would a clear, evenhanded, rigorous, and humane mind like Einstein's have thought about all this? Einstein, a very conscious Jew who felt the connection to his people by a thousand threads, was very much in favor of the dream of a Jewish homeland, but his dream differed greatly from Theodor Herzl's dream of a state *exclusively* for the Jews. Thanks to Fred Jerome's rigorous examination of Einstein's writings and statements on Israel and Palestine, we need not speculate what Einstein *would* have said. This volume clearly demonstrates that Einstein, right from the beginning, championed what was in accord with elementary morality: The creation of a "Jewish home" in Palestine would turn into a crime if it resulted in the dispossession of the native Arab population; classical colonialism as practiced earlier by the European nations would turn the Arabs of Palestine into permanent enemies of the colonialist Jewish invaders; an irreconcilable conflict, however, was still avoidable on the basis of setting up a country in which both Jews and Arabs were accorded the same civil and national rights. And sometimes, Einstein even went further in saying that a socialist (or

social-democratic) solution of the conflict between the Jewish immigrants and the bulk of the Palestinian-Arab people
could be achieved on the basis of getting rid of the masters—
and their respective imperial designs—on both sides on the
basis of equality.

When the UN decided to release Palestine from the British
Mandate into "independence," and to privilege the minority
(one-third) Jewish population with 56 percent of the best territory, while the original two-thirds majority of Arab inhabitants of Palestine were assigned only 44 percent, all this came
to naught, for the time being at least, and with grave consequences.

Einstein, who was not a political expert and had never
claimed to be one, all the same sticks out from all the self-
proclaimed or otherwise hyped political commentators in
having referred to all these points right from the start. Here
is the voice of a man who was not ready to be pressured into
conformity by his own community or anyone else, even after
this community had suffered the abyss of its own holocaust
at the hands of the Nazis.

The sense of elementary justice that pervades everything
that Einstein said on this conflict is what makes this book
special. Interested—or naïve and deluded—parties will often
tell you that the Israel/Palestine conflict is insoluble and in-
tractable. It is not, if justice and equal rights for both sides,
as always propagated by Einstein, are to be the principles.
Understood in this way, the present book makes a major
contribution to solving and healing one of the most toxic
conflicts of our time. But let there be no illusions: As in
Einstein's own day, the just principles advocated by particularly clear-sighted persons like him will never prevail until

the "small," ordinary people Einstein throughout his life felt so much sympathy with and whom he thought should be in the center of the historical process will also raise their voices.

The time, as ever, to do this is now.

—Michael Schiffmann
Heidelberg (December 27, 2008)

As might be expected, there is in Professor Einstein's nationalism no room for any kind of aggressiveness or chauvinism. For him the domination of Jew over Arab in Palestine, or the perpetuation of a state of mutual hostility between the two peoples, would mean the failure of Zionism.

—Leon Simon, *Einstein on Zionism*

EINSTEIN ON ISRAEL
AND ZIONISM

PROLOGUE

"Though everybody knows me, there are very few people who really know me," Einstein said toward the end of his life. In a conversation with a close friend, the scientist reportedly added, "I am a revolutionary."[1] In disentangling himself from his look-alike media myth, Einstein—the real Einstein—spoke and wrote frequently and eloquently to explain and advocate for his views on what he considered the critical issues in society as well as in science.[2] His work includes hundreds of pages of statements (letters, articles, essays, and interviews, both published and unpublished) on Zionism and Israel.

Those who have heard or read anything at all about Einstein's politics probably know that Einstein was asked to become president of Israel in 1952 after the death of Chaim Weizmann, the country's first president. Israel's offer was widely publicized then—and since. But very few people know that when Einstein turned down the presidency, he said, "I would have to say to the Israeli people things they would not like to hear."[3] Nor do they know the statement by Israeli prime minister Ben-Gurion: "Tell me what to do if he says yes! I've had to offer him the post because it was impossible not to, but if he accepts we are in for trouble."[4]

For most people, Einstein is the kindly, twinkle-eyed, absentminded genius lost in a faraway universe of complex equations, a jigsaw puzzle of squiggles on the blackboard. In the press coverage of Einstein, the who, what, where, when, and (especially) why of history have not made it out of journalism school. "The Unknown Einstein," proclaimed the cover of a recent "special issue" of a popular science magazine. Yet, for the most part, the magazine left Einstein's politics alone—and still unknown.

My two previous books on the scientist—*The Einstein File: J. Edgar Hoover's Secret War Against the World's Most Famous Scientist* and *Einstein on Race and Racism*, written with coauthor Rodger Taylor—helped to fill a void with material about critical aspects of Einstein's life that no one had mentioned before (such as his twenty-year friendship with Paul Robeson).*

In *Einstein on Israel and Zionism*, unlike those two books, rather than filling in the blanks (where most people had no information whatever), I focus on correcting a widely accepted story told and retold primarily by the mainstream media (see Epilogue)—that Einstein was a major supporter, a "champion" of the state of Israel.

This book is also unlike the two previous books in that Einstein is not only the book's subject, but also the book's primary author. My role has been mainly to provide a

---

*The Einstein-Robeson friendship will be featured in an upcoming major motion picture, produced by Danny Glover and his Louverture film company.

platform for Einstein's frequently expressed but little-known (and in some cases never before published) views on this issue, more critical today than it was during Einstein's lifetime.

In addition to Einstein's writings on the subject, virtually unknown is Einstein's 1952 interview and meeting with Mohamed Heikal. As a journalist, I had known Heikal's name for some time—for twenty years he was editor of Egypt's influential daily *Al-Ahram*—but had never heard of any Heikal-Einstein connection.

When I first learned of their 1952 meeting in Princeton,[5] I wondered how I'd missed it in my previous reading. But as I went back over the indices and contents in the Einstein biographies, monographs, and archive files, Heikal's name was nowhere to be found. Nor did my calls to Einstein scholars—professors, physicists, biographers, and historians—uncover any memory of a Heikal-Einstein meeting.

My thoughts quickly turned to the almost universal lack of knowledge Rodger Taylor and I had encountered a few years earlier when researching Einstein's friendship with Paul Robeson for our book *Einstein on Race and Racism*. But in that case, though no Einstein biographies mentioned Robeson, at least a few of my historian and physicist friends had known who Robeson was and that he and Einstein had had some connection.

Fortunately (for many reasons), Heikal is still alive and definitely kicking, and in 2006 was willing to meet.[6]

. . .

The absence of Einstein's interview with Mohamed Heikal, the best-known journalist in the Arab world, from all Einstein biographies is probably not an oversight or a question of space—e.g., "We wanted to include it but just couldn't fit it in." It seems much more likely that the Heikal meeting, which involved much more than an interview, didn't fit the Einstein image, the media myth described above. For the same reason, many of the essays and letters of Einstein that appear here have rarely, if ever, been previously published.

Einstein had mixed feelings about Zionism. While supporting the goal of a Jewish "homeland" within Palestine, he never wavered from arguing forcefully for equal rights and equal power for the Arabs, whom he called "kinfolk" of the Jews. In the words of one of his earliest editors and translators, "Professor Einstein's nationalism [has] no room for any kind of aggressiveness or chauvinism. For him the domination of Jew over Arab in Palestine, or the perpetuation of a state of mutual hostility between the two peoples, would mean the failure of Zionism."[7]

Arranged chronologically, the book details Einstein's ambiguous relationship with various Zionist leaders and with Zionism, describing his support for cultural centers for Jews (cultural Zionism) even as he steadfastly opposed the establishment of a Jewish state "with borders and an army."

For the list of Einstein's correspondents and their short biographies, see page 253.

THE BACKSTORY

To understand how and how much Einstein and Zionism crossed paths, it is useful to review briefly where each of those paths began in the late nineteenth century and the routes they followed until they intersected.

EARLY EINSTEIN

At first glance, it would have seemed unlikely that the adolescent Einstein would get involved with Zionism or even with anything specifically related to the concepts of Judaism. *Irreligious*[1] is the word Einstein used to describe his parents. He grew up in a German Jewish, middle-class, small-business[2] family that—like most German Jews—did its best to assimilate into German society.

For a few childhood years Einstein became involved with formal religion (Judaism), but, as he later explained, his "deep religiosity" came to an abrupt end at the age of twelve. "Through the reading of popular books I soon reached the conviction that much in the stories in the Bible could not be true. The consequence was a positively fanatic [orgy of] freethinking coupled with the impression that youth is intentionally being deceived by the state through lies; it was a crushing impression. Suspicion against every kind of authority grew out of this experience, a skeptical attitude . . . which has never again left me. . . ."[3]

He did not go to synagogue, and (except for those few childhood years) had little interest in his or any religion. Indeed, during the first forty years of Einstein's life, religion played little if any part in his activities. With the publication in Berlin in 1915 of his general theory of relativity, Einstein, by the age of thirty-eight, had produced all of his great theories, which revolutionized our understanding of the universe.

Einstein first left Germany at the age of fifteen, mainly to avoid being drafted into the Prussian Army. He became a Swiss citizen and finished school in Switzerland.

When he couldn't find an academic position—at least partly because of anti-Semitism[4]—Einstein worked for several years as a patent clerk, during which time he developed three of his most famous theories, including the world's most widely known equation, $E = mc^2$.

He did ultimately receive university appointments, in both Zurich and Prague, and in 1913 the Germans, who were flexing their political and military muscles and recognized the value of science and technology in achieving international domination, made him an offer he could not refuse (research facilities, finances, and independence). The offer was made by two leading German physicists, Max Planck and Walter Nernst, who came to see Einstein in Zurich, but they made it clear that their offer was backed by the German government.[5]

When World War I began shortly after Einstein moved to Berlin, he was one of the very few professors in that country who refused to support Germany's war effort. But because he was Einstein and his presence in Berlin lent such prestige to Germany, he was not harried, deported, or arrested by the government, as were other pacifists.

Nonetheless, as soon as he arrived in Germany, anti-Semitism became a part of what he saw and felt around him. During and after World War I (1914–1918), Jews from Eastern Europe, tired of the persecution and pogroms, the killings, the ghettoes, and the scarcity of jobs, fled by the thousands to Western Europe and (even more) to the United States. Many of them carried hunger in their stomachs and Bolshevism in their bookbags.

For those two reasons, especially the latter, the Jews were not welcomed in the West.

"When I came to Germany [in 1914] . . . I discovered for the first time that I was a Jew," Einstein wrote some years later, "and I owe this discovery more to Gentiles than Jews. . . . I saw worthy Jews basely caricatured, and the sight made my heart bleed. I saw how schools, cartoons, and innumerable other forces of the Gentile majority undermined the confidence even of the best of my fellow-Jews, and felt that this could not be allowed to continue."[6]

In Germany, where virtually every able-bodied young male German was needed for the army, most Jews found work during the war. But when the war ended—after the country's surrender in 1918 and the return home of the defeated army—there was a sharp rise in anti-Semitic attacks throughout Germany, and the government considered a proposal to send the Jews "back where they came from." (Such plans for the mass expulsion of Jews from Germany continued into the 1930s.[7])

Before the end of 1919, Einstein wrote to his friend Paul Ehrenfest in Holland, "Anti-Semitism is strong here and political reaction is violent."[8]

Those who knew Einstein's character were probably not surprised that it was in reaction to these attacks that he recognized—and asserted—his Jewish identity: "Until seven years ago I lived in Switzerland, and as long as I lived there," Einstein explained, "I was not aware of my Jewishness, and there was nothing in my life that stirred my Jewish sensibility and stimulated it. This changed as soon as I took up residence in Berlin." Einstein went on to describe "the plight of many young Jews":

> I saw how anti-Semitic surroundings prevented them from pursuing regular studies and how they struggled for a secure existence. This is especially true of East European Jews, who are constantly subject to harassment. I do not believe they constitute a large number in Germany. Only in Berlin are there perhaps a greater number. Yet their presence has become a question that occupies the German public more and more. Meetings, conferences, newspapers press for their quick removal or internment. The housing shortage and economic depression are used as arguments to justify these harsh measures. Facts are assiduously overstated in order to influence public opinion against East European Jewish immigrants.

> *East European Jews are made the scapegoats for the malaise in present-day German economic life, which is in reality a painful after-effect of the war. Opposing these unfortunate refugees, who have escaped the hell that is Eastern Europe today, has become an effective political weapon that is successfully used by demagogues.*

When the new German government publicly contemplated deporting the Jews back to the east, Einstein stood up for them:

> *I pointed out* [in the *Berliner Tageblatt*] *the inhumanity and irrationality of these measures.*
>
> *Together with a few colleagues, Jews and non-Jews, I held university courses for East European Jews. . . .*
>
> *These and similar experiences have awakened my Jewish-national feelings. I am not a Jew in the sense that I call for the preservation of the Jewish or any other nationality as an end in itself. I rather see Jewish nationality as a fact, and I believe every Jew must draw the consequences from this fact. I consider raising Jewish self-esteem essential, also in the interest of a natural coexistence with non-Jews.*[9]

It should be clear from this that being Jewish, to Einstein, wasn't simply something one was, off in a corner by oneself. Quite the opposite. In a 1938 article titled "Why Do They Hate the Jews?" he wrote: "The bond that has united the Jews for thousands of years, and that unites them today is, above all, the democratic ideal of social justice, coupled with the ideal of mutual aid and tolerance among all men."[10]

To avoid any misunderstanding, it's important to note that Einstein never became a practicing religious Jew. Einstein's identification with the persecuted Jews and his desire to stand up for them was consistent with the resistance to religious and political persecution—and to racism—that characterized his entire life.[11]

At a luncheon one day in 1930 at the London home of his friend Lord Herbert Samuel, Einstein mentioned that he was frequently attacked in Germany, "parce que je suis Rouge et Juif" ("because I am Red and Jewish"). Samuel, who knew "that Einstein's politics were pink rather than red," declared, "Mais pas très Rouge" ("But not very Red"). Einstein replied, "Et pas très Juif."[12]

Nevertheless, Einstein himself had been the target of that postwar German anti-Semitism. In 1920, when the whole world was hailing his name and inviting him to visit, a small group of Germans organized a series of public meetings in Berlin to denounce the theory of relativity as a "Jewish perversion," and went on to attack Einstein with thinly veiled anti-Semitic insults. The meetings were sponsored by the Working Party of German Scientists for the Preservation of Pure Science—a mouthful of a title. Einstein scornfully renamed the group "Anti-Relativity, Inc."[13] The most prominent name associated with the anti-Einstein attacks was the Nobel Prize–winning scientist Philipp Lenard.

Years later, as Hitler's chief scientist, Lenard would write, "Science, like every other human product, is racial and conditioned by blood." And, focusing on the main target, "The most important example of the dangerous influence of Jewish circles on the study of nature has been provided by Mr. Einstein with his mathematically botched up theories."[14] (While Lenard, in 1920, led the public attack on relativity and Einstein, reportedly one secret financial backer of the effort to discredit Einstein was the notoriously anti-Semitic American industrialist Henry Ford.*)

How much did these attacks turn Einstein toward Zionism? Nothing brings out nationalist feelings and the sense of ethnic pride or racial identity as much as being attacked for being a member of a "minority" group.[15] Try being black in the white man's world of the United States and see how long you can maintain that "race doesn't matter" or "race is not an issue."

In 1921 Zionist leader Chaim Weizmann sent a telegram to Kurt Blumenfeld, a top Zionist recruiter who had already won Einstein's sympathy for "Zionist efforts," ordering him "to stir up Einstein," and to convince Einstein to accompany him (Weizmann) on his fundraising trip to America. Blumenfeld read the telegram aloud (in part) to Einstein. "It seems more than likely that Lenard and 'Anti-Relativity,

---

*In 1923, when Henry Ford announced he might become a candidate for U.S. president, a little-known Nazi Party leader in Germany named Adolf Hitler told the *Chicago Tribune*: "I wish I could send some of my shock troops to Chicago and other big American cities to help" (Higham, *Trading with the Enemy*, p. 155). Hitler was a fan of Ford's booklet *The International Jew: The World's Foremost Problem*. The booklet first appeared as a series of articles in Henry Ford's newspaper, misnamed *The Dearborn Independent*. In *Mein Kampf*, asserting that the Jews were the "controlling masters" of American production, Hitler added: "only a single great man, [Henry] Ford, to their [the Jews'] fury, still maintains full independence." In 1938, the year of *Kristallnacht* (the night of November 10 when rampaging Nazi gangs assaulted and murdered Jews throughout Germany and Austria), Ford accepted the Grand Cross of the German Eagle, the highest Nazi award given to non-Germans. "The German Foreign Office believed that Ford was a financial supporter [of the anti-Einstein efforts]" (Brian, *Einstein: A Life*, 110).

Inc.' were in [Einstein's] mind as he listened to Weizmann's telegram,"[16] according to Einstein biographer Ronald Clark.

Einstein himself wrote that the torrent of German anti-Semitism at the end of the First World War not only "awakened" his "Jewish-national feelings," but was also "my major motive for joining the Zionist movement."[17]

In fact, however, Einstein never actually enrolled in any Zionist organization, and while he expressed sympathy for certain Zionist projects, he also dissociated himself from others.

EARLY ZIONISM

The undeclared winners of the First World War may well have been the Zionists. In 1917, as the war was heading toward its end with victory for the British, French, and U.S. Allies in sight, the British government issued the Balfour Declaration, stating that:

> *His Majesty's government view with favour the establishment in Palestine of a national home for the Jewish people, and will use their best endeavours to facilitate the achievement of this object, it being clearly understood that nothing shall be done which may prejudice the civil and religious rights of existing non-Jewish communities in Palestine, or the rights and political status enjoyed by Jews in any other country.*

At the end of World War I, in 1918, the British and French were still the dominant world powers. In dividing up the spoils of war won from Germany and the Ottoman Empire, the British and French made sure they took over the choice colonies, especially in the Middle East, the British taking Egypt and Palestine (including what would become Jordan). The League of Nations, to no one's surprise, gave its approval. Thus, the British were assigned responsibility for the "Mandate" over Palestine—which was ideal for the Zionists.

Setting up a new Israeli state seemed simple enough. The same power that issued the Balfour Declaration not only recognized the Zionist claims to Palestine but had the League of Nations' authority as well as the military power to enforce those claims.

But things hadn't always been so simple for the Zionists.

Zionism emerged in the second half of the nineteenth century as a response by Jews to persecution by autocratic regimes in most Eastern European states. In the late 1870s, Jewish philanthropists such as the Montefiores and the Rothschilds responded to the persecution in Eastern Europe by sponsoring agricultural settlements for Russian Jews in Palestine.[18] From 1882 to 1903, some twenty-five thousand Jews migrated from Eastern Europe to settle in Palestine. This is generally considered the "first wave" of Jewish immigration, or the first *Aliyah*, a Hebrew word meaning "ascent," which implies the act of spiritually ascending to the Holy Land. During the "second Aliyah," or wave of immigration (1903 to 1914), 40,000 to 50,000 Jews entered Palestine—whose total Arab population was more than 650,000. Far more Jews resettled in the United States and Western Europe during these periods.[19]

The birth of the Zionist movement is sometimes traced

to the year 1894 when, after a blatant frame-up of a trial,
a French general staff officer who was Jewish, Alfred
Dreyfus, was convicted of treason and sentenced to life at
the notorious penal colony on Devil's Island in French
Guiana. The Dreyfus Affair profoundly shocked European
bourgeois Jews, and much of the world.* Theodor Herzl,
an Austro-Hungarian[20] Jewish journalist, described the
Dreyfus Affair as a turning point in his life: Prior to the Affair, he had been anti-Zionist; afterward, he became ar-
dently pro-Zionist. Herzl believed that only through the
establishment of a Jewish nation-state would Jews become
a people like all other peoples and anti-Semitism cease to
exist.

Political Zionism, whose goal was transforming Palestine** into a Jewish state, was founded by Herzl, who in

---

*Two years later, in 1896, the real culprit was brought to light and identified: a
French Army major named Ferdinand Walsin Esterhazy. However, French high-
level military officials dismissed or ignored this new evidence, which exonerated
Dreyfus. Thus, in January 1898, military judges unanimously acquitted Esterhazy
on the second day of his trial. French military counterintelligence officers fabri-
cated false documents designed to secure Dreyfus's conviction as a spy for Germany. They were all eventually exposed, in large part due to a resounding public
intervention by writer Emile Zola (J'Accuse) in January 1898. The case had to be
reopened, and Dreyfus was brought back from Guiana in 1899 to be tried again.
The intense political and judicial scandal that ensued divided French society between those who supported Dreyfus (the Dreyfusards) and those who condemned
him (the anti-Dreyfusards).

Eventually, all the accusations against Dreyfus were demonstrated to be base-
less. He was exonerated and reinstated as a major in the French Army in 1906. He
later served during the whole of World War I, ending his service with the rank of
lieutenant-colonel.

**In recent history the area called Palestine includes the territories of present-day
Israel and Jordan. From 1517 to 1917 most of this area remained under the rule
of the Ottoman Empire and was part of what was then called Syria. After the Allies' victory in World War I, Palestine became a British Mandate.

1896 published what may be considered the Zionist "manifesto": *Der Judenstaat (The Jewish State: An Attempt at a Modern Solution of the Jewish Question)*, and in 1897 organized the First Zionist Congress in Basel, Switzerland, which called on Jews to colonize Palestine.

But Herzl's Zionist plans had one major problem: How do you take over a territory and make it a Jewish nation when there are more than half a million indigenous people who have been living and farming in that place for hundreds of years and who consider it their home?

Over the years, some Zionists have argued that there were virtually no Arabs living in Palestine. Thus, they developed the slogan "A land without people [Palestine] for a people without land [Jews]."[21] But more than half a million people, families with homes and schools and mosques and farms, would have become immediately obvious to any visitor.[22] One widely reported story is that when Max Nordau, one of Herzl's earliest disciples, first visited Palestine and found Arabs living there, "he came running to his master crying: 'I didn't know that—but then we are committing an injustice.'"[23]

For the most part, the "problem" of how Zionists could settle already-settled land was the issue Herzl and the other early political Zionists faced. Morality aside, how could such a takeover happen? The Jews had no planes, no tanks, and no guns to speak of. To Herzl, the answer was obvious: the Zionists would become a cat's-paw for a big power seeking to expand its colonization to the East—not simply to the Middle East but through the Middle East to India and China. Herzl and the early Zionist leaders set out to arrange such a deal, offering to provide service to and an outpost for what was then a rapidly expanding Western colonialism. Herzl took the direct approach to every possible big-power "sponsor" who might protect the Zionists, who would, in turn, help that power expand its international empire.

If historians were to vote for the one man who most represented European colonialism, the heavy favorite might well be Cecil Rhodes (the founder of Rhodesia). In 1902 Herzl wrote to Rhodes, asking him to support the project for Jewish settlement in Palestine:

> You are being invited to help make history. That cannot frighten you, nor will you laugh at it. It is not in your accustomed line; it doesn't involve Africa, but a piece of Asia Minor, not Englishmen but Jews. But had this been on your path, you would have done it by now. How, then, do I happen to turn to you, since this is an out-of-the-way matter for you? How indeed? Because it is something colonial.[24]

Moses Hess, who, before Herzl, was perhaps the first to spell out the basic Zionist philosophy in *Rome and Jerusalem*, published in 1862, thought that the Jewish colonization of Palestine could and should be achieved in collaboration with the French colonization of Syria and other areas of the Middle East. In "the founding of Jewish colonies in the land of their ancestors," Hess writes, "France will undoubtedly lend a hand."

Leaving no doubt, either, about his own point of view, Hess declares: "the soldiers of civilization, the French, are gradually sweeping away the dominance of the barbarians."[25] And still more clearly: "Do you doubt that France will help the Jews to found colonies which may extend from Suez to Jerusalem and from the banks of the Jordan to the coast of the Mediterranean? Our lost fatherland [will] be rediscovered on the road to India and China that is now being built in the Orient."[26] But while there was some interest among the French colonialists, this early French-Jewish alliance didn't work out.

Meanwhile, Herzl was still promoting his plan. He saw Zionism—and did his best to sell Zionism—as a means for major profit-making. Indeed, the first version of *The Jewish State* was titled *Address to the Rothschilds*, and intended for the private use of the multimillionaire Rothschild family.[27] Herzl, the son of a rich banker-broker, had first attempted to woo Baron Maurice de Hirsch; when that failed, he turned to the Rothschilds.

Herzl proposed that the Rothschilds establish a private company to "organize trade and commerce in the new country." The company, to be controlled by major financial and banking groups, would put their credit "at the service of the National Idea," and in return would reap enormous profits: "One million would produce fifteen millions; and one billion, fifteen billions."[28]

But Herzl "was a child of his age," as David Hirst puts it. "It was the heyday of European imperialism, and Herzl knew that the brutal force of reality would make nonsense of his *Altneuland* [a book he had written about an idyllic Jewish utopia]. He knew—indeed, he had written—that immigration into an already populated country would soon turn the natives against the newcomers. . . . Violence was implicit in Zionism from the outset." Hirst then spells out the essence of Herzl's position:

The prophet of Zionism saw that coercion and phys-
ical force were inevitable. . . . To his diaries, not
published until 26 years after his death in 1904, he
confided the beliefs which in his public utterances he
had been careful to omit: that military power was an
essential component of his strategy and that ideally
the Zionists should acquire the land by armed con-
quest. True, the Jews had no military means of their
own, but Herzl sought to enlist, among the imperial
powers of the age, a sponsor which did.[29]

In making his pitch to the big powers, Herzl invariably
made it clear that he and the Zionists he represented shared
the big powers' racism toward the "under-developed" world
of "barbarians": "For Europe we would form part of the
rampart against Asia, serving as an outpost of civilization
against barbarism. As a neutral State we would remain in
contact with all Europe which would have to guarantee
our existence."[30]

Besides offering Zionism as a tool to Rhodes (who declined the offer) and to British colonialism in Africa, Herzl
met in 1901 with Turkish officials in Constantinople who
at that time controlled Palestine. Herzl tried (unsuccess-
fully) to get the Turks to grant him a charter for a Jewish-
Ottoman Colonization Association in Palestine. Herzl also
met with and tried to sell his program to heads of other
Western nations, including the notoriously anti-Semitic
German kaiser, who was closely allied with the Ottoman
Turks. The kaiser "made anti-Semitic remarks in his presence to which the Zionist leader offered no objection."
Herzl met, too, with Russian minister Wenzel von Plehve,

whom Palumbo calls "the most notorious Jew-hater of his age."[31] These meetings all proved fruitless. Herzl's Zionism still urgently needed adoption by someone of power.

Indeed, the 1897 Zionist Congress organized by Herzl in Basel spelled it out: Besides voting predictably to promote Jewish immigration to Palestine, perhaps the most important action the congress took was its unanimous pledge to work toward "obtaining the consent of [foreign] governments [who would help] to reach the goals of Zionism."[32]

As we've seen, the initial attempts by Herzl and Hess failed, but persistence, in this case, finally paid off for the Zionists. The significant "government consent" for these objectives was the Balfour Declaration of 1917, promising British support for "the establishment in Palestine of a national home for the Jewish people," and pledging to "use their best endeavours to facilitate the achievement of this object."

After decades of failing to convince any major power to become its political and military sponsor, the Zionists finally succeeded in being adopted by the British.

But the British superpower was not in the business of charity, of making donations to Israel. Supporting Zionism and a Jewish settlement in the Middle East clearly had a direct value to the British and other colonial powers as they sought to extend their grasp further into Africa and Asia.*

"With the approach of World War I, Britain sought justification for a permanent military presence in Palestine,"

---

*A symbolic coincidence: The year 1882, usually cited as the start of the first wave of Jewish immigration to Palestine, is the same year that British troops occupied Egypt (not to leave until 1955).

historian Baylis Thomas explains, adding, "[British] support of Jewish claims in Palestine . . . created tensions and the justification needed."[33]

In addition to Britain's two longstanding strategic goals in the Middle East—the protection of the Suez Canal and the protection of the Gulf, both vital links to India—there was now a new and even more powerful motive for controlling the area: oil.

The Balfour Declaration also coincided neatly with the decision of the British government in 1916, under new prime minister Lloyd George, to take over complete control of Palestine. Until then, Palestine had been under the joint control of England, France, Russia, and Italy. As Thomas points out, for the British to take total control:

> An "idealistic" rationale was needed for cutting out France and the other allies from Palestine. The Zionists held the answer. If an attempt was made to impose a Jewish state on Palestine, this would predictably elicit Arab hostility which, in turn, could justify a British military/peacemaker presence in Palestine. And if it happened to come to pass that a Jewish state was established in Palestine, then this, too, would serve British ends [both] as a defense of the Suez Canal against [Arab] attacks . . . and as a station on the future air routes to the East.[34]

The Balfour Declaration, which several Zionists (including Leon Simon) helped to draft, at the invitation of the British Foreign Office, has two major qualifications concerning the Zionist goal of a Jewish state. First, it calls for a Jew-

ish "home" or "homeland" within Palestine, and *not a state.*
(This is a difference that people like Einstein felt was significant.) Second, it specifically promises to protect the "civil
and religious rights of existing non-Jewish communities in
Palestine." These two are clearly related, since if an outside
force (e.g., Zionists) were to set up a state against the wishes
of the Arab population, this would clearly violate "the civil
and religious rights of existing non-Jewish communities in
Palestine."

Yet a reading of even a sampling of Zionist writings
makes it clear that most Zionists, at least the political Zionists (who were the dominant force in the Zionist movement), had every intention, from the start, of establishing a
state in Palestine, if not, indeed, of turning all of Palestine
into a Zionist state.

The Arabs were wary of the Balfour Declaration from
the start, but officially they greeted it initially as a policy
they could live with, opening the door to a Jewish community with which they might be friendly. Theoretically, at
least, and even physically, there was room for two communities. But as the Zionist aims became clearer, so did Arab
resistance. (See chapter 2.)

Zionist leaders generally avoided stating their goals
openly, but just two years after the Balfour Declaration
was signed, Chaim Weizmann slipped and told a London
conference:

> I trust to God that a Jewish state will come about, but
> it will come about not through political declarations,
> but by the sweat and blood of the Jewish people. [The
> Balfour Declaration] is the golden key which unlocks

> *the doors of Palestine and gives you the possibility to*
> *put all your efforts into the country. . . . We . . . desire*
> *to create in Palestine such conditions, political, eco-*
> *nomic and administrative, that as the country is devel-*
> *oped, we can pour in a considerable number of*
> *immigrants and finally establish such a society in*
> *Palestine that Palestine shall be as Jewish as England*
> *is English or America is American.*[35]

Zionist officials were apparently nervous about letting these comments reach the public since, according to David Hirst, "These revealing passages were omitted from later editions of the book in which they appear."[36]

But one Zionist position was spelled out with no deletions by Vladimir Jabotinsky, the leading Revisionist (right-wing) Zionist, especially during the 1920s and 1930s (the right wing is often the most blunt):

> *Our colonization must . . . proceed in defiance of*
> *the will of the native population. This colonization*
> *can therefore continue and develop only under the*
> *protection of a force independent of the local*
> *population—an iron wall which the native popula-*
> *tion cannot break through.*
>
> *This is the sum total of our policy towards the*
> *Arabs. . . . What is the Balfour Declaration for?*
> *What is the Mandate for? To us they mean that*
> *an external power has committed itself to creating*
> *such security conditions that the local population,*
> *however much it would have wanted to, would be*

*unable to interfere administratively or physically with
our colonization.*[37]

By the end of World War I, the British Army (led by
Field Marshall Edmund Allenby) had defeated the Ottoman forces (Persian and Turkish) to take control of a
vast area that included Palestine. The Balfour Declaration,
explains Einstein biographer Ronald Clark, "meant the
transformation of Zionism from a pious hope to a practical
possibility." It became an even more "practical possibility"
with the "peace" settlement and redivision of the world at
Versailles. Little wonder that Clark writes: "The hopes of
the Jews looked high."[38]

Soaring on Balfour wings—the Declaration not only promised the Jews "a national home" in Palestine, but British
troops, ships, and guns to protect their unsettling new
settlement—the Zionist leadership decided in 1919 to reach
out to recruit Jewish intellectuals. Einstein's name was on
the list, and Zionist recruiter Blumenfeld succeeded in
bringing the soon-to-become-famous scientist at least
partly into the Zionist caravan. At his meeting with Blumenfeld in 1919, Einstein said, "I am, as a human being,
an opponent of nationalism. But as a Jew, I am from today
a supporter of the Jewish Zionist efforts."[39]

As Ronald Clark pointed out some forty years ago,
anti-Semitism was probably the principal factor influencing
Einstein's Zionist conversion (at least as much as Blumenfeld's persuasion):

[Einstein] had emerged in the autumn of 1920 a different man from the almost lighthearted professor [of] only 24 months earlier. . . . Now he was not only a scientist but one who might genuinely be able to influence the tide of world affairs.

And by now he had watched the tide of anti-Semitism begin to rise and had felt it lapping round his own feet in Berlin and Bad Nauheim. It seems more than likely that Lenard and the "Anti-Relativity Company" were in his mind.[40]

Einstein made his only visit to Palestine while he and his second wife, Elsa, were returning from a trip to Japan in early February 1923. On his trip to the United States in 1921, Einstein had helped to raise money for the Hebrew University, and now he would make the university's inaugural address. While in Jerusalem they stayed in the home of the British high commissioner Sir Herbert Samuel, a Jew, with whom Einstein became lifelong friends. On February 7 in University House on Mount Scopus, Einstein lectured on the theory of relativity. The chairman of the Palestine Zionist Executive concluded his introduction with a dramatic pronouncement: "Mount the platform which has been waiting for you for 2,000 years."[41]

Blumenfeld may well have come courting Einstein at just the right historical moment. He would eventually write numerous articles and essays on his "success" in recruiting Einstein, emphasizing his cleverness or, as Clark puts it, "the skill with which he brought Einstein into the Zionist camp." In Blumenfeld's own words, utilizing Einstein for publicity purposes "was only successful if I was able to get under his skin in such a way that eventually he believed that words had not been put into his mouth but had come forth from him spontaneously."[42]

But despite Blumenfeld's claims, Einstein was only a sometimes ally. Had Blumenfeld been a candidate running for office, seeking Einstein's vote, it would have been relatively easy. Einstein could have said, as with so many candidates, "I like some of the things he's saying, he's eloquent, decent enough, I'll vote for him." However, Blumenfeld wanted a lot more than a vote from Einstein. The trouble— for Blumenfeld—was that Einstein's endorsement came with a battalion of *if*s and *but*s that made Einstein an increasingly critical "supporter."

To some extent, Blumenfeld knew that Einstein had not been really—or fully—recruited. In 1921, after he persuaded Einstein to accompany Zionist leader Chaim Weizmann to America (see below), Blumenfeld sent Weizmann a warning:

> *Einstein, as you know, is no Zionist, and I ask you not to try to make him a Zionist or to try to attach him to our organization. . . . Einstein, who leans to socialism, feels very involved with the cause of Jewish labor and Jewish workers. . . .*
>
> *I heard . . . that you expect Einstein to give speeches. Please be quite careful with that. Einstein . . . often says things out of naïveté which are unwelcome by us.*[43]

Perhaps Blumenfeld was not quite as clever as he claimed. Perhaps Einstein was the clever one (he has a reputation in that area)—more clever than naïve, a term Blumenfeld used frequently to describe him. Perhaps Einstein allowed himself to be semipersuaded or to be persuaded to support only those aspects of Zionism that he already liked—what might be called Einstein's "other Zionism."

1

FIGHTING ANTI-SEMITISM

1919–1929

November 2, 1917: The Balfour Declaration, supporting "a national home for the Jewish people" in Palestine, is approved by the British Cabinet, in the form of a letter from British foreign secretary Arthur James Balfour to Lord Walter Rothschild.

1919: The King-Crane Commission is assigned by U.S. president Woodrow Wilson to report on the Middle East. It finds that the majority of Arabs overwhelmingly oppose a Jewish homeland, fearing it will lead to an exclusively Jewish state; also that the Zionist plan would mean "a practically complete dispossession"[1] of the Arabs in Palestine. The King-Crane Report is then ignored by England, France, and by Wilson.

April 5, 1920: The San Remo Conference of World War I winners, under League of Nations auspices, "assigns" Britain as the Mandatory power over Palestine.

1921: The formation of Haganah is announced. The Jewish underground military organization is to become the basis of the Israeli Defense Forces.

1922: As "suggested" by the San Remo Conference, the League of Nations gives Britain the Mandate for Palestine. The U.S. Congress and President Warren Harding approve the Balfour Declaration. The first British census of Palestine shows 757,182 people, 11 percent Jewish. The Palestinian Fifth National Congress votes in favor of an economic boycott of Zionists.

1924: The United States passes the Immigration Restriction Act, effectively banning immigration from Asia and Eastern Europe.

1925: The Hebrew University of Jerusalem officially opens.

1928: Britain recognizes the independence of Transjordan, which—by arrangement with the British—occupies most of the territory of the Palestine Mandate.

As the SS *Rotterdam* arrived in New York Harbor from Europe on April 2, 1921, New York State's former governor Jimmy Walker and the city's future mayor Fiorello LaGuardia were among the officials on hand to welcome the ship's celebrity passengers, Albert Einstein and his (second) wife, Elsa. But when the ship docked, dozens of reporters unceremoniously pushed past the reception committee dignitaries and rushed onto the ship, flashbulbs popping, newsreel cameras grinding, and questions flying, mostly about the theory of relativity.

It was Einstein's first visit to the United States. The scientist had become the world's first international media star less than two years earlier (eight years before Lindbergh). In May 1919, during a solar eclipse, British scientists had measured a deflection of starlight around the sun, thus confirming the general theory of relativity. It wasn't long before the media and a war-weary world, hungry for peacetime heroes, discovered Einstein.

On November 7, the London *Times* announced:

REVOLUTION IN SCIENCE, NEW THEORY OF THE
UNIVERSE. NEWTONIAN IDEAS OVERTHROWN.

Three days later, *The New York Times* joined in:

LIGHTS ALL ASKEW IN THE HEAVENS,
EINSTEIN THEORY TRIUMPHS

In the next few years, Einstein would win the Nobel Prize, speak to audiences in scores of countries, and be honored and celebrated throughout the world. One trip would take the Einsteins to China, Japan, Palestine, and Spain, to be cheered by hundreds of thousands of people.

In New York, several thousand people, besides the dignitary-packed reception committee, had come to see and cheer the suddenly famous scientist. The front page of the next morning's *New York Times* headlined:

EINSTEIN EXPLAINS RELATIVITY
Thousands Wait Four Hours to Welcome
Theorist and His Party to America[2]

Einstein had already begun his traveling and speaking—
in Leyden, Prague and Vienna—but his arrival in New York
marked his first trip outside of Europe, and for the moment,
on the *Rotterdam*, he had his hands full with reporters: "Can
you explain the Relativity Theory?" "Is it true that only a
dozen people around the world can understand it?"

Einstein denied the "rumor" that only twelve people in
the world understood his theory, and did his best to provide a
preliminary, popular explanation: "If you will not take the
answer too seriously, and consider it only as a kind of joke,
then I can explain it as follows: Formerly, people believed that
if all *material* things disappeared from the Universe, time and
space would be left. But according to the relativity theory,
time and space disappear together with the other things."

When Einstein had some trouble understanding and
speaking in English, at first Elsa attempted to help, but when
she didn't do too well, either, Chaim Weizmann, president
of the World Zionist Oranization, who was traveling with
the Einsteins, volunteered to translate.[3] The Zionist leader
was coming to the United States to raise funds for a Hebrew
University in Jerusalem and to promote Zionism among
American Jews,[4] and Einstein had been persuaded to accompany Weizmann, although he had some hesitations about it.

Einstein's mixed feelings about the trip may be seen in
two of his letters, written just a few weeks before depart-
ing. On March 8, he wrote to Maurice Solovine that he
was "not going entirely willingly to America," but only to

help raise money for the Hebrew University, adding: "I am to play the role of a little tin god and a decoy." And a day later, to Fritz Haber: "Of course, they don't need me for my abilities but only because of my name [which] they hope will have a fair amount of success with the rich kinsmen of Dollar-land. Despite my emphatic internationalism, I believe I am always obliged to stand up for my persecuted and morally oppressed kinsmen."[5]

Einstein's ambivalence about the trip with Weizmann extended—over the years—to his feelings about Weizmann himself,[6] and—more to the point of this book—to Zionism in general.

March 22, 1919
Excerpt from a Letter to Paul Ehrenfest

At present, the political scene disappoints me very much. . . . One doesn't know where to look to find any joy in the activities of humankind. The thing that makes me most happy is the realization of the Jewish state* in Palestine. It seems to me that our fellow tribesmen are after all more sympathetic (or at least less brutal) than these abominable Europeans.[7]

December 30, 1919
On Jewish Immigration to Germany,[8]
in *Berliner Tageblatt*

Among the German public, voices are increasingly heard demanding legal measures against East European Jews. It is

---

*The word *state* here may well have been a random use by Einstein. It certainly did not reflect his position, as the reader will see in the pages that follow.

claimed there are 70,000 Russian, i.e., East European Jews, in Berlin alone; and these East European Jews are alleged to be profiteers, black marketeers, Bolsheviks, or elements that are averse to work. All these arguments call for the most sweeping measures, i.e., herding all immigrants into concentration camps or expelling them.

Measures that devastate so many individuals must not be triggered by slogan-like assertions, even less so as objective re-examination has shown that we have here a case of agitation by demagogues. It does not reflect the actual situation and is not a suitable means for counteracting existing wrongs. Agitation against East European Jews in particular raises suspicion that calm judgment is being clouded by strong anti-Semitic instincts and, at the same time, that a *specific* method of influencing the mood of the people is chosen which diverts from the true problems and from the real causes of the general calamity.

As far as is known, an official inquiry by the authorities that would undoubtedly reveal the invalidity of the accusations has not been conducted. It may very well be true that 70,000 Russians live in Berlin; but according to competent observers, only a small fraction of them are Jews, while the overwhelming majority are of *German descent*. According to authoritative estimates, not more than 15,000 Jews have immigrated from the East since the signing of the peace treaty. Almost without exception they were forced to flee by the horrible conditions in Poland and to seek refuge here *until they are given an opportunity to emigrate elsewhere.* Let us hope that many of them will find a true homeland as free sons of the Jewish people in the newly established Jewish Palestine.

It is quite likely that there are Bolshevik agents in Germany, but they undoubtedly hold foreign passports, have at their disposal ample funds, and cannot be arrested by any administrative measures. The big profiteers among the East European Jews have certainly, long ago, taken precautions to elude arrest by officials. The only ones affected would be *those poor and unfortunate ones,* who in recent months made their way to Germany under inhumane privations, in order to look for work here. Only these elements, certainly harmless to the German national economy, would fill the concentration camps, and there perish physically and spiritually. Then one will complain about the self-made "parasitic existences" who no longer know how to take their place in a normally functioning economy. The misguided policy of suddenly laying off thousands of East European Jewish laborers—who were coerced into coming to Germany during the war—and thus depriving them of their means of livelihood, leaving them with nothing to eat and systematically denying them job opportunities, has indeed forced people into the black market to keep themselves and their families from starving. The German economy, too, is certainly best served if the public supports the efforts of those who try to channel East European Jewish immigrants into productive work (as, e.g., the often mentioned Jewish Labor Bureau does). Any "order of expulsion"—now so vigorously demanded—would only have the effect that the worst and most harmful elements remain in the country, while those willing to work would be driven into bitter misery and despair.

The public conscience is so dulled toward appeals for humanity that it no longer even senses the horrible injustice which is here being contemplated. I refrain from going into details. But it is disturbing when even leading politicians do not consider how much their proposed treatment of East European Jews will damage Germany's *political and economic position*. Has it already been forgotten how much the deportation of Belgian laborers undermined the moral credibility of Germany? And today, Germany's situation is incomparably more critical. Despite all efforts, it is extremely difficult to re-establish damaged international relations; in all nations only a few intellectuals among the peoples of the world are initiating some first attempts; the hope for new economic connections (e.g., the material help of America) is still very weak today. The expulsion of the East European Jews— resulting in unspeakable misery—would only appear to the whole world as new evidence of "German barbarism," and provide it with a pretext, in the name of humanity, to hamper Germany's reconstruction.

Germany's recovery can really not be accomplished by the use of force against a small and defenseless portion of the population.

April 3, 1920
From *About Zionism*

When an intimidated individual or a careerist among my brethren feels inclined or forced to identify himself as a son of his forefathers, he usually describes himself— provided he was not baptized—as a "*German citizen of the Mosaic faith.*" There is something comical, even tragic-comical in this designation, and we feel it immediately. Why? It is quite obvious. What is characteristic about this man is not at all his religious belief—which usually is not that great, anyway—but rather his being of *Jewish nationality*. And this is precisely what he does *not* want to reveal in his confession. He talks about religious faith instead of kinship affiliation, of "Mosaic" instead of "Jewish" because the latter term, which is much more familiar to him, would emphasize affiliation to his kith and kin. Besides, the broad designation "German citizen" is ridiculous because practically everybody you meet in the street here is a "German citizen." Then, if our hero is no fool—and that is rather rare indeed—there must be a certain intention behind it. Yes, of course! Frightened by frequent slander he wants to assert that he is a good and dutiful German citizen, even though all his life he has been bedeviled—often not just a little—by "German citizens" because of his "Mosaic faith."

For brevity's sake, I have used the term "*Jewish nationality*" above, sensing that it could meet with resistance. Nationality is one of those slogans that cause vehement reaction in contemporary sensibilities, while reason treats the concept with less confidence. If somebody finds this word inappropriate for our case, he may choose another one, but I can easily circumscribe what it means in our case.

When a Jewish child begins school, he soon discovers that he is different from other children, and that they do not treat him as one of their own. This being different is . . . in no way based only upon the child's religious affiliation or on certain peculiarities of tradition. Facial features already mark the Jewish child as alien, and classmates are very sensitive to these peculiarities. The feeling of strangeness easily elicits a certain hostility, in particular if there are several Jewish children in the class who, quite naturally, join together and gradually form a small, closely knit community.

With adults it is quite similar. Due to race [Rasse]* and temperament as well as traditions (which are only to a small extent of religious origin) they form a community more or less separate from non-Jews. Aside from social difficulties, due to the changing intensity of anti-Semitism over the course of time, a Jew and a non-Jew will not understand each other as easily and completely as two Jews. It is this basic community of race and tradition that I have in mind when I speak of "Jewish nationality."

In my opinion, aversion to Jews is simply based upon the fact that Jews and non-Jews are different. It is the same feeling of aversion that is always found when two nationalities have to deal with one another. This aversion is a consequence of the *existence* of Jews, not of any particular qualities. The reasons given for this aversion are threadbare and changing. . . . there is no shortage of reasons; and the feeling of aversion toward people of a foreign race with whom one, more or less, has to share daily life, will emerge by necessity.

Herein lies the psychological root of all anti-Semitism, but by no means does it justify the agitation of the anti-Semites. A feeling of aversion may be natural, but to follow it unre-

---

*Stachel has explained Einstein's changing or developing views on the idea of Jews as a "race": "While he lived in Germany . . . Einstein seems to have accepted the then-prevalent racist mode of thought, often invoking such concepts as 'race' and 'instinct,' and the idea that the Jews form a race. . . . After living in the United States for several years, and presumably after he became aware of the campaign by Franz Boas and his fellow anthropologists against the concepts of racial purity and racial instinct, exploited so devastatingly by the Nazis, Einstein rejected any racial or other biological sanction for Judaism" (Stachel, *Einstein from B to Z*, 68–69).

servedly indicates a low level of moral development. A no-
bler individual will guide his actions by reason and insight
and not by dull instinct.

But how is it with society and with the state? Can it
tolerate national minorities without fighting them? There is
no state today that does not regard tolerance and the protection of national minorities as one of its duties. Let us
hope the state takes these duties seriously. This involves
halting its practice of demanding that Jews in many cases
abandon principle and abase themselves (Baptism) in order
to obtain government employment. . . .

The methods used by Jews to fight anti-Semitism are
quite diverse. I have already characterized the assimilatory
one, that is, to overcome anti-Semitism by dropping nearly
everything Jewish and appealing to the civil rights of Jews.
This method is not calculated to raise the reputation of the
Jewish people in the estimation of the non-Jewish world; besides, it is useless and morally questionable. Another method
of combating anti-Semitism, occasionally used by Jews who
have not yet broken with everything Jewish, is to draw a
sharp dividing line between *East European Jews* and *West
European Jews*. Everything evil blamed on Jews as a totality
is heaped on the East European Jews and, thus, of course
granted as an actually existing fact. The result of this not
merely bad but also foolish procedure is, of course, just the
opposite of what was intended. Anti-Semites have no intention of clearly distinguishing between East European and
West European Jews as some West European Jews might
wish; instead, they interpret this strange kind of defense as
an admission and unfairly accuse those West European Jews
of betraying their own people. It is not difficult to prove, in

both general and individual cases, that most West European Jews are nothing but former East European Jews; and vice versa for all East European Jews. And since the major concern of anti-Semites is to prove that Jewish inadequacies and vices have not been acquired during a few generations, but can allegedly be shown to have existed through the entire history of the Jewish people, the inference from East European Jews to West European Jews appears logically justified. And here we do not even take into consideration that East European Jewry contains a rich potential of the greatest human talents and productive forces that can well bear comparison to the higher civilization of West European Jews. . . .

It cannot be the task of the Jews to obtain "immunity" from the anti-Semites by accusing any part of their own people. This attitude reveals a severe misconception of judgment on the Jewish people we will never accept. As Jews we know the faults of our people better than others do, and we alone are called upon and able to remedy this. This can only be achieved, however, if we follow our Jewish duty: that we always view the Jewish people as a living whole and that standing shoulder to shoulder with our brethren we work for a Jewish and human future for our people.

April 3, 1920
Excerpt from a Response to an Invitation to a Meeting of the Central Association of German Citizens of the Jewish Faith[9]

. . . I would gladly attend if I believed that such an endeavor might meet with success. First, however, anti-Semitism and servility among our own Jewish people should be fought through education. More dignity and more independence in our own ranks! Only when we have the courage to regard ourselves as a nation, only when we respect ourselves, can we win the respect of others, or the respect of others will then follow. Anti-Semitism as a psychological phenomenon will always be with us as long as Jews and non-Jews are thrown together. Where is the harm in that? It may be that our survival as a race is thanks to anti-Semitism; that, in any case, is what I believe.

. . . I am neither a German citizen nor do I believe in anything that might be described as "Jewish faith." But I am a Jew and am glad to belong to the Jewish people, though I do not regard it in any way as chosen. Let us leave anti-Semitism to the goy, and save our love for kith and kin. . . .

March 8, 1921
Excerpt from a Letter to Maurice Solovine
I am not going entirely willingly to America, but am doing so only in the interests of the Zionists, who are obligated to ask for dollars for education in Jerusalem, and on this occasion I am to play the role of a little tin god and a decoy. If our places could be changed, I would willingly let you go in my place.

. . . I am not a jingo, and I firmly believe that the Jews, given the smallness and dependence of their colony in Palestine, will be immune from the folly of power.

March 9, 1921
Letter to Fritz Haber
Dear friend Haber:
What happened to me with regard to this journey to America, which can't be canceled anymore under any cir-

cumstances, is this. A couple of weeks ago, when no one even thought about any political entanglements, a local Zionist appreciated by me visited me and brought along a telegram by Prof. Weizmann informing me that the Zionist Organization asks me to join several German and English Zionists on a trip to America to deliberate about school affairs in Palestine. Of course, they don't need me for my abilities but only because of my name, whose advertising powers they hope will have a fair amount of success with the rich kinsmen of Dollar-land. Despite my emphatic internationalism, I believe I am always obliged to stand up for my persecuted and morally oppressed kinsmen as far as it is in any way in my powers. I thus happily agreed without pondering it for more than five minutes, even though just before I had declined all offers from American universities. So this was much more an act of loyalty than one of disloyalty. Most of all, the prospect of the creation of a Jewish university fills me with particular joy, after I have recently seen innumerable examples of the perfidious and unloving treatment of superb young Jews over here, truncating all their educational possibilities. I could also mention some other events during the last year that must push any Jew with self-esteem to take Jewish solidarity more seriously than would formerly have seemed indicated and natural. Just think of Röthe, Wilamowitz-Möllendorff and the infamous Nauheim brigade, which got rid of the fool Weyland only for opportunistic reasons.* No rational person can accuse me

---

*These were among the anti-Semites who had been attacking Einstein in Berlin.

of infidelity with regard to German friends. I have turned down many alluring calls to Switzerland, to Holland, to Norway, and to England without even in a single case pondering whether I should accept them. Incidentally, I did this not out of attachment to Germany, but rather to my dear German friends, of whom you are one of the most excellent and benevolent. For me as a pacifist, an attachment to the German political entity would be unnatural. But on the other hand there are considerations of tact dictated by the moment; at the present moment, these bring about a conflict-ridden situation which it was, however, impossible to predict.

The situation is aggravated by the fact that a couple of weeks ago, I accepted an invitation for a lecture at the University of Manchester, which, incidentally, leaves the choice of the date pretty largely to me. A few weeks ago, no rational German would have endorsed a rejection; today, my acceptance looks like a provocative act against Germany,* but certainly without any guilt on my part. Should the cloudy political situation continue, I would perhaps be able to abstain from the visit to Manchester; I would certainly meet with the understanding of the colleagues there if I explained the reasons to them as friendly and as honestly as possible. I should also add that a scientific corporation is not at all identical with the state. If scholars took their own profession more seriously than their political passions, they would organize their actions

_____

*Increasing nationalism within Germany after World War I was already (in 1921) taking the form of hostility to England and its wartime allies who had defeated Germany.

more in accord with cultural than with political considerations. It must even be said that the English behave much better than our colleagues here with regard to this. They are mostly Quakers and pacifists. How excellent a stand they took with regard to me and the theory of relativity!

. . . All this is cura posterior. But there is no way around going to America, since I have definitely agreed and the places on the steamship have already been procured. It is only a self-evident duty I fulfill with this. . . .

Yours,
Einstein

June 18, 1921
Letter to Paul Ehrenfest

Dear Ehrenfest,

The journey to America and England was so exhausting that all I'm able to do right now is just vegetate. My activities for the Jerusalem University were very successful. Zionism really represents a new Jewish ideal that can give the Jewish people a renewed joy in its existence. Financially, the university seems secured to such an extent that the medical faculty, which is particularly important for the construction work, can be started soon. It was not the rich, but members of the middle class who have made this possible, the 6,000 Jewish doctors in America in particular. I am very glad to have followed Weizmann's invitation. In several places, however, a high-tensioned Jewish nationalism shows itself that threatens to degenerate into intolerance and bigotry; but hopefully this is only an infantile disorder. For the reestablishment of international relations among scientists my journey has also been positive. Everywhere I went I

found alacrity, affectionate reception, and a peaceful disposition. England in particular has made an excellent impression on me in every regard; as long as this country retains
the leadership, everything will go relatively well.

Affectionate regards to you all, including the Malt-
schickes [kids].

Yours,

Einstein

June 21, 1921
"How I Became a Zionist," in *Jüdische Rundschau*[10]

Until a generation ago, Jews in Germany did not regard
themselves as part of the Jewish people. They simply
thought of themselves as members of a religious community, and many still do today. In fact they are far better assimilated than Russian Jews. They have attended mixed
schools and have accommodated themselves to both the
everyday and cultural life of the Germans. Yet in spite of
the equal rights they enjoy formally, strong social anti-
Semitism remains. Especially the educated class supports
the anti-Semitic movement. They have even constructed a
"science" of anti-Semitism, while the intellectuals of Russia, at least prior to the war, were usually philo-Semitic and
made frequent and honest attempts to fight the anti-Semitic
movement. This has a number of causes. To some degree,
the phenomenon is based on the fact that Jews exert an influence on the intellectual life of the German people altogether out of proportion to their numbers. While in my
opinion the economic position of the German Jews is vastly
overestimated, Jewish influence on the press, literature, and
science in Germany is very pronounced and obvious to even

the casual observer. There are many individuals, however, who are not anti-Semites and are honest in their argumentation. They regard Jews as a nationality distinct from Germans and feel that increasing Jewish influence threatens their national character. Although the percentage of Jews in England, for instance, is perhaps not much less significant than in Germany, English Jews certainly do not exercise a comparable influence on English society and culture. Yet the highest civil-service positions are accessible to them there, and a Jew can become Lord Chief Justice or Viceroy of India, something almost unthinkable in Germany.

Anti-Semitism is frequently a question of political calculation. Whether or not somebody admits to his anti-Semitism is often merely a question of which political party he belongs to. A socialist, even if he is a convinced anti-Semite, will not admit to or act on his conviction because it does not fit into the program of his party. Among conservatives, however, anti-Semitism often stems from the desire to exploit instincts that already exist in the population. In a country like England, where Jewish influence is less and the sensitivity of non-Jews is therefore far less, it is the existence of old, deep-rooted liberal traditions that hinders the rapid growth of anti-Semitism. . . . I say this without knowing the country personally. Nevertheless, the attitude toward my theory adopted by English science and the press has been characteristic. In Germany, for the most part, a newspaper's political orientation dictated its judgment of my theory; the attitude of English scientists on the other hand demonstrated that their sense of objectivity is not clouded by a political point of view. I should add that the English have actually influenced the development of our science to a great degree and have gone about testing the theory of relativity with great energy and with remarkable success. While anti-Semitism in America assumes only a social guise, it is political anti-Semitism that is far more common in Germany. The way I see it, the racial particularity of Jews will necessarily influence their social relations with non-Jews. I believe the conclusion which Jews should draw from this is to acknowledge their particular lifestyle and cultural contributions. For the time being they should display a certain dignified restraint and not be so eager to mix socially, which non-Jews desire only a little or not at all. On the other hand, anti-Semitism in Germany also has consequences that, from a Jewish point of view, should be welcome. I believe German Jewry owes its continued existence to anti-Semitism. Religious forms, which in the past hampered Jews from mixing with and integrating into their surroundings, are now in the process of disappearing due to growing affluence and improved education. Thus, nothing which leads to separation in social life remains but this antagonism to the surroundings called anti-Semitism. Without this antagonism, the assimilation of Jews in Germany would proceed quickly and unimpeded.

I have observed this in myself. Until seven years ago I lived in Switzerland, and as long as I lived there I was not aware of my Jewishness, and there was nothing in my life that would have stirred my Jewish sensibility and stimulated it. This changed as soon as I took up residence in Berlin. There I saw the plight of many young Jews. I saw how anti-Semitic surroundings prevented them from pursuing regular studies and how they struggled for a secure existence. This is especially true of East European Jews, who are constantly subject to harassment. I do not believe they constitute a large number in Germany. Only in Berlin are there perhaps a greater number. Yet their presence has become a question that occupies the German public more and more. Meetings, conferences, newspapers press for their quick removal or internment. The housing shortage and economic depression are used as arguments to justify these harsh measures. Facts are assiduously overstated in order to influence public opinion against East European Jewish immigrants. East European Jews are made the scapegoats for the malaise in present-day German economic life, which is in reality a painful after-effect of the war. Opposing these unfortunate refugees, who have escaped the hell that is Eastern Europe today, has become an effective political weapon that is successfully used by demagogues. When the government contemplated measures against East European Jews, I stood up for them in the *Berliner Tageblatt*, where I pointed out the inhumanity and irrationality of these measures.

Together with a few colleagues, Jews and non-Jews, I held university courses for East European Jews, and I would like to add that our activity met with the official recognition and full support of the Ministry of Education.

These and similar experiences have awakened my Jewish-national feelings. I am not a Jew in the sense that I call for the preservation of the Jewish or any other nationality as an end in itself. I rather see Jewish nationality as a fact, and I believe every Jew must draw the consequences from this fact. I consider raising Jewish self-esteem essential, also in the interest of a natural coexistence with non-Jews. This was my major motive for joining the Zionist movement. Zionism, to me, is not just a colonizing movement directed toward Palestine. The Jewish nation is a living fact in Palestine as well as in the Diaspora, and Jewish national feelings must flourish everywhere that Jews live. Under today's living conditions members of the same clan or peoples must have a lively awareness of their kinfolk in order not to lose their sense of self and their dignity. It was the unbroken vitality of the masses of American Jewry that first made it clear to me how sickly German Jewry is.

We live in an age of exaggerated nationalism and, as a small nation, must take this fact into account. But my Zionism does not preclude cosmopolitan views. My point of departure is the reality of Jewish nationality, and I believe that every Jew has an obligation toward his fellow Jews. Zionism has a varied significance. It opens the prospect for a dignified human existence to many Jews who presently languish in Ukrainian hell or degenerate economically in Poland. By leading Jews back to Palestine and restoring a healthy and normal economic existence, Zionism represents a productive activity that enriches all of society. The main point, however, is that Zionism strengthens Jewish dignity and self-esteem, which are critical for existence in the Diaspora. Moreover, in establishing a Jewish center in Palestine it creates a strong bond that gives Jews a sense of self. I have always found repulsive the undignified addiction to conformity of many of my peers.

The founding of a free Jewish community in Palestine will again put Jewish people in a position where they can bring their creative abilities to fruition without hindrance. The establishment of the Hebrew University and similar institutions will not only allow the Jewish people to bring about its own national renaissance, it will also give it the opportunity of contributing to the spiritual life of the world on a freer basis than ever before.

June 27, 1921
Address to a Zionist Meeting in Berlin

For the last two thousand years the common property of the Jewish people has consisted entirely of its past. Scattered over the wide world, our nation possessed nothing in common except its carefully guarded tradition. Individual Jews no doubt produced great work, but it seemed as if the Jewish people as a whole had not the strength left for great collective achievements.

Now all that is changed. History has set for us a great and noble task in the shape of active cooperation in the building up of Palestine. Eminent members of our race are already at work with all their might on the realization of this aim. The opportunity is presented to us of setting up centers of civilization which the whole Jewish people can regard as its work. We nurse the hope of erecting in Palestine a home of our own national culture which shall help to awaken the Near East to new economic and spiritual life.

The object which the leaders of Zionism have before their eyes is not a political but a social and cultural one. The community in Palestine must approach the social ideal of our forefathers as it is laid down in the Bible, and at the same time become a seat of modern intellectual life, a spiritual center for the Jews of the whole world. In accordance with this notion, the establishment of a Jewish university in Jerusalem constitutes one of the most important aims of the Zionist organization.

During the last few months I have been to America in order to help raise the material basis for this University there. The success of this enterprise was a natural one. Thanks to the untiring energy and splendid self-sacrificing spirit of the Jewish doctors in America we have succeeded in collecting enough money for the creation of a Medical Faculty, and the preliminary work is being started at once. After this success I have no doubt that the material basis for the other faculties will soon be forthcoming. The Medical Faculty is first of all to be developed as a research institute and to concentrate on making the country healthy, a most important item in the work of development. Teaching on a large scale will only become important later on. As a number of highly competent scientific workers have already signified their readiness to take up appointments at the University, the establishment of a Medical Faculty seems to be placed beyond all doubt. I may add that a special fund for the University, entirely distinct from the general fund for the development of the country, has been opened. For the latter, considerable sums have been collected during these months in America, thanks to the indefatigable labors of Professor Weizmann and other Zionist leaders, chiefly through the self-sacrificing spirit of the middle classes. I conclude with a warm appeal to the Jews in Germany to contribute all they can, in spite of the present economic difficulties, for the building up of the Jewish home in Palestine. This is not a matter of charity but an enterprise which concerns all Jews and the success of which promises to be a source of the highest satisfaction to all.

July 1, 1921
"On a Jewish Palestine," in *Jüdische Rundschau*

Rebuilding Palestine is for us Jews not merely a matter of charity or a colonial issue but rather a problem of paramount importance for the Jewish people. Palestine is not primarily a refuge for East European Jews but rather the incarnation of a reawakening national feeling of community of all Jews. Is it opportune and necessary to revive and strengthen this feeling of community? I believe I must answer this question with an unqualified "yes," based not only on spontaneous emotions but on sound reason.

Let us briefly cast a glance at the development of German Jews during the last one hundred years. A century ago, our ancestors, with few exceptions, lived in the ghetto. They were poor, politically disenfranchised, separated from non-Jews by a wall of religious traditions, daily lifestyle, and legal restraints. In their intellectual development they were limited to their own literature, and only faintly influenced by the tremendous revival that European intellectual life experienced during the Renaissance. For the most part ignored, these modestly living people had one advantage over us: every one of them belonged with every fiber of his being to a community that completely absorbed him, in which he felt himself a fully-fledged member, and in which no one demanded anything of him that ran counter to his natural way of thinking. Our ancestors were physically and intellectually rather atrophied, but in social respects they enjoyed an enviable spiritual equilibrium. Then came emancipation. Suddenly an individual had undreamed-of opportunities of development. Individuals rapidly established contact with the higher economic and social strata.

Eagerly they absorbed the magnificent achievements that the arts and sciences had created in the West. They threw themselves with ardor into this development, making lasting contributions of their own. In the process they appropriated the external forms of life of the non-Jewish world, and increasingly turned a blind eye to their religious and social traditions, and adopted non-Jewish habits, customs, and ways of thinking. It seemed as if they would be absorbed into the numerically larger, politically and culturally better organized host nations, so that after a few generations no visible trace would remain. Complete dissolution of the Jewish nation in Central and Western Europe appeared inevitable.

Things turned out differently. There seem to be instincts in racially distinct nationalities that counterbalance their assimilation. The accommodation of Jews in language, morals, and even religious forms to the European nations among whom they live could not extinguish the alienation that exists between Jews and their European host nations. In the last analysis this instinctive feeling of alienation is the source of anti-Semitism. Well-meaning tracts thus cannot eradicate it. Nationalities do not want to mix; they prefer to go their own way. A satisfactory situation can only be achieved through mutual tolerance and respect.

Toward this end it is especially important that we Jews again become conscious of our nationality and that we regain the self-respect that we need for a prosperous existence. We must learn to rededicate ourselves to our forefathers and to our history, and as a people we must accept those cultural duties that serve to strengthen our feeling of community. It is not enough to take part as mere individuals in the cultural development of mankind, we must also tackle tasks that only national unity can solve. This is the only way that Jewry can become socially sound.

I ask you to view the Zionist movement from this perspective. Today, history has delegated to us the task of actively participating in the economic and cultural rebuilding of the land of our fathers. Enthusiastic and highly gifted men have laid the groundwork, and many admirable kinsmen are prepared to devote themselves completely to this labor. May every one of you fully appreciate the importance of this task and contribute to its success to the best of your abilities!

May 1, 1923
"My Impression of Palestine," in *New Palestine*

I cannot begin these notes without expressing my heartfelt gratitude to those who have shown so much friendship toward me during my stay in Palestine. I do not think I shall ever forget the sincerity and warmth of my reception—for they were to me an indication of the harmony and healthiness which reigns in the Jewish life of Palestine.

No one who has come into contact with the Jews of Palestine can fail to be inspired by their extraordinary will to work, and their determination which no obstacle can withstand. Before that strength and spirit there can be no question of the success of the colonization work.

The Jews of Palestine fall into two classes—the urban workers and the village colonizers. Among the achievements of the former, the city of Tel Aviv made a singularly profound impression on me. The rapidity and energy which has marked the growth of this town has been so remarkable that Jews refer to it with affectionate irony as "Our Chicago."

A remarkable tribute to the real power of Palestine is the fact that the Jewish elements which have been resident in the country for decades stand distinctly higher, both in the matter of culture and in their display of energy, than those elements which have only recently arrived.

And among the Jewish "sights" of Palestine none struck me more pleasantly than did the school of arts and crafts, Bezalel, and the Jewish workingmen's groups. It was amazing to see the work that had been accomplished by young workers who, when they entered the country, could have been classified as "unskilled labor." I noted that beside wood, other building material is being produced in the country. But my pleasure was tempered somewhat when I learned of the fact that the American Jews who lend money for building purposes exact a high rate of interest.

To me there was something wonderful in the spirit of self-sacrifice displayed by our workers on the land. One who has actually seen these men at work must bow before their unbreakable will and before the determination which they show in the face of their difficulties—from debts to malaria. In comparison with these two evils the Arab question becomes as nothing. And in regard to the last I must remark that I have myself seen more than once insurance of friendly relations between Jewish and Arab workers. I believe that most of the difficulty comes from the intellectuals and, at that, not from the Arab intellectuals alone.

The story of the struggle against malaria constitutes a chapter by itself. This is an evil which affects not only the rural, but also the urban population. During my visit to

Spain some time ago, we submitted to the Spanish Jews a proposition that they send, at their expense, a specialist on the subject of malaria to Palestine, and that this specialist should carry on his work in connection with the work of the University of Jerusalem. The malaria evil is still so strong that one may say that it weakens our colonization work in Palestine by something like a third.

But the debt question is particularly depressing. Take for instance the workers of the colony of Degania. These splendid people groan under the weight of their debts, and must live in the direst need in order not to contract new ones. One man, even of moderate means, could, if he were large-hearted enough, relieve this group of its heartbreaking burden. The spirit which reigns among the land and building workers is admirable. They take boundless pride in their work and have a feeling of profound love for the country and for the little localities in which they work.

In the matter of architectural taste, as displayed in the buildings, in the town, and on the land, there has been not a little to regret. But in this regard the engineer, Kaufmann, has done a great deal to bring good taste and a love of beauty into the buildings of Palestine.

To the government considerable credit must be accorded for its construction of roads and paths, for its fight against malaria and, in general, for its sanitary work as a whole. Here the government has no light task before it. One can hardly find another country which, being so small, is so complicated by virtue of the divisions among its own population as well as by virtue of the interest taken in it by the outside world.

The greatest need of Palestine today is for skilled labor.

No academic forces are needed now. It is hoped that the completion of the Technical College will do a great deal toward meeting the need of the country for trained workmen.

I am convinced that the work in Palestine will succeed in the sense that we shall create in that country a unified community which shall be a moral and spiritual center for the Jewries of the world. Here and not in its economic achievement lies, in my opinion, the significance of this work. Naturally we cannot neglect the question of our economic position in Palestine, but we must at no time forget that all this is but a means to an end. To me it seems of secondary importance that Palestine shall become economically independent with the greatest possible speed. I believe that it is of infinitely greater importance that Palestine shall become a powerful moral and spiritual center for the whole of the Jewish people. In this direction the rebirth of the Hebrew language must be regarded a splendid achievement. Now must follow institutions for the development of art and science. From this point of view we must regard as of primary importance the founding of the university which, thanks largely to the enthusiastic devotion of the Jewish doctors of America, can begin its work in Jerusalem. The university already possesses a journal of science which is produced with the earnest collaboration of Jewish scientists in many fields and in many countries.

Palestine will not solve the Jewish problem, but the revival of Palestine will mean the liberation and the revival of the soul of the Jewish people. I count it among my treasured experiences that I should have been able to see the country during the period of rebirth and re-inspiration.

February 8, 1924
Letter to Erich Mendelsohn
Dear Mr. Mendelsohn,

On Saturday 16, this month, at 8:30 P.M. sharp Mr. Blumenfeld will give a speech in my apartment on the mental, political, and economic preconditions for the colonization of Palestine by the Jews.

After the speech, we want to have tea together and enter into a thorough discussion with Mr. Blumenfeld.

With the highest esteem,

A. Einstein

February 17, 1925
Excerpts from "Mission," in *Jüdische Rundschau*

The existence of different nationalities and consequently of mutually antagonistic nationalisms, both within and without Europe, must be considered a misfortune in my opinion. Must we state again that a certain type of nationalism represents a real danger for peace and an inexhaustible source of injustice and sorrow?

On the other hand, there is a fact that cannot be ignored: The Jews are almost everywhere treated as members of a group that is clearly characterized nationally. This seems regrettable to Jews, like myself, who consider membership in the human species as the ideal, possible to attain, even though difficult. . . .

The Jews must also put their nationality to use. May they do it so as to further the welfare of all!

They must develop those virtues and faith which are indispensable to one who wishes to serve all of humankind. Since, at least for the present moment, the Jewish nationality is not going to vanish, Jews must justify their existence. They must, without being ridiculously arrogant, restore their awareness of the human values which they embody. They must re-learn the mission that they can accomplish, re-learn it through studying their past and through a better understanding of the spirit of their race.*

By remembering a past filled with glory and sorrow and by opening their eyes to a healthier, dignified future, Zionism teaches self-knowledge and instills courage. It restores the moral force which allows Jews to live and act in dignity. It frees the soul from the unforgivable future of exaggerated modesty which only oppresses and makes one unproductive. Finally Zionism reminds Jews that the centuries they have lived through in sorrow together enjoins upon them the duty of solidarity.

Inspired by the mystique of Zionism, perhaps they will finally be able to fulfill the tasks that are incumbent upon them, and which demand the high-principled exertions and single-minded labor of Israel. Only at this price will those who believe in fraternal bonds among people of all nations be able to usefully spread words of wisdom and humanity, which are needed more today than ever.

For this reason, I cannot see the Zionist movement as an outgrowth of the poisonous views that destroy the enjoyment and thinking of life.

A Jew who strives to impregnate his spirit with humanitarian ideals can call himself a Zionist without contradiction.

---

*See footnote on page 36.

One must be thankful to Zionism for the fact that it is the only movement that has given many Jews a justified pride, that it has once again given a despairing race the necessary faith, if I may so express myself, given new flesh to an exhausted people. . . .

Zionism is in the process of creating in Palestine a center of Jewish intellectual life, and for that reason we will always be thankful to its leaders. This moral homeland will, I hope, succeed in bringing more vitality to a people that does not deserve to die. I have already observed the first signs of this moral resurgence.

Thus, I can assert that Zionism, which appears to be a nationalistic movement, has, when it comes down to it, a significant role to play for all mankind.

March 20, 1926
Letter to Kurt Blumenfeld in Berlin

Dear Mr. Blumenfeld:

Before I decide in the matter touched upon in your letter, I would like to have a piece of information categorically necessary for my good conscience: an annual balance sheet of the Zionist Organization, which should show:

1. How much money was collected in the individual countries?
2. How much of this money was spent outside of Palestine?
3. How much of it in Palestine?
4. How is the money consumed in Palestine split between management, land acquisition, and other needs?

You know how much I appreciate the educational achievements of Zionism. As an enterprise, I don't know it well enough to support it with a good conscience.

Respectfully yours,

AE

April 9, 1926
Excerpt from Einstein's Response to Don Levine*

Although I believe that it is only in Palestine that work of lasting value can be achieved, and that everything that is done in the Diaspora countries is only a palliative . . . nevertheless . . . the efforts being made to colonize Jews in Russia must not be opposed because they aim at assisting thousands of Jews whom Palestine cannot immediately absorb. . . . On this ground, these efforts seem worthy of support.

1927
"The Jews and Palestine," in *About Zionism*
(Published in 1930)

The Palestine problem, as I see it, is twofold. There is first the business of settling the Jews in the country. This demands external assistance on a large scale; it cannot be successfully accomplished unless the national resources of Jewry are laid under contribution. The second task is that of stimulating private initiative, especially in the commercial and industrial spheres.

The deepest impression left on me by Zionist work in

*Levine had asked: What is your view of the present Jewish colonization movement in Russia? And how would it affect the Palestine colonization?

Palestine is that of the self-sacrifice of the young men and women workers. Gathered here from all sorts of different environments, they have succeeded, under the influence of a common ideal, in forming themselves into closely-knit communities and in working together on lines of systematic co-operation. I was also most favourably impressed by the spirit of initiative shown in the urban development. There is something here that almost suggests an avalanche. One feels that the work is being borne along on the wings of a strong national sentiment. Nothing else could explain the extraordinarily rapid advance, especially on the sea-coast near Tel-Aviv.

At no time did I get the impression that the Arab problem might threaten the development of the Palestine project. I believe rather that, among the working classes especially, Jew and Arab on the whole get on excellently together. The difficulties which are as it were inherent in the situation do not rise above the threshold of consciousness when one is on the spot. The problem of the rehabilitation and sanitation of the country seems incomparably more difficult.

It is a common thing for Jews to miss the significance of the Palestine question: they do not see what it has to do with them. It is indeed easy to ask what it matters to a scattered nation of so many millions whether a million or a million and a half of them are settled in Palestine. But for me the importance of all this Zionist work lies precisely in the effect that it will have on those Jews who will not themselves live in Palestine. We must distinguish in this connection between internal and external effects. The internal effect, in my opinion, will be a healthier Jewry: that is to say, the Jews will acquire that happiness in feeling themselves at one, that sense of being self-sufficient, which a common ideal cannot fail to evoke. This is already evident in the younger generation of our day—not among the young Zionists only—and distinguishes it, greatly to its advantage, from earlier generations, whose endeavours to be absorbed in non-Jewish society produced an almost tragic emptiness. That is the internal effect. The external effect I see in the status which a human group can attain only by collective and productive work. I believe that the existence of a Jewish cultural centre will strengthen the moral and political position of the Jews all over the world, by virtue of the very fact that there will be in existence a kind of embodiment of the interests of the whole Jewish people.

2

YEARS OF CRISIS

1929–1939

1928: The British propose a parliament for Palestine that would have equal representation from Jewish and Arab populations (and some appointees by the British). At first, the Arabs—who were between 80 and 90 percent of the population—reject the proposal, and the Zionists are inclined to accept it. But when, in 1928, the Arabs accept it, the Zionist leadership rejects it.

August 1929: A sharp increase in fighting in Palestine begins with attacks by Arabs against Jews in Hebron and Safed and attacks against Arabs by British troops. Violent incidents actually began in 1928, continuing for at least two years with casualties on both sides.*

---

*One major cause of the Arab attacks was the failure of the British Mandate government to implement the system of equal representation that it had promised. "The Palestinian uprising in 1929 was the direct result of Britain's refusal to implement at least their promise of parity after the Palestinians had been willing to set aside the democratic principle of majoritarian politics, which Britain has championed as the basis for negotiations in all the other Arab states within its sphere of influence" (Pappe, *Ethnic Cleansing*, 14).

1930: Second British census reports Palestine's population at 1,035,154, with 16.9 percent Jewish.

Mid-April 1936: Palestinian rebellion begins, opening with a six-month general strike and continuing until 1939. The 1936–39 uprising eventually forces the British to station more troops in Palestine than in the entire Indian subcontinent.

1937: The British Peel Commission declares that there is no common ground between Jews and Arabs and that the British Mandate has been a failure, and recommends the partitioning of Palestine. The Arabs denounce that plan. The World Zionist Organization accepts "with major qualifications."

In the summer of 1930, Norman Bentwich, a Jewish and British lawyer appointed by the British as attorney general for the Mandate government of Palestine, visited Einstein at his summer cottage in Caputh, just outside of Berlin, to seek advice from the man who was soon to achieve the status of a semisaint among Jews around the world.

The previous year had seen a sharp increase in fighting in Palestine, beginning in August 1929, including attacks by Arabs against Jews in Hebron and Safed, and attacks against Arabs by British soldiers. The specifics of each incident varied, of course,* and included a number of widely

---

*In one case, a Jewish teenager was killed in a fight between Jewish and Arab youth on a football field. "The fight seems to have been started by the Jewish boys," according to American journalist Vincent Sheehan (David Hirst, *The Gun and the Olive Branch*, 190, citing Sheehan, *Personal History*, 392–408).

reported religious disputes over the Wailing Wall and the Al Aqsa Mosque.

But fundamentally the fighting was caused by conditions resulting from the steadily growing Jewish settlement in Palestine under the rules—and the guns—of the British Mandate.

> *The ordinary Arab in Palestine in these years was faced with a steeply escalating increase in his cost of living brought about by the economic transformation of the area by the Jews [including] vast tracts of Jewish workingmen's quarters erected by Jewish building societies. Sometimes, too, he had the experience of being driven away from work sites by Jewish pickets, and he resented the fact that when he was allowed to work, the government paid the Jewish workman double the rate it paid him.[1]*

With more Jews arriving every year to settle additional lands (often bought from Arab absentee landlords), with the approval and protection of the British authorities and with no end in sight, Arab rebellions against Zionists in Palestine increased, as more and more Arabs saw their land being settled by Jews and felt their future threatened. Armed battles between Arabs and Jews erupted throughout the summer of 1929, with hundreds killed on both sides.

"The 1929 riots can be understood," Israeli historian Simha Flapan explains, "only against the background of the serious economic crisis in the country as a whole and in the Arab population in particular. The British Commission of Enquiry following the disturbances revealed for the first time the gravity of the problem of landlessness among Arab peasants. In more than one hundred villages they visited, the Commission found that 29.8 per cent of rural families had no land at all and an additional 40 per cent [had] holdings smaller than the minimum required for subsistence."[2]

While this report and others sharply swayed British public opinion toward sympathy with the Arabs, the "solution" proposed by Zionist leaders, and especially Weizmann, was the deportation of all Arabs to Jordan, a plan that only aggravated Arab suspicions and hostility toward the Zionists.

Weizmann rejected Arab proposals to negotiate as well as several proposals for a binational state or self-government in Palestine, arguing, in Flapan's words, "that democracy was not appropriate for backward peoples." Weizmann himself put it no less chauvinistically: "In most non-European countries Parliamentary government has proved a sheer farce," adding that Arabs "are too primitive and too much under the influence of Bolshevik and Catholic agitation to understand what we are bringing them."[3]

Among those arguing most publicly for a binational state were Hugo Bergmann, a founder of Brit Shalom, an organization advocating reconciliation and cooperation between Jews and Arabs, and Judah Magnes, head of the Hebrew University of Jerusalem. Weizmann, in an angry letter to Einstein, denounced both of them and complained that Einstein ("even you") was sympathetic to their views.*

When the Zionists denounced the Arab attacks, the British authorities responded by arresting some thirteen

---

*See Einstein-Weizmann letters of 1929, pages 78–83.

hundred Arabs. In all, the British sentenced twenty-eight people to death, twenty-six of them Arabs. (After numerous appeals and interventions, only three—all Arabs—were hanged.)[4] It was exactly what the British had expected—and possibly hoped for—a "peacekeeping" pretext for maintaining troops in the area.* The details of the fighting are complex, and, as always, versions vary. At least one observer, Vincent Sheehan, wrote, "I was bitterly indignant with the Zionists for having, as I believed, brought on this disaster."[5]

It was not yet a full-fledged Palestinian rebellion[6]—that would begin seven years later. But the 1929 events were clear signs of what was to come, the opening shots of a decade of Arab resistance to both the British Mandate and the Zionists. In the thirties, Jews, many escaping Nazi-controlled areas of Europe, continued to immigrate to Palestine under that protective umbrella of British troops on duty throughout the Mandate. As Arab resentment simmered and flared up from place to place, bands of Palestinian peasant guerrillas appeared around the country. Finally the resistance caught fire in the flames of the insurrection of 1936–1939.

The rebellion began with a general strike that continued for six months (until October 1936), making it one of the longest general strikes in history.[7] By the second year of the

---

*"Britain had two immediate strategic concerns in the Middle East—the protection of the Suez Canal and of the Gulf. Both were vital links with India . . . and the Gulf region now had the additional value of oil" (Mansfield, *History of the Middle East*, 149). (See also Kiernan, *The Arabs*, 247.) "Oil had been the chief reason for the inclusion of the Mosul region within the area controlled by Britain" (Khalidi, *Resurrecting Empire*, 99).

rebellion, guerrilla bands of peasants from different parts of the country succeeded in controlling much of the hill country and many towns throughout Palestine. As one British official put it, "By September 1938, the country was to all practical purposes, non-existent."[8]

With war clouds menacing Europe, the British government was hard-pressed to find troops to repress a rebellion in Palestine. Ironically, it was Chamberlain's deal with Hitler—denounced as appeasement throughout the world— that allowed the British to redeploy massive numbers of troops from Europe to crush the Palestinian uprising. "Peace in our time," Chamberlain's hollow words as he and his British troops stood by and let the Nazis take Czechoslovakia, appear doubly harsh and ironic when we consider that the British Empire needed those thousands of troops to brutally prevent their Arabian "loyal subjects" from taking power in Palestine. No peace was intended for the Palestinians.[9] The Arab guerrillas, British Vice-Marshall Pierce wrote, "were not out for loot. They were fighting what they believed to be a patriotic war in defence of their country."[10] How ironic that for all their condemnation of Chamberlain's appeasement, the Western powers never once criticized, or even mentioned, British aerial and artillery bombardment of Palestinian villages by the very troops withdrawn from Europe.

After reconquering Palestine with twenty thousand additional troops,[11] the British huddled and conferenced and tried to come up with policies that would prevent such rebellions from recurring. At first a white paper proposed partition of Palestine, but that didn't seem workable. After several attempts, the British came up with the McDonald

White Paper, which declared that Palestine should not become a Jewish state and that they would admit seventy-five thousand more Jewish immigrants over the next five years but then no more.

The white paper was denounced by the Zionists, who intensified their opposition, and the British did in fact soften their stand. The McDonald White Paper was also condemned by Arab sources: "The White Paper of 1939 which has been subjected to so much criticism . . . as an act of appeasement to the Arabs . . . was no such thing,"[12] according to one leading Arab writer, Edward Atiyah.

Besides being alarmed by the fighting and the future it foretold, Bentwich had an additional problem—as a Jewish attorney general appointed by the British in a land that was overwhelmingly Arab, he was, to no one's surprise, not trusted by the vast majority of people in the region.[13] At the same time, ironically, he had many disagreements with the Zionist leadership. (The books he would eventually write include a biography of Judah Magnes, the leading political organizer of the cultural Zionists, and other Jews who opposed establishing the state of Israel.)

It was, then, not particularly surprising when Bentwich went to visit Einstein in Berlin in 1930—the Jewish press was still overflowing with headlines about the Arab attacks. What was surprising was the message Bentwich brought back from Einstein: "[Einstein said] he would not remain associated with the Zionist movement unless it tried to make peace with the Arabs, in deed as well as in word. The Jews should form committees with the Arab peasants and workers, and not try to negotiate only with the leaders."[14]

During the thirties, the rising tide of fascism in Germany, Japan, Italy, and Spain preoccupied Einstein and most of the democratic forces around the world. Nonetheless, echoes of Einstein's commitment to friendship with the Arabs resound in a number of essays and letters the scientist wrote during that period when Zionist leaders were publicly denouncing the Arab attacks as "massacres." A few examples can be seen in his letters of 1929 and 1930 to Asis Domet, Heinrich York-Steiner, and Hugo Bergmann. The letter to Bergmann ends on an almost bitter note: "*What saddens me is less the fact that the Jews are not smart enough to understand this, but rather, that they are not just enough to want it*"[15] (emphasis in the original).

Perhaps most significantly, less than a year after the Hebron events, Einstein made headlines around the world for publicly opposing the death sentences of the Arabs arrested there.*

At the same time—during the 1930s—and unrelated to

---

*"Einstein Calls for Commutation of Death Sentences for 25 Arabs Who Participated in the Riots of August 1929," *New York Times*, June 1, 1930. Sayen contends, "The riots of 1929 profoundly disturbed Einstein. He was furious that the British authorities had been unable to protect the Jewish victims. . . . He was contemptuous of the barbarity of the rioters, yet at the same time he joined with War Resisters International in calling for amnesty for the condemned Arab rioters because he felt that right-wing Jewish youth shared the blame. Publicly and privately, he appealed to Arabs and Jews to find a way to settle their differences and put an end to the almost total lack of contact between the two communities. He felt the two cultures could complement each other, and he suggested that Jewish children should learn Arabic" (Sayen, *Einstein in America*, 105).

the events in Palestine, Einstein expressed support for two little-known projects that would have relocated Jews to new communities in China and in Peru. Both projects were counter to the policies of the Zionists, who saw only Palestine as the Jewish homeland.

But in Einstein's life, the decade of the thirties was most important because it marked his leaving Germany* and his move to the United States where, among other things, he met with Dr. F. I. Shatara, president of the Arab National League in the United States, in an unsuccessful attempt to start a series of peace talks. In 1933 Einstein was given a position at the new Institute for Advanced Study[16] in Princeton, New Jersey, which is where the Einsteins settled and where he would live the last twenty-two years of his life.

Still, as the decade of the thirties drew to a close and violence between Jews and Arabs intensified again in Palestine, before World War II brought about some changes (see following chapter), Einstein again spelled out his position on Jewish-Arab relations. Shortly after a 1939 attack in Palestine by Arabs against Jews, he declared: "There could be no greater calamity than a permanent discord between us and the Arab people. Despite the great wrong that has been done us, we must strive for a just and lasting compromise with the Arab people. Let us recall that in former times no people lived in greater friendship with us than the ancestors of these Arabs."[17]

---

*The Einsteins had left Germany in December 1932, just a month before Hitler came to power, for a temporary visit to the United States, where Einstein had a visiting professorship at Caltech in Pasadena. It was not until after the Nazis had seized power and raided their Berlin home, seized their property, and put a price on his head, that Einstein decided to stay permanently in the United States.

1929
Address to the Sixteenth Zionist Congress*
(July 28–August 14, 1929)

We all feel this is a great day for all of us. Allow me to say how I see and feel the greatness of this day. The Jewish tragedy of our age lies in the fact that the Jewish people is scattered and splintered. The individual Jew nowadays is isolated as such and suffers as a result of his isolation. This suffering has become a tragedy. How is it possible to find a solution for this tragic situation other than by establishing a home of our own? The man who realized that with unusual clarity was Theodor Herzl.

What Herzl saw was simplicity in itself, yet no one had realized it before him. Only a small group of people had concentrated around him. He realized that the Jewish people alone is capable of creating the movement that would break through that individual isolation. With the healthy instinct of a political genius, Herzl felt that that could be achieved through the rebuilding of Eretz Yisrael. Almost all opposed Herzl, in the fear that the idea might prove injurious to their status in the countries of their domicile—possibly might lead to a complete loss of status. Herzl, who knew that this was not the case, entered upon that onerous task which proved to be impossible from the political point of view, with a small group of faithful followers. Nowadays we have come to realize that Herzl had set them on the road to redemption. We must recognize

---

*Note the way Einstein begins the last sentence of his address: "We, the others . . ." These words indicate that at the time of this speech, Einstein clearly did not consider himself to be a Zionist.

that with all our hearts and express our deep admiration of his memory.

We must not lose sight of the fact that the rebuilding of Eretz Yisrael is an important and onerous obligation for all Jews and that this task also implies a great gift to us, and for that we must be indebted not only to the two great leaders, Herzl and Weizmann, but also to that courageous and enthusiastic minority that calls itself Zionist. We, the others, owe these people our national solidarity, and I believe that these people have the moral right to exert the strongest influence on the work that we who are gathered here, wish to do.

August 1929
"Jew and Arab," in *About Zionism*

Shaken to its depths by the tragic catastrophe in Palestine, Jewry must now show that it is truly equal to the great task it has undertaken. It goes without saying that our devotion to the cause and our determination to continue the work of peaceful construction will not be weakened in the slightest by any such set-back. But what has to be done to obviate any possibility of a recurrence of such horrors?

The first and most important necessity is the creation of a modus vivendi with the Arab people. Friction is perhaps inevitable, but its evil consequences must be overcome by organized co-operation, so that the inflammable material may not be piled up to the point of danger. The absence of normal contact in every-day life is bound to produce an atmosphere of mutual fear and distrust, which is favourable to such lamentable outbursts of passion as we have witnessed. We Jews must show above all that our own history of suffering has given us sufficient understanding and psychological insight to know how to cope with this problem of psychology and organization: the more so as no irreconcilable differences stand in the way of peace between Jews and Arabs in Palestine. Let us therefore above all be on our guard against blind chauvinism of any kind, and let us not imagine that reason and common-sense can be replaced by British bayonets.

But one demand we must certainly make of the Mandatory Power, which is responsible for the well-being of the country. Adequate protection must be afforded to those who are engaged in peaceful work. The measures devised for their protection must have regard on the one hand to the scattered position of the Jewish settlements, and on the other hand to the need for helping to smooth over national differences. It goes without saying that there must be adequate participation of Jews in the police force. The Mandatory Power cannot escape the reproach that this duty has not been fully carried out, quite apart from the fact that the responsible authorities misjudged the true state of affairs in the country.

The greatest danger in the present situation is that blind chauvinism may gain ground in our ranks. However firm the stand we make for the defense of our lives and property, we must not forget for a single moment that our national task is in its essence a supra-national matter, and that the strength of our whole movement rests in its moral justification, with which it must stand or fall.

Two Letters to Asis Domet
September 27, 1929

Dear Mr. Asis Domet!

Of course I remember you very well, and I have read the article of yours that appeared in the *Berliner Tageblatt* at the end of August with great interest. Generally, I completely share your opinion that it is necessary to work for the creation of an Arab-Jewish community that brings those two tribally related peoples closer to each other while excluding nationalist fanatics. As for your drama, I will study it in the very near future, and after that, you will be hearing from me again.

Yours with the most amicable regards

December 5, 1929

Dear Mr. Asis Domet!

A couple of months ago, I read, with great interest, your Palestinian drama. Its content, however, is so offensive for England that a participation in its performance would inevitably have generated harmful animosity. Because of a lapse on my part, at the time I forgot to inform you about this. Your article in the *Berliner Tageblatt*, occasioned by the beginning of the unrest in Palestine, I have read with great interest. In the main point, my opinion is the same as yours, namely, that it must be left to the Jews and Arabs to turn their coexistence in Palestine into a harmonious and pleasant affair, and that basically one should not rely on England's help in this regard.

Unfortunately, the poor state of my health doesn't allow me to visit the theater at such a late time. Therefore I'm sending back the three theater tickets with best thanks.

Yours with amicable regards

September 27, 1929
Excerpt from a Letter to Hugo Bergmann

Dear Mr. Bergmann,

To me, the events in Palestine seem to have proven once more how necessary it is to create a real symbiosis between Jews and Arabs in Palestine. By this I mean the existence of continuously functioning, mixed, administrative, economic, and social organizations. The separate coexistence is bound from time to time to lead to dangerous tensions. In addition, all Jewish children should be obligated to learn Arabic.

With kind regards,

AE

October 8, 1929
Letter to Willy Hellpach

Dear Mr. Hellpach:

I have read your article on Zionism and the Zurich Congress and feel, as a strong devotee of the Zionist idea, that I must answer you, even if only shortly.

The Jews are a community bound together by ties of blood and tradition, and not of religion only: the attitude of the rest of the world toward them is sufficient proof of this. When I came to Germany fifteen years ago I discovered for the first time that I was a Jew, and I owe this discovery more to Gentiles than Jews.

The tragedy of the Jews is that they are people of a definite historical type, who lack the support of a community to keep them together. The result is a want of solid foundations in the individual which amounts in its more extreme forms to moral instability. I realized that salvation was only possible for the race if every Jew in the world should become attached to a living society to which he as an individual might rejoice to belong and which might enable him to bear the hatred and the humiliations that he has to put up with from the rest of the world.

I saw worthy Jews basely caricatured, and the sight made my heart bleed. I saw how schools, cartoons, and innumerable other forces of the Gentile majority undermined the confidence even of the best of my fellow-Jews, and felt that this could not be allowed to continue.

Then I realized that only a common enterprise dear to the heart of Jews all over the world could restore this people to health. It was a great achievement of Herzl to have realized and proclaimed at the top of his voice that, the traditional attitude of the Jews being what it was, the establishment of a national home or, more accurately, a center in Palestine, was a suitable object on which to concentrate our efforts.

All this you call nationalism, and there is something in the accusation. But a communal purpose without which we can neither live nor die in this hostile world can always be called by that ugly name. In any case it is a nationalism whose aim is not power but dignity and health. If we did not have to live among intolerant, narrow-minded, and violent people, I should be the first to throw over all nationalism in favor of universal humanity.

The objection that we Jews cannot be proper citizens of the German state, for example, if we want to be a "nation," is based on a misunderstanding of the nature of the state which springs from the intolerance of national majorities. Against that intolerance we shall never be safe, whether we call ourselves a people (or nation) or not.

I have put all this with brutal frankness for the sake of brevity, but I know from your writings that you are a man who stands to the sense, not the form.

Albert Einstein

November 19, 1929
Letter to Heinrich York-Steiner

Dear Mr. York-Steiner!

First of all, I want to express to you my highest appreciation for your wonderful book, which I have read in total and whose thrust I fully endorse. It is very pleasing that this book meets with so much interest.

I have written various things on the occasion of the most recent conflicts with the Arabs, and thus I do not know what exactly you are alluding to. But in any case, you can reprint whatever you deem suitable.

I have come across Zionism only after my move to Berlin, in the year 1914 at the age of 35, after having lived in a completely neutral environment before. Since that time, I've been clearly aware that, in order to maintain, or rather, win back a decent existence, we Jews urgently need a reanimation of communal feeling. The only endeavor that leads us closer to this goal, I see in Zionism.

The time has come to take care that this movement avoid the danger of degenerating into blind nationalism. In my view, one must first of all strive to achieve the insight that resentment towards the Arabs must be replaced by psychological understanding and an honest will to cooperate with them. Overcoming this difficulty will, in my opinion, be the very criterion on which the conclusion that our community has a right to exist in a higher sense depends. Unfortunately, I must openly confess that I think that the attitude of our Zionist officialdom as well as the majority of public expressions in this connection . . . leave much to be desired.

Yours with affectionate and respectful regards

Einstein-Weizmann Letters of 1929

November 25, 1929

Dear Mr. Weizmann:

I thank you very much for your letter and can imagine that you are beset with difficult problems. At the same time I have to tell you frankly that I am concerned about the position of our leading personalities. Recently, Brodetsky has again treated the Arabic problem in a lecture with such superficiality, which has led to the present state of affairs. The economic and psychological problems of the Judeo-Arabic symbiosis were completely bypassed, handled as but an episode of conflict. This was even more out of place, since the discerning listeners would be totally convinced of the insincerity of such a point of view. I am enclosing a letter from Hugo Bergmann who, in my opinion, covers the essentials. If we are not able to find a way to honest cooperation and honest pacts with the Arabs, then we have learned nothing during our two thousand years of suffering, and deserve the fate which will befall us. Above all, in my opinion, we must avoid relying too much upon the English. Should we namely not be able to come to a real co-operation with the leading Arabs, we will be dropped by the English, perhaps not formally but still de facto. And they will with their traditional pious raise of eyebrows bewail our debacle amongst protestations of their innocence, without raising a finger for us.

With kindest regards

Yours,

A. Einstein

London, November 30, 1929

Dear Professor Einstein,

With heavy heart I reach for the pen to answer your last letter. I do not know how the speech by Brodetsky sounded, but what I have read in the *Rundschau* I believe cannot be objected to. It is possible that Brodetsky, who lacks the nuances of the German language, could not make himself completely clear. What are then the important facts? The Arabs have attacked us unexpectedly, wanted to destroy our settlement work, have murdered and plundered, and now we are pressed from all sides to seek ways and means to conclude a pact with the Arabs.

Already at the 12th Congress have we declared solemnly how we contemplate our living-together with the Arabs; everything which we accomplished in the land testifies to peace in our actions and thinking. Why did they attack us? Does anyone believe today that it is possible to negotiate with the Mufti [see footnote on page 136] or the Arab Executive? They would laugh at us, if we were to make attempts of rapprochement, despite what Bergmann writes in his articles. The present Arab leaders, murderers and thieves, only want one thing—to chase us into the Mediterranean!

I believe that negotiation with the Arabs is possible only under one condition, namely if the (English) government makes it clear to the Arabs that it has the firm intention to carry out the Mandate. If it does not do this, then the Arabs will believe—rightly so—that we are forsaken by England, and then they will not have much interest to unite with us. They do not yet understand, or do not want to understand, what we offer them and what a real friendship between them and us can offer the world. For that they are too primitive and also under the influence of factors, such as Bolshevistic and Catholic agitations. The Arab people has not yet spoken. For the people today speak corrupt Levantines, like the Mufti and suchlike. I have said it clearly to Ramsay Macdonald, and also have written it, that we are prepared to go to the negotiating table, but that he—Macdonald—has to make it clear to them that the Mandate, the National Homeland, etc. are chosen judges. If they will accept this, we will also accept a Palestinian Parliament, but it must be one which is not a dagger in our back. One of two things: either we come to Palestine in the name of our just right, or we are foreigners who creep in through their good manners and money. If the world does not recognize our just right, then this is a mistake of the world and a misfortune for us, and I know that the world has misunderstood us for 2000 years. We do not want to rule over anyone, but also not bow down to anyone or be ruled by anyone—enough of this!

The little Palestine was the only piece of ground where we could stand upright. Now come the Magneses, the Bergmanns and break up our united front, represent the matter so as if we do not want peace. Today they are quoted by NEAR EAST AND INDIA—a paper unfriendly to us—and a contrast between them and us constructed, only because we do not want to negotiate with murderers at the still open graves of the Hebron and Safed victims, because we believe in another tactic. The hypocrite—the Tartuffe—Magnes relinquishes readily the Balfour Declaration. He has not bled for it, he has only won by it. Believe me, I know the Palestinean Arabs. If we give in now, we can pack up and have to tell ourselves and the people: "The business does not succeed now, and we will wait and pray and mourn and hope in better days and a more just mankind, which will also understand the Jews."

You know from my past that I was never a hot-head, I have always preached to the Zionists the most unpopular realities. I also believe in an agreement with the Arabs; it is necessary for us, it is necessary for the Arabs and the English, but all three partners must act together and each give something. Until now we have given everything. . . . And this at the fresh graves of our brothers. The Arabs have not even expressed any regrets about the attacks. Now, of course, Bergmann and Magnes, and even you (and this hurts me most deeply!) are quoted against us and out of the mouths of murderers we are told: "Yes, if all Zionists were like Bergmann, etc." For centuries all enemies of the Jews have used this phrase and divided us through "separateness." We—I—who has fought all my life for peace and moderation, am the Hugenberg, and Magnes the Stresemann!

I hope better days will come, but now this is a dark period, and what makes my life most bitter is the feeling that your faith in us, in the justice of our cause has been shattered.

With a heavy heart,
Your most faithful
Chaim Weizmann

December 1929

Dear Weizmann!

I was very alarmed by your echo, because it showed me that I unwittingly caused harm with my letter. It never once entered my head to oppose you, and I opened my mouth only once, when I was compelled to by the delegate of the International Society against Anti-Semitism. I am very sorry that you spent so much time on a letter to me, from which I see that you do not assess my attitude correctly. It does not come into my mind that one should negotiate with the instigators.

I did not dislike Brodetsky's lecture because of its content, but because of what was missing: a causal psychological consideration of the events, and an honest reflection about preventative politics. Nothing is gained by recrimination, carrying on to the end, and leaning on England. It is true, the opponent has committed crimes. He was instigated, this is also true. But this analysis is superficial, and it is dangerous to be satisfied with it.

I know that Bergmann's words easily degenerate into accusations against us. But on this point he seems to be right: Without honest cooperation with the Arabs there is no peace and no security. This is for the long range politics and not for the present time. I really believe that one has missed much in this connection, but one should reflect upon it, and not fight against each other. In the last analysis—even if we were not practically defenseless—it would not be worthy of us to want to maintain a nationalism a la Prussienne. Do not answer me now; unfortunately you need your strength now too much. I will be silent, as much as I can, and will not meddle into anything.

I am returning your letter, which I have read carefully, to you, because my secretary is anyhow very much overworked. While I wish you and Palestine very soon and from my heart happier times I am with cordial greetings

Yours,

A. Einstein

December 4, 1929

Letter to Einstein from Selig Brodetsky,

Executive of the Zionist Organization, London

Dear Professor Einstein,

Ever since I addressed the meeting in Berlin at which I had the honour of having you among my audience, I have been very much affected by your remark to me at the end of my speech expressing obvious disapproval of my statement on the Arab question. I know, of course, that my German is sufficiently weak to account for my views being misunderstood. I therefore write you a few lines in order to make clear what I intended to say.

During the greater part of my speech, I endeavoured to make clear that our work in Palestine must be based upon a friendly attitude towards our Arab neighbours. I pointed out many respects in which our work had obviously benefited the Arabs, and I even said that I welcomed the fact that our health work in Palestine had produced the effect of causing the Arab population to grow in numbers faster than ever before, faster than the growth of the Jewish population with all the immigration which is taking place. I pointed out that the Arabs in Palestine will be our neighbours in the future, as they have been in the past, that Jews and Arabs will have to live side by side, that we Jews have no desire to do anything which can be interpreted as pushing the Arabs out of Palestine, or suppressing their own individuality as a people. I emphasized that the future of Palestine was dependent upon the two peoples, the Jews and the Arabs, living together in peace, each enjoying the fullest possible rights individually and collectively.

If, therefore, you characterize my remarks as being like those of Mussolini, then I must take it that you referred to the couple of sentences in which I ventured to lay down one or two fundamental principles. I said that our work in Palestine is quite impossible without the recognition and guaranteeing of the principles of the Mandate and the Balfour Declaration, namely:—the right of the Jewish people to bring as many immigrants into Palestine as the economic capacity of the country and the financial sacrifices of the Jewish people will allow, without such immigration being restricted by any political consideration; and further the right of the Jews who go to Palestine to build the Jewish National Home upon the basis of a national life. I said that if these principles are accepted by the Arabs, then the question of how to arrange for the Jews and Arabs to live side by side is one of comparative detail, and one upon which there should be no difficulty for an agreement to be arrived at between us and the Arabs.

It may be that I am not using exactly the same words as I used in Berlin two weeks ago, but the report in the *Rundschau* of this part of my speech is exact, and I leave it to you to judge whether you can characterize such remarks as being in any way chauvinistic.

I happen, personally, to be very advanced in my general political views. I am not only a Socialist; I am a firm believer in the fundamental necessity of peace. I do much work on behalf of the principles underlying the League of Nations, and in every way possible I do what I can in favour of peace ideals. In connection with Zionism, I have, ever since the emergence of the Revisionist party, fought this party and its militaristic ideals on every possible occasion; so much so that in England I am known as an outspoken opponent of any form of chauvinism and militarism in connection with the Zionist movement.

But chauvinism is not to be confused with calm firmness. If we wish to have a Jewish national home in Palestine, then the fundamental principles, without which such a home would be impossible, must be safeguarded and guaranteed. Otherwise, we would be simply leading the Jewish people astray, making them believe that we are building up in Palestine something which is to be of value to the future life of the whole people, while, in fact, we would be creating in Palestine a particularly impoverished Jewish minority, with no such status or rights as would distinguish it from Jewish minorities in countries like Hungary and Poland. I am absolutely opposed to legions of Jewish soldiers in Palestine. I want peace in Palestine, and I want to prevent the creation of a spirit of civil war between Jews and Arabs in the country. But this cannot mean that, as the result of disgraceful butchery, the Arabs are to receive such concessions from us or from the British Government as will, on the one hand, encourage them to use similar methods in the future, and will, on the other hand, make our own work so difficult as to be almost impossible.

The Arabs have stated quite clearly that they want self-government in order to prevent Jewish immigration into Palestine. It is therefore clear that unrestricted self-government given to the Arabs, especially as the result of their August attacks upon us, would be suicide on our part.

I hope you will appreciate the fact that you cannot characterize as the language of a Mussolini, a clear but firm statement that we must have the principles of the Jewish National Home and of Jewish Immigration recognized and guaranteed before concessions to the Arabs can be made.

I venture to trouble you to this extent because, as I need hardly say, any opinion expressed by yourself is one that carries the greatest weight with everybody, whilst I, in particular, have such a profound respect for your unrivalled intellectual achievements and for your noble idealism, that I am very anxious not to give you a false impression of my views upon a matter which is of such great concern to all Jews.

Will you kindly give my cordial greetings to Mrs. Einstein and my apologies for not having been able to greet her in person when I was in Berlin, as she disappeared before I could do so.

I am, with kindest regards,
Yours sincerely,
Selig Brodetsky

December 14, 1929
Response to Brodetsky

I'm sorry that my criticism affected you as it did. What I have against your talk is less what you have done but more what you have left unsaid. What's missing, specifically, is an analysis of the cause of the reaction of the Arab world against us—without which the question, in my conviction, cannot be solved. I believe it is my duty to express my opinion. But I have neither the time nor strength to participate in your polemic. I'm happy that we have no power. If national pigheadedness proves strong enough, then we will knock our brains out as we deserve.

Two Letters to the Editors of *Falastin**
February 1, 1930

Sir:

One who, like myself, has cherished for many years the conviction that the humanity of the future must be built up on an intimate community of the nations, and that aggressive nationalism must be conquered, can see a future for Palestine only on the basis of peaceful co-operation between the two peoples who are at home in the country. For this reason I should have expected that the great Arab people would show a truer appreciation of the need which the Jews feel to re-build their national home in the ancient seat of Judaism; I should have expected that by common effort ways and means would be found to render possible an extensive Jewish settlement in the country.

I am convinced that the devotion of the Jewish people to Palestine will benefit all the inhabitants of the country, not only materially, but also culturally and nationally. I believe that the Arab renaissance in the vast expanse of territory now occupied by the Arabs stands only to gain from Jewish sympathy. I should welcome the creation of an opportunity for absolutely free and frank discussion of these possibilities, for I believe that the two great Semitic peoples, each of which has in its way contributed something of

---

Falastin, one of the leading Arab publications in English, described by its editors as the "Arab National Organ," had published an article several months earlier that was critical of the Zionists.

lasting value to the civilization of the West, may have a great future in common, and that instead of facing each other with barren enmity and mutual distrust, they should support each other's national and cultural endeavours, and should seek the possibility of sympathetic co-operation. I think that those who are not actively engaged in politics should above all contribute to the creation of this atmosphere of confidence.

I deplore the tragic events of last August not only because they revealed human nature in its lowest aspects, but also because they have estranged the two peoples and have made it temporarily more difficult for them to approach one another. But come together they must, in spite of all.

Albert Einstein[18]

March 15, 1930

Sir:

Your letter has given me great pleasure. It shows me that there is good will available on your side, too, for solving the present difficulties in a manner worthy of both our nations. I believe that these difficulties are more psychological than real, and that they can be got over if both sides bring honesty and good will to the task.

What makes the present position so bad is the fact that Jews and Arabs confront each other as opponents before the mandatory power. This state of affairs is unworthy of both nations and can only be altered by our finding a *via media* on which both sides agree.

I will now tell you how I think that the present difficulties might be remedied; at the same time I must add that this is only my personal opinion, which I have discussed with nobody. I am writing this letter in German because I am not capable of writing it in English myself and because I want to bear the entire responsibility for it myself. You will, I am sure, be able to get some Jewish friend of concil-iation* to translate it.

A Privy Council is to be formed to which the Jews and Arabs shall each send four representatives, who must be in-dependent of all political parties.

Each group is composed as follows:

A doctor, elected by the Medical Association;
A lawyer, elected by the lawyers;
A working men's representative, elected by the trade
    unions;
An ecclesiastic, elected by the ecclesiastics.

These eight people are to meet once a week. They un-dertake not to espouse the sectional interests of their pro-fession or nation but conscientiously and to the best of their power to aim at the welfare of the whole population of the country. Their deliberations shall be secret and they are strictly forbidden to give any information about them, even in private. When a decision has been reached on any subject in which not less than three members on each side concur, it may be published, but only in the name of

---

*Einstein's reference to a "friend of conciliation" reflects his view that despite Arab resentments and anger, some among the Arab population want to find a way to work things out peacefully with the Jews.

the whole Council. If a member dissents he may retire from the Council, but he is not thereby released from the obligation to secrecy. If one of the elective bodies above specified is dissatisfied with a resolution of the Council, it may replace its representative by another.

Even if this "Privy Council" has no definite powers, it may nevertheless bring about the gradual composition of differences, and secure a united representation of the common interests of the country before the mandatory power, clear of the dust of ephemeral politics.

Exchange of Letters About Peru* with Max Warburg
April 24, 1930

Dear Professor Einstein,

The project "Social economy-based suggested organization of the Peruvian concession for settlement of needy and displaced Jews from the Eastern territories" has been vetted by two knowledgeable sources. Please find enclosed two copies of the evaluations, one part of a letter from a friend, the other from Professor Sapper of Würzburg.

---

*From 1930 to 1931, Einstein supported an initiative to settle one million Jews from Eastern European countries in Peru. To wit, this correspondence with Max Warburg. "The Peru initiative was an international one," according to Barbara Wolff, archivist at the Einstein Archives in Jerusalem, "or it was at least in contact with French and American groups. Others who sympathized with this project included Franz Oppenheimer and Emil Bernhard Cohn." Einstein was interested in the possibilities of setting up Jewish settlements in a number of places besides Palestine. See his support for the "China project" and the American Committee for Birobidjan. In all these cases, the Zionist leadership opposed Einstein, arguing that Palestine should be the only international homeland for Jews. Besides Warburg, Einstein wrote to the Jewish Colonization Association in Paris about Peru, and was surprised by their negative response. "It seems," says Barbara Wolff, "this project ran up against the Zionist-only initiatives."

Please handle the enclosures with utmost confidentiality. I am also enclosing an essay by Mr. Karl Sapper, which I will ask you to remit to me after your perusal as well. I have reached the conclusion that this suggested project is not viable and must not find our support. I had already got this impression from a cursory reading, but felt the necessity to have the entire proposal examined first by competent sources. The way things stand now, we cannot afford to be splintered. I am therefore of the opinion that we should focus our attention on Palestine, unless we are able to settle Jews permanently in their various countries of residence.

Yours truly,

Max Warburg

August 5, 1930

Dear Mr. Warburg!

In the two evaluations, I was primarily impressed by the comment on the great distance between the markets, or rather the convenience of public transportation. On the other hand, the climate of the region under consideration should, as a result of its altitude, not be tropical. Far be it from me to have any opinion whatsoever regarding the suitability of the territory in question. However, I am convinced that, in light of the difficult situation in the East, we should not discard any potential possibility *without investigation*. It would not be a risky undertaking to send over a few trusted people to study the area. Professor Oppenheimer deems the exploration of the region justified, based on research on the quality of the region under consideration. Of course I am also convinced that Palestine is of great *moral* significance for the Jews of the entire world. However, that land is surely not suitable for taking in masses of people.

This letter is merely a justification for my having troubled you in this matter.

All best wishes,

Albert Einstein

November 21, 1930
Excerpt from a Letter to Einstein in Berlin from the Jewish Colonization Association in Paris

Monsieur:

We have been advised by M. S. Rainach to whom we sent your letter of the 18th, to let you know the reasons for which the Council of the JCA believes it should not support the proposals for Jewish colonization in Peru. . . . We have also had several conversations with promoters of the project and let them know how we see things.

After having profoundly examined the whole question, our Council has reached the following conclusions:

1. The colonization plan would require considerable capital to prepare the immigrants and settle them in Peru;
2. It would be overwhelmingly difficult to enlist the number of people required to make the plan work—some 6000 families would be needed—and the work would be extremely difficult and physically grueling;
3. Adapting to the harsh climate of that region would be extremely difficult. . . . the heat and lack of re-

any settlement other than Palestine could be no longer called "zionism" and defeats the purpose of dipping under the mosque.

sources all contribute to our great doubts that any
success would be possible.

We regret that under such conditions we are unable to
take part in this project, and we hope that you will carefully consider the contents of this letter. Please consider the
contents of this letter as confidential.

November 28, 1930
Excerpt from Einstein's Response

I almost have the impression that the JCA aims at making it appear Jewish colonization is not advisable.

May 16, 1930
Letter to Bernard Lecache

Dear Mr. Lecache:

I have read your book with extraordinary interest and
am pleased about the great sense of justice that France,
again and again, continues to display in all matters, including those of concern to the Jews. Overwhelmed by other
correspondence, I unfortunately am opening your amiable
letter only today, which prevents me from sending the
timely message expected of me.

With regard to the question of Palestine, my most eager
wish would be that, by policies preserving the legitimate
interests of the Arabs, the Jews might succeed in proving
that the Jewish people has managed to learn something
from its own past, long ordeal.

With kind regards

June 19, 1930
Letter to Hugo Bergmann*

Dear Mr. Bergmann,

I completely agree with everything you have written me. But there is one point where I must make an exception. In case of conflict, a unified parliament can have disastrous consequences for the minority. It is necessary to find some way to guarantee our minority its existence and cultural self management. But apart from this, as I just said, I agree with you entirely. Only direct cooperation with the Arabs can create a dignified and safe life. If the Jews don't comprehend this, the whole Jewish position in the complex of Arab countries will become step by step untenable. *What saddens me is less the fact that the Jews are not smart enough to understand this, but rather, that they are not just enough to want it* [emphasis in original].

With kind regards,

AE

December 3, 1930
**Cable to the Zionist Organization of America, as
Reported in *The New York Times* (December 3, 1930)**

EINSTEIN ATTACKS BRITISH ZION POLICY

With all the nations involved in the present crisis, the Jewish problem is again felt in all its acuteness. We Jews

---

*Some months earlier, in a letter to Einstein, Bergmann had supported Einstein's call for equality between Arabs and Jews and asserted that the Jews should give the Arabs a chance to share in electrification of Palestine and should encourage more Arab schools, adding: "The difficulties in achieving this, are almost entirely on the Jewish side."

are everywhere subject to attacks and humiliations that result from the exaggeration of nationalism and racial vanity, which, in most European countries, expresses itself in the form of aggressive anti-Semitism. In such a time [there is] no other way than united participation in the rebuilding of the Jewish national home in Palestine. . . .

By means of modern methods of reconstruction, Palestine offers ample room for Jews and Arabs [to] live side by side in peace and harmony in a common country. I believe that the setbacks of last year must strengthen within us the recognition of our duty to improve . . . our relations with the Arab people and to convince them of the advantages Zionism creates for them.

December 6, 1930
On Board the SS *Belgenland** as Reported in *The New York Times* (December 7, 1930)

EINSTEIN SAYS JEWS SHOULD SEEK TRUCE
Urges Them to Treat Directly with Arabs in
Settling Differences
Non-Zionists Attack Him

DEC. 6—"Jews should seek to reach a direct understanding with the Arab masses and thus diminish the Palestine government's [British Mandate's] function as the arbiter of Jewish-Arab interests," Prof. Albert Einstein said today.

"I believe it possible to reach such an understanding," said Prof. Einstein.

---

*The Einsteins were on their way to the United States, where Einstein had a winter appointment as a guest faculty member at Caltech in Pasadena.

December 13, 1930
Excerpt from "The Jewish Mission in Palestine,"*
NBC Radio Address

In the first place, we must pay great attention to our relations with the Arab people. . . . avoid . . . those dangerous tensions which can be exploited to provoke hostile action against us. . . . [O]ur upbuilding of Palestine . . . serves also the real interests of the Arab population.

. . . For our community is not, and must never become, a political one; this is the only permanent source whence it can draw new strength and the only ground on which its existence can be justified.

December 24, 1930
**Letter to Rabbi Louis J. Newman, Congregation
Rodeph Sholom, New York City**

Very dear Mr. Newman,

I absolutely agree with you with regard to the road that should be taken in Palestine. I think that the creation of a mixed counseling entity which would consist of influential and well-meaning Jews and Arabs and would meet regularly within certain intervals would have to constitute the first practical step in this direction. It would be very kind of you if you would get into contact with Mrs.

---

*Two days after their ship arrived in New York, Einstein gave an address (*The Fight Against War*, 33–34) on NBC radio from Rockefeller Center. The speech was "organized by" Avukah, the American Student Zionist Foundation, which had a cultural Zionist outlook.

Irma Lindheim, 1 West 67th Street in New York, who pursues a similar goal and also has various connections to Arabs.

Yours respectfully

1931*
Excerpt from "Address on the Reconstruction of Palestine"

Today we can look back at these ten years with joy. . . . The latest pronouncements of the British government indicate a return to a juster judgment of our case.**

But we must never forget what this crisis has taught us—namely that the establishment of satisfactory relations between the Jews and the Arabs is not England's affair but ours.

We—that is to say, the Arabs and ourselves—have got to agree on the main outlines of an advantageous partnership which shall satisfy the needs of both nations. [This] is no less important and no less worthy of our efforts than the promotion of the work of construction itself. Remember that Switzerland represents a higher stage of political development than any national state, precisely because of the greater political problems which had to be solved before a stable community could be built up out of groups of different nationality.

---

*While visiting the United States.
**The British had just overturned the Passfield White Paper, a document published in October 1930 that sought to sharply weaken British support for the Jews in Palestine. Under pressure from the Jews, the British reversed themselves and adopted a new "interpretation" that returned to their previous support for the Jews.

February 16, 1931

Excerpt from an Address at the Ambassador Hotel in Los Angeles

A decade or two ago* a group of far-sighted men, among whom the unforgettable Herzl stood out . . . came to the conclusion that we needed a spiritual center in order to preserve our solidarity in difficult times. Thus arose the idea of Zionism and the work of settlement in Palestine. . . .

The difficulties we have been through have also brought some good in their train. They have shown us once more how strong is the bond which unites the Jews of all countries. . . . The crisis has also purified our attitude to the question of Palestine, purged it of the dross of nationalism. It has been clearly proclaimed that we are not seeking to create a political society but that our aim is . . . a cultural one in the widest sense of the word. That being so, it is for us to solve the problem of living in a neighborly spirit, side by side with our kinfolk and brethren, the Arabs, in a noble, open and generous manner.

July 11, 1932

Letter to Edward M. Freed, New York City

Dear Sir,

I am in favor of Zionism as it is the only endeavor capable of uniting the Jews of the entire globe.

To what extent the Jews are a racial community, that is without interest. It is sure that they share a common des-

---

*A relatively common error—it was actually some three decades earlier. Even geniuses make mistakes.

tiny . . . they are a community of destiny, and that they are in urgent need of mutual assistance.

I am not a nationalist and I do not wish any discrimination of the Arabs in Palestine. The Jewish immigration to Palestine in the framework of suitable limits can't do harm to anyone. It [the immigration] does not need to be based on any historical titles.

May 30, 1932
Letter to Samuel David Leidesdorf

Among the Zionist organizations, "Working Palestine" is the one whose work benefits in the most direct way the most valuable stratum of the people down there, namely those who by the work of their hands transform the desert into flowering settlements. Those workers are a selection, based on voluntary participation, from the whole Jewish people, an elite consisting of strong, conscious, and unselfish people. They are no uneducated manual laborers who sell the work of their hands to the highest bidder, but educated, spiritually alert, and free people whose peaceful battle with a neglected soil is to the direct and indirect benefit of the whole Jewish people. To alleviate their harsh lot as much as possible means the salvation of most valuable human lives, for the struggle of the first settlers on soil not yet sanitized is a hard and dangerous endeavor and a grave personal sacrifice. How true this is can be appraised only by those who have seen it with their own eyes. Anyone who helps to improve the equipment of these people supports the work in an effective manner.

This working class alone is also the only force which is capable to create healthy relations to the Arab people, which is the most important political task of Zionism. Administrations come and go, but in the life of and between peoples, human relations are finally the decisive factor. For that reason, support for "Working Palestine" also means both the promotion of a humane and dignified politics in Palestine and an effective fight against those narrow-minded nationalist sub-currents from which the political world in general, and, in a weaker form, the smaller political world of the Palestine work, is suffering today.

March 16, 1933
As Reported in *The New York Times*

EINSTEIN HONORED AT A DINNER HERE
Attack Upon Nationalism
as a Menace to Civilization
Marks Address to 1,000
He Will Shun Germany

. . . He declared upon his arrival yesterday that he "does not intend to put foot on German soil as long as conditions in Germany are as at present."

Q: "Have any personal threats been made against you?"

A: "I do not know of any," Dr. Einstein replied.[19]

Q: "Will you remain permanently out of Germany?"

A: "I have no definite intentions. It all depends on the situation."

Dr. Einstein combined an attack on nationalism as "a grave danger for the whole of western civilization" with a tribute to German culture, whose true representatives, he said, are now being subjected "to unworthy treatment" in their own country. He felt, however, that this was only temporary and was but a repetition of the not infrequent eclipse of cultural forces in other countries in times of political and social disturbance.

Q: "What is your view now of German culture?"

A: "Germany's contribution to the culture of mankind is so vital and significant that you cannot imagine the world without it. This must be specially emphasized at the present time when the genuine exponents of this culture are receiving unworthy treatment in their own country. This, by the way, has been the case not infrequently in many countries. The truly cultural forces are only a small part of the population everywhere, and this part has practically no direct influence upon political events."

In his address at the dinner Dr. Einstein denounced nationalism as moved by "powers inimical to life."

"To combat it is the inescapable duty of every well-intentioned and perceiving person of our time," he said. "As I myself am no nationalist, the meaning of a people, in my opinion lies in this—that it achieves something for humanity. The only worthy attitude of an individual, as of a nation is this—to serve a greater whole and to strive for improvement and ennoblement." *but that needs to start at home!*

Dr. Einstein pleaded for support of the Hebrew University in Palestine, saying that this institution was now all the more necessary because of the obstacles being placed for Jews in Eastern Europe in the sciences and the practices of scientific professions.

"In the course of the years I have heard much that is sad regarding this spiritual misery," Dr Einstein said, "and it is unfortunately not easy to say where the western boundary of this Eastern Europe is to be sought. In any case this boundary is indefinite and the psychical misery of the Jews is not lighter than the physical. Many talented Jews are lost to culture because the way to learning is barred to them. It will be one of the foremost aims of the university in Jerusalem to alleviate this misery. May it contribute to the attainment by the Jewish people of a spiritual and moral height which will be worthy of its past."

February 13, 1934
Letter About China* to Dr. Maurice William**
Dear Sir,

Your plan seems to me to be full of hope and reasonable, and its realization must be attempted with energy. The

---

*See footnote to correspondence with Max Warburg on Peru, page 90.
**New York dentist Maurice William campaigned in 1934 to have German Jewish refugees from Hitler moved to China (see Maurice Sokolow, "Dentist Who Changed History," *Harper's*, December 1943). On January 30, 1934, Dr. William sent Einstein a copy of his proposal, "China: A Possible Solution to the German-Jewish Situation," along with a note: "Mr. Emile Hilb has informed me that you would like me to send you some information about the possibilities of finding a new home in China for German Jews."

greatest challenge will be finding work opportunities in China. Those who have access to the collected money are the ones who have the responsibility to do so. Such difficulties are certainly surmountable but I can't help with this as I don't understand anything about the organization of these things. However, I can help search for suitable personalities if I'm convinced that the people there will really find a mode of living.

With friendly greetings

May 21, 1934
Excerpt from a Message to the United Jewish Appeal Meeting at the Hotel Commodore, New York City

If we Jews, as a scattered people, have sustained our existence through almost two millennia without any means of external power, we owe this to the fact that the teachings of our fathers have remained alive in us. The core of these teachings is understanding and help for all human beings, particularly for our Jewish brethren, connected to us by tradition as well as common fate. In order to save precious life, precious cultural goods, as well as the standing of the Jewish people in the world, such help is now necessary for the German Jews who, under the prevailing circumstances, are unable to help themselves. . . .

American Jews, you are called to show that the spirit of our fathers lives on in you, unbroken. You are called to show that love is stronger than hatred and persecution.

EINSTEIN'S EXCHANGES WITH THE
REVISIONIST (RIGHT-WING) ZIONISTS

April 20, 1935
Excerpt from "The Goal of Jewish-Arab Amity,"
Address at the Manhattan Opera House to the
National Labor Committee for Palestine, as
Reported in *The New York Times* the Following Day

JEWISH-ARAB AMITY URGED BY EINSTEIN

If Palestine is to become a Jewish national centre, then the Palestinian settlement must develop into a model way of life for all Jewry through the cultivation of spiritual values. I am convinced that the Histadrut is the embodiment of the best energies working in this direction. It is the strongest bulwark against all tendencies to poison the life of the community. It forms the most effective check on Revisionism, a movement which seeks to lead our youth astray with phrases borrowed from our worst enemies, and hinders the labor of most devoted pioneers.

Under the guise of nationalist propaganda Revisionism seeks to support the destructive speculation in land; it seeks to exploit the people and deprive them of their rights. Revisionism is the modern embodiment of those harmful forces which Moses with foresight sought to banish when he formulated his model code of social law.

Furthermore, the state of mind fed by Revisionism is the most serious obstacle in the way of our peaceable and friendly cooperation with the Arab people, who are racially our kin.

April 23, 1935

Excerpt from a Letter to Beinish Epstein, Leader of the Revisionist Zionist Party*

You certainly know better than I do that my characterization of the aims of the revisionist party was appropriate.

They borrow from the Fascists . . . methods that I abhor deeply, and use them to serve the interests of those who, relying on their ownership of the means of production, disfranchise and exploit the nonowners [*die Nichtbesitzenden*].

I am convinced that it is the duty of everyone who is serious about Zionism to fight your party with all available means.

It is my opinion that [the success] of your party would signify the bankruptcy of the Zionist objectives.

In my eyes, the revisionist approach to the Arabic problem is as ignoble as it is dangerous.

I can't understand why you want to hear all that from me; actually, you know it better and more precisely than I do.

April 28, 1935

Letter from Elias Ginsburg of the Zionist-Revisionist Organization of America

Dear Prof. Einstein:

Mr. Beinish Epstein has turned over your letter of the 23rd to me. I read and reread it and could not believe my own eyes. That a man of your responsibility and standing should permit himself to make such irresponsible and groundless accusations is beyond my understanding.

---

*This letter is in response to Epstein's initial approach on behalf of the Revisionist Party.

Since these accusations are made under your signature, I take it that you either have in your possession or you can readily lay your hands on documents and data which would corroborate them. If so, I must ask you to be good enough to either mail me copies of that evidence or else show me the originals and in that case, I am prepared to come to Princeton to scan them.

What I am particularly interested in seeing is the proof that we advocate a policy toward the Arabs which is "un-würdig und gefährlich [undignified and dangerous]," "that we seek to support a destructive speculation in land and to exploit the people and to deprive them of their rights."

Upon failing to receive such evidence within one week from the day of this writing, I shall be obliged to call you to a Court of Honor where you will be required to present that evidence.

Trusting to hear from you soon, I am

Cordially yours,

Elias Ginsburg, Chairman/ Central Committee

April 29, 1935
Letter to Salman Rubaschow of the League for Labor Palestine in New York City

Dear Mr. Rubaschow:

I am sending you a copy of the letter from Mr. Ginsburg; it seems that the calm in the little anthill is now a little bit disturbed. For now, I won't answer, but I'd like to ask you to collect material that enables us to answer effectively when a suitable opportunity arises.

Yours with affectionate regards,

AE

May 7, 1935
Letter from Elias Ginsburg

Dear Prof. Einstein:

Though instead of the seven days given to you in our registered letter of the 26th ultimo, we have waited for a full 10 days, no reply from you has reached us.

We hereby call upon you to appoint an unbiased judge, one who is not affiliated directly or indirectly with any of the Zionist factions, to examine your charges and the evidence in their support. . . . We shall . . . select one equally unbiased [and they] will elect their chairman and the three of them will constitute the Court of Honor whose decision will be binding on you and us. . . .

Your failure to retract [your statements] or to accept our invitation to appear before a Court of Honor will place you before the American people in a highly uncomplimentary light and your future public utterances will receive the evaluation they merit.

Sincerely yours,

Elias Ginsburg, Chairman, Central Committee

May 10, 1935
Letter from Salman Rubaschow

Dearest Professor:

It is only now, after my return from New York, that I have gotten your letters, and I greatly regret that, because of my absence, they have been left unanswered.

Your clear and decisive response to Mr. Epstein was a true joy for all of us. But this arrow has hit its goal only after it has itself caused such a stir.

As I see, [the Zionist Revisionist group] has already

pushed ahead and communicated this to its readers via
Ginsburg's last letter. It seems to me that it is high time by
now to allow ourselves to also publish your letter to Epstein. Should all of this really go to court, it will be an excellent opportunity for you to clearly and publicly state
your views once more. There will be no lack of material
which supports our claims. The staff of the *Jewish Frontiers*, which has published your Seder speech in its authentic
form, will assemble the necessary material and keep it at
the ready for that purpose. Of course in my view, and if
you agree, the only acceptable venue is the court of honor
appointed by the World Zionist Organization.

May 12, 1935
Letter to Salman Rubaschow
Dear Mr. Rubaschow:

After close consideration, I think it would be tactically
unwise of me to get involved in any argument with these
folks before any forum. This would only serve to provide
them with an opportunity for political advertisement, and
would be welcome nourishment for the anti-Semites. The
one thing perhaps useful to ponder is whether I should not
base my claims every now and then on the use of your material from the Jewish press. But even this seems doubtful to me
since the juxtaposition of argument and counterargument
would tend to weaken, rather than strengthen, the original
impression. Perhaps one could leave it at repeating my words
and supporting them without any commentary by some typ-
ical public pronouncements of revisionist politicians.

Yours with kind regards,

AE

June 26, 1935
Address at a Fundraising Dinner Sponsored
by United Jewish Appeal in New York City, as
Reported in *The New York Times* the Following Day

EINSTEIN FINDS JUDAISM IN PERIL

The basic nature of Judaism automatically imposes upon us as a community two kinds of obligations. First, we must be alert and prepared for sacrifice on the side of all those aspirations which have a moral goal similar to that described above; secondly, we must keep our community healthy and creative so that it may conserve and increase its value for the achievement of the great goal of humanity.

In such times as these, consideration for the preservation of Jewry comes foremost. Today it is our duty to put all available Jewish forces, if possible exclusively, at the disposal of the current relief activities. Particularly essential is it to provide help for the upbuilding of Palestine, for this work showed itself in this time of persecution as a refuge and as a moral support unparalleled among all other organizations, no matter how meritorious they may be.

Without Palestine, the horrors of recent years would have been even more terrible and the demoralization of the Jewish people far greater. With special gratitude, therefore, we remember Theodor Herzl today and the prophetic insight with which he foresaw the threatening danger in all its magnitude. He died early, a sacrifice to his superhuman efforts in the battle against misunderstanding and indifference. May our present generation prove to be at least worthy of him.

March 10, 1936

Statement to the Keren Kajemeth (Jewish National Fund) Celebration in Philadelphia

I have to protect my time as a miser surrounded by thieves protects his money, since otherwise it will be the end of all serious work. But all the same, they have succeeded in getting me to stand before you here today. How have they been able to enforce this? I will give away the secret, if you don't tell anyone I did. They said to me: The Jews of Philadelphia are the worst Jews in all of America; that's why you have to come to us. This argument finally convinced me.

But since I am pretty much the brooding type and don't like to employ a vague expression, I have to tell you more precisely what I mean by a bad Jew. A bad Jew is a person who neglects his duty toward the Jewish community. Such negligence, however, is a crime, since the Jewish community is a community of fate beleaguered by powerful enemies, which has an urgent need that all its individuals stick together in order to avoid its destruction. This is true, not only for the community, but also for its individual members, whose only protection and foothold is in their community.

Think of the fate of the German Jews, who by and large have also been bad Jews. Just think about what their future fate would be today, were it not, and had it not been, for the existence of the good Jews.

The thought about this last episode in our history, so rich in similar episodes, automatically evokes the thought of Palestine, which is now the only sanctuary for many of the expelled German Jews. They owe this solely to the fact that a good part of the Jewish people consist of good and

self-confident Jews who haven't sought and found salvation in gutless flight, but rather, in self-sacrificing work.

I assure you: There is not one good Jew who doesn't
stand behind the construction work in Palestine. On the
other hand, one can grow old and gray while doing religious lip service, and be a bad Jew all the same. However,
fidelity to the formal tradition and fidelity to the people go
for the most part hand in hand.

I, for one, harbor the hope to be hearing in a few years
from now: There is no need for you to come to Philadelphia. For here, the only Jews are good Jews.

April 17, 1938
Address for the Third Seder, National Labor
Committee for Palestine, as Reported in
The New York Times

3,000 HEAR EINSTEIN AT SEDER SERVICE
Against Palestine State
Division Might Give Rise to "Narrow Nationalism"
That Is Being Fought, He Holds

. . . Professor Einstein spoke in German at the Seder of
the National Labor Committee for Palestine, attended by
representatives of Jewish labor and civic and cultural life.

. . . While urging continued effort in the upbuilding of
Palestine as a Jewish homeland, he expressed himself as opposed to the British proposal for a division of Palestine between Jews and Arabs and the creation of a separate Jewish
State. He feared that the setting up of a political Jewish State
in Palestine might lead to the development of a "narrow

nationalism within our own ranks, against which we have already to fight strongly even without a Jewish state."

April 29, 1938
Excerpt from "Our Debt to Zionism"
. . . To be a Jew . . . means first of all to acknowledge and follow in practice those fundamentals in humaneness laid down in the Bible. . . .

We meet today because of our concern for the development of Palestine. . . . [O]ne thing, above all, must be emphasized: Judaism owes a great debt of gratitude to Zionism. The Zionist movement has revived among Jews the sense of community. . . .

Now the fateful disease of our time—exaggerated nationalism, borne up by blind hatred—has brought our work in Palestine to a most difficult stage. . . . [We must have] armed protection against fanatical Arab outlaws.

. . . Everyone knows that the riots are artificially fomented by those directly interested in embarrassing not only ourselves but especially England. Everyone knows that banditry would cease if foreign subsidies were withdrawn. . . .

Just one more personal word on the question of partition: I should much rather see reasonable agreement with the Arabs on the basis of living together in peace than the creation of a Jewish state. . . . [T]he essential nature of Judaism resists the idea of a Jewish state with borders, an army, and a measure of temporal power. . . . I am afraid of the inner damage Judaism will sustain—especially from the development of a narrow nationalism within our own ranks, against which we have already had to fight strongly, even without a

Jewish state. . . . A return to a nation in the political sense of the word would be equivalent to turning away from the spiritualization of our community which we owe to the genius of our prophets. If external necessity should after all compel us to assume this burden, let us bear it with tact and patience.

April 21, 1938
Letter from F. I. Shatara, President of the Arab National League

My dear Professor Einstein:

Permit me to congratulate you for your address delivered on April 17th, at Seder Service, Hotel Astor, New York City. The warning that you have uttered against the dangers inherent in Political Zionism finds ample substantiation in the current unfortunate events in Palestine. At a time when most Jewish leaders seem to have yielded to emotional romanticism, it is refreshing to hear from a clear-headed leader and thinker who has the courage to tell the truth no matter how unpopular the truth may be.

It is my humble opinion that if Zionists will follow your advice, the historic friendship between the Jews and Arabs will be restored, peace will reign in Palestine, and the two cousin races can then collaborate towards the upbuilding of a Semitic civilization.

This is a great task, which requires a great leader like yourself. If you will lend your efforts and prestige towards solving the Palestine problem, you will have rendered a service to humanity which will rival your immortal service to science.

Very truly yours,

F. I. Shatara

May 16, 1938
Reply from Einstein

Dear Dr. Shatara,

As I was traveling, my answer to your letter from 21 April was delayed. I was happy to receive your letter because the pitiful situation in Palestine can only improve through better communication and understanding. I think it would be most useful if the two of us could talk and try to strike common ground. If we should understand each other we can try to ask others closer to the conflict to join our discussion. If we don't reach a common ground, we won't have lost anything.

I would like to invite you here to Princeton for a visit as we would definitely not be disturbed.

Yours sincerely

May 24, 1938
Letter to F. I. Shatara

Dear Dr. Shatara:

Thank you for your kind offer. No interpreter is needed and for a first talk we are better alone. I propose next Monday afternoon (May 30th). The choice of the hour is up to you and it would be kind if you would inform me about it.

Very sincerely yours

May 30, 1938
Excerpt from a Letter to Samuel Leidesdorf

Dear Mr. Leidesdorf,

... Today, I was visited by the Arab Dr. F. I. Shatara (153 Clinton Street, Brooklyn). As a person, he has made a very good impression on me, and he has an optimistic stance toward the problem. He is in favor of striving for a—for now temporally limited—agreement, some sort of ceasefire for a couple of years, during which time the definite negotiations could then take place.

The plan is that initially, we list three or four men from either side, which we would then have to bring together for an informal conference. I think one person we should bring into this right from the start is Mr. Chaim Greenberg of the Histadrut, who has made a pretty favorable impression on me. Otherwise, people could get the impression that the Jewish Committee is the only force behind this effort. If you pick out the other two persons, a first meeting of our members could take place. I am attaching a few papers that Mr. Shatara left with me. You can give these to the men envisaged so far, provided that discretion in the whole affair is reliably guaranteed. Anyway, for now this is no more than mutual enlightenment about the ideas being present on the other side. Shatara assured me that Roosevelt would actively support an attempt at reconciliation for Palestine. He is apparently very interested in this.

Yours with affectionate regards

May 31, 1938
Excerpt from a Note to Otto Nathan
Dear Nathan,

Recently, I was visited by a very sympathetic Arab who wanted to initiate a peace action in Palestine. I will tell you about it later on.

With affectionate regards

July 1, 1938

Letter from Maurice Hexter at the Federation for the Support of Jewish Philanthropic Societies, New York City

Dear Professor Einstein,

The meeting which I told you would take place yesterday with Dr. Waldman, Secretary of the American Jewish Committee, Dr. Shatara, Dr. Amateau and myself, was very good.

I have the feeling, although it is only an inference, that Dr. Shatara has not been in touch with the Supreme Arab Committee, but has only been in touch with Dr. Tannous. We told Dr. Shatara that we attach great value to a meeting taking place between representatives of both sides, without any terms of reference, in order to see to what extent the area of conflict might be reduced. We further told Dr. Shatara that, unless the extremists of both sides could be brought to some sort of agreement, there would be no agreement, and that, in our judgment an agreement reached only between Jews in America with Christian Arabs (both he and Dr. Tannous are Christian Arabs) would not get us very far. We require agreement with the Moslems not only because they are the majority in Palestine and the surrounding territories, but because their group is the more extreme.

We suggested to Dr. Shatara the following procedure, which he thought worthwhile. He is to get in touch with the Mufti to see whether the latter would participate in such a conference, provided Dr. Weizmann and his group also agree. We are to get in touch with Dr. Weizmann to determine whether he and his group will participate in such a conference, provided the Mufti is ready to do so. Inasmuch as the Mufti probably will not be prepared to disclose his answer before he knows what the answer of Dr. Weizmann is, it was suggested that the answer of the Mufti be sent to Professor Hocking, or some other American whom he trusts, and that Dr. Weizmann's reply be sent to you.

We have still to determine who is to write to Dr. Weizmann. The thought went through our minds that you would be the best one to do so, and I would be grateful for your views on this matter.

Faithfully yours,

Maurice B. Hexter

July 5, 1938

Excerpt from a Letter to Maurice B. Hexter

Dear Mr. Hexter,

If it is your absolute wish, I will write to Mr. Weizmann. . . . Incidentally, he [Weizmann] has written me a letter where he complains about the very same speech delivered by me that caused Mr. Shatara to get into contact with me. . . .

I tend to think that it would be important as well as promising to get into contact with the people of Labor-Palestine, e.g., Mr. Chaim Greenberg, who, in my view, is a considerate and just man. The Labor-Palestine people's political influence is undoubtedly quite significant, and it seems to me that this group has a relatively independent stance towards the official Zionist administration, and that it should be more accessible to an effort at reconciliation than the political administration of Zionism. If we could win over this group, with its aid we would be in a better position to influence Weizmann and his friends with any prospect of success.

With kind regards,

AE

July 7, 1938
Letter from Maurice B. Hexter

Dear Professor Einstein:

Your letter of July 5th reached us this morning, and I confess there is a good deal in what you say. I will discuss your letter with Mr. Waldman and then advise you further. In the meantime, I think it would be excellent if you were to get in touch with Mr. Greenberg and sound him out as to the proposed demarche. I think it better that you get in touch with Mr. Greenberg rather than either Mr. Waldman or myself. At the same time, I would like to advise you that Mr. Shatara has not yet sent me the letter which he was to have done before sending it on to his Arab friends.

With kindest regards,

Cordially yours,

Maurice B. Hexter

July 12, 1938
Letter to Chaim Greenberg at *Jewish Frontier*

Dear Mr. Greenberg:

You certainly remember my speech, received with a certain skepticism in your circle, with the remarks about the Jewish state. As you know, as a reaction to this speech, I received a letter from the President of the Arab National

League in New York, Dr. Shatara, upon which, based on your words of recommendation, I had a conversation with him in Princeton. My personal impression of Dr. Shatara was that of an absolutely trustworthy and sympathetic person. We agreed that an attempt should be made to bring together people as influential and well-oriented as possible from both the Jewish and the Arab side to a meeting that aims at drafting a proposal for a preliminary agreement between Arabs and Jews in Palestine that avoids a partition of the country. The idea is that as a first measure, one should try to find five people on the Jewish and five people on the Arab side that then should hold the said conference.

Following the suggestion of Mr. Leidesdorf, the first thing I did was to address the former assistant of Felix Warburg, Mr. Maurice Hexter, suggesting to him to admit you into our confidence. He very readily agreed. Since I am located in a somewhat uncomfortable distance from New York, I would suggest that you give Mr. Hexter a call and have a preliminary talk with him. (71 West 47 Str., Bryant 9-7130.) Provided that you want to deal with the matter at all, you will then certainly be able to agree with him on the question of who might be the additional two or three personalities on our side you would like to join this effort.

With kind regards

July 12, 1938
Letter to Maurice Hexter

Dear Mr. Hexter,

Attached, you'll find the copy of a letter I have written to Mr. Greenberg. Perhaps you should not bother to wait for a call from him, since I do not know what sorts of internal and external resistance the man has to overcome.

With kind regards

August 2, 1938
Letter from F. I. Shatara to Einstein at Peconic, Long Island

My dear Professor Einstein:

I have not written to you previously because I knew that Dr. Hexter was keeping you informed of developments.

The Syrian Government is sending two delegates to the World's Fair. At last night's meeting of the Arab-Jewish group it was suggested to hold an informal and private conference between Jewish leaders, Arab leaders, and the two delegates, who will doubtless be able to give accurate information as to the possibilities of an agreement. Accordingly, I have this morning cabled Fakhry Baroody, the chief delegate, to ask him if he would be willing to participate in such a conference, and suggested that he discuss this with the Mufti and other Arab leaders before sailing August 8. If such a conference would be held here, I believe it will open a way for other effective measures.

I shall let you know as soon as I receive a reply as we are all counting on you to take an active part should this conference materialize.

Trusting that you are enjoying the summer and with kindest regards,

Very cordially yours,

F. I. Shatara

P.S. After dictating this letter, we received word that Fakhry Baroody left Syria and so the cable was not sent.

October 30, 1938
Address at the Opening of Congress House for Refugees

During the world war, the great Dutch physicist H. A. Lorentz once said to me: "I am happy to belong to a nation that is too small to commit great follies." By scattering us all over the world, fate has brought the Jewish people into a similar situation. We are a minority everywhere and have no violent means of defense at our disposal to protect our community against our numerous enemies and opponents—fortunately. The role that armies and the diplomatic corps supported by them play for other nations, for us is played by mutual aid and a tradition of appreciation and nurturing of intelligence and rationality. In former times, this tradition was primarily sustained by the religious form that permeated the whole life, a form whose inevitable gradual liberalization must be carefully compensated by an education towards social responsibility if the body of our people is to be kept healthy and vigorous.

With regard to his behavior toward society, the individual belonging to a small minority has an incomparably more difficult task to solve than any other person. How shall he behave vis-à-vis the Jewish community and vis-à-vis the wider community of all other human beings? An exhaustive conceptual answer to this question does of course not exist. Life is an art and no science, and in each individual case the decision must be left to the healthy intuition of the individual and the sympathetic understanding of the moment. The problem is made even more difficult by the fact that the best and finest Jews, the prophets together with Jesus Christ, as well as our best philosophical teachers, were for the most part cosmopolitans whose ideal was guided by the human condition in general. How can fidelity to the Jewish community be combined with a general humanistic outlook, with the concept of world citizenship?

In a humanity in which the ideals of charity and philanthropy were alive and common property, concern about the Jewish community would be superfluous; it would be limited to the sustenance of the religious and cultural traditions. But actually, we live in a world in which the Jewish people is surrounded by prejudice and threatened in its existence by hostile powers. The ignoble onslaught against us doesn't stop at any border—it is one partial symptom of an economic and political disease of all of Western humanity. This onslaught doesn't rage against us alone, but against the dignity and rights of the individual in general, against all expressions of a more subtle spirituality, an onslaught against anything that makes life rich and livable for people of a more dignified nature.

In such a time, internal cohesion and mutual aid among all Jews of all countries is the inescapable imperative. If only all Jews were ready to learn from the misapprehensions of the German Jews in the course of the last twenty years! For most German Jews, an international Jewish community did not so much as exist. In their own eyes, they were Germans and only Germans. For them, the "Eastern Jew" was nothing but a foreigner. If he was given any help at all, it was done in a condescending manner that was not exactly pleasant for the recipient of the benefaction. These German Jews slavishly copied even those ways of life of the Germans most alien to them, simply to make their environment forget their Jewish pedigree. How have I suffered under the lack of pride and dignity among these German Jews, something they themselves weren't even conscious of! A single political thunderstorm was sufficient to destroy all their illusions. In one stroke, they lost all those precarious goods whose acquisition they had bought by sacrificing their inner dignity and their peculiar traditional character. Materially and mentally broken, their only remaining protection lies in the help by those of the Jews in other countries who haven't lost their peculiar character through such a ruinous sort of assimilation.

I call on you to learn from the fate of the German Jews, and to preserve, by creating suitable institutions, the independence that you will need in the hour of affliction. You shouldn't have any confidence that this hour will never come, but should rather treat the international community of all Jews as sacred and untouchable. That way you will also render the best service to the recovery of the general international situation, because cleanliness and honesty are what is lacking most anywhere.

For these reasons, it is with particular joy and satisfaction that I welcome the work of unselfish help created by the women's department of the Jewish Congress through the establishment of the home for newly arriving exiled Jews. I have the highest esteem for the tireless work of Mrs. Stephen Wise, who has set up this house with love and expertise. None of those accommodated there will ever again forget what the brotherly solidarity of Jews who have remained upright means.

I call on you to see to it that this benedictional work can be continued, and that it can time and again anew encourage and bring comfort and aid to our persecuted brothers.

November 11, 1938

"Why Do They Hate the Jews?" in *Collier's Magazine*

I should like to begin by telling you an ancient fable, with a few minor changes—a fable that will serve to throw into bold relief the mainsprings of political anti-Semitism:

The shepherd boy said to the horse: "You are the noblest beast that treads the earth. You deserve to live in untroubled bliss; and indeed your happiness would be complete were it not for the treacherous stag. But he practiced from youth to excel you in fleetness of foot. His faster pace allows him to reach the water-holes before you do. He and his tribe drink up the water far and wide, while you and your foal are left to thirst. Stay with me! My wisdom and guidance shall deliver you and your kind from a dismal and ignominious state."

Blinded by envy and hatred of the stag, the horse agreed. He yielded to the shepherd lad's bridle. He lost his freedom and became the shepherd's slave.

The horse in this fable represents a people, and the shepherd lad a class-A clique aspiring to absolute rule over the people; the stag, on the other hand, represents the Jews.

I can hear you say: "A most unlikely tale! No creature would be as foolish as the horse in your fable." But let us give it a little more thought. The horse had been suffering the pangs of thirst, and his vanity was often pricked when he saw the nimble stag outrunning him. You, who have known no such pain and vexation, may find it *difficult* to understand that hatred and blindness should have driven the horse to act with such ill-advised, gullible haste. The horse, however, fell an easy victim to temptation because his earlier tribulations had prepared him for such a blunder. For there is much truth in the saying that it is easy to give just and wise counsel—to others!—but hard to act justly and wisely for oneself; I say to you with full conviction: We all have often played the tragic role of the horse and we are in constant danger of yielding to temptation again.

The situation illustrated in this fable happens again and again in the life of individuals and nations. In brief, we may call it the process by which dislike and hatred of a given person or group are diverted to another person or group incapable of effective defense. But why did the role of the stag in the fable so often fall to the Jews? Why did the Jews so often happen to draw the hatred of the masses? Primarily because there are Jews among almost all nations and because they are everywhere too thinly scattered to defend themselves against violent attack.

A few examples from the recent past will prove the point: Toward the end of the nineteenth century the Russian people were chafing under the tyranny of their government. Stupid blunders in foreign policy further strained their temper until it reached the breaking point. In this extremity the rulers of Russia sought to divert unrest by inciting the masses to hatred and violence toward the Jews. These tactics were repeated after the Russian government had drowned the dangerous revolution of 1905 in blood—and this maneuver may well have helped to keep the hated regime in power until near the end of the World War.

When the Germans had lost the World War hatched by their ruling class, immediate attempts were made to blame the Jews, first for instigating the war and then for losing it.

In the course of time, success attended these efforts. The hatred engendered against the Jews not only protected the privileged classes, but enabled a small, unscrupulous and insolent group to place the German people in a state of complete bondage.

The crimes with which the Jews have been charged in the course of history—crimes which were to justify the atrocities perpetrated against them—have changed in rapid succession. They were supposed to have poisoned wells. They were said to have murdered children for ritual purposes. They were falsely charged with a systematic attempt at the economic domination and exploitation of all mankind. Pseudo-scientific books were written to brand them an inferior, dangerous race. They were reputed to foment wars and revolutions for their own selfish purposes. They were presented at once as dangerous innovators and as enemies of true progress. They were charged with falsifying the culture of nations by penetrating the national life under the guise of becoming assimilated. In the same breath they were accused of being so stubbornly inflexible that it was impossible for them to fit into any society.

Almost beyond imagination were the charges brought against them, charges known to their instigators to be untrue all the while, but which time and again influenced the masses. In times of unrest and turmoil the masses are inclined to hatred and cruelty, whereas in times of peace these traits of human nature emerge but stealthily.

Up to this point I have spoken only of violence and oppression against the Jews—not of anti-Semitism itself as a psychological and social phenomenon existing even in times and circumstances when no special action against the Jews is under way. In this sense, one may speak of latent anti-Semitism. What is its basis? I believe that in a certain sense one may actually regard it as a normal manifestation in the life of a people.

The members of any group existing in a nation are more closely bound to one another than they are to the remaining population. Hence a nation will never be free of friction while such groups continue to be distinguishable. In my belief, uniformity in a population would not be desirable, even if it were attainable. Common convictions and aims, similar interests, will in every society produce groups that, in a certain sense, act as units. There will always be friction between such groups—the same sort of aversion and rivalry that exists between individuals.

The need for such groupings is perhaps most easily seen in the field of politics, in the formation of political parties. Without parties the political interests of the citizens of any state are bound to languish. There would be no forum for the free exchange of opinions. The individual would be isolated and unable to assert his convictions. Political convictions, moreover, ripen and grow only through mutual stimulation and criticism offered by individuals of similar disposition and purpose; and politics is no different from any other field of our cultural existence. Thus it is recognized, for example, that in times of intense religious fervor different sects are likely to spring up whose rivalry stimulates religious life in general. It is well known, on the other hand, that centralization—that is, elimination of independent groups—leads to one-sidedness and barrenness in science and art because such centralization checks and even suppresses any rivalry of opinions and research trends.

JUST WHAT IS A JEW?

The formation of groups has an invigorating effect in all spheres of human striving, perhaps mostly due to the struggle between the convictions and aims represented by the different groups. The Jews too form such a group with a definite character of its own, and anti-Semitism is nothing but the antagonistic attitude produced in the non-Jews by the Jewish group. This is a normal social reaction. But for the political abuse resulting from it, it might never have been designated by a special name.

What are the characteristics of the Jewish group? What, in the first place, is a Jew? There are no quick answers to this question. The most obvious answer would be the following: A Jew is a person professing the Jewish faith. The superficial character of this answer is easily recognized by means of a simple parallel. Let us ask the question: What is a snail? An answer similar in kind to the one given above might be: A snail is an animal inhabiting a snail shell. This answer is not altogether incorrect; nor, to be sure, is it exhaustive; for the snail shell happens to be but one of the material products of the snail. Similarly, the Jewish faith is but one of the characteristic products of the Jewish community. It is, furthermore, known that a snail can shed its shell without thereby ceasing to be a snail. The Jew who abandons his

faith (in the formal sense of the word) is in a similar position. He remains a Jew.

Difficulties of this kind appear whenever one seeks to
explain the essential character of a group.

The bond that has united the Jews for thousands of years
and that unites them today is, above all, the democratic
ideal of social justice, coupled with the ideal of mutual aid
and tolerance among all men. Even the most ancient religious scriptures of the Jews are steeped in these social ideals,
which have powerfully affected Christianity and Mo-
hammedanism and have had a benign influence upon the
social structure of a great part of mankind. The introduction of a weekly day of rest should be remembered here—
a profound blessing to all mankind. Personalities such as
Moses, Spinoza and Karl Marx, dissimilar as they may be,
all lived and sacrificed themselves for the ideal of social justice; and it was the tradition of their forefathers that led
them on this thorny path. The unique accomplishments of
the Jews in the field of philanthropy spring from the same
source.

The second characteristic trait of Jewish tradition is the
high regard in which it holds every form of intellectual as-
piration and spiritual effort. I am convinced that this
great respect for intellectual striving is solely responsible
for the contributions that the Jews have made toward the
progress of knowledge in the broadest sense of the term. In
view of their relatively small number and the considerable
external obstacles constantly placed in their way on all
sides, the extent of those contributions deserves the admiration of all sincere men. I am convinced that this is not

due to any special wealth of endowment, but to the fact that the esteem in which intellectual accomplishment is held among the Jews creates an atmosphere particularly favorable to the development of any talent that may exist. At the same time a strong critical spirit prevents blind obeisance to any mortal authority.

I have confined myself here to these two traditional traits, which seem to me the most basic. These standards and ideals find expression in small things as in large. They are transmitted from parents to children; they color conversation and judgment among friends; they fill the religious scriptures; and they give to the community life of the group its characteristic stamp. It is in these distinctive ideals that I see the essence of Jewish nature. That these ideals are but imperfectly realized in the group—in its actual everyday life—is only natural. However, if one seeks to give brief expression to the essential character of a group, the approach must always be by the way of the ideal.

WHERE OPPRESSION IS A STIMULUS

In the foregoing I have conceived of Judaism as a community of tradition. Both friend and foe, on the other hand, have often asserted that the Jews represent a race; that their characteristic behavior is the result of innate qualities transmitted by *heredity* from one generation to the next. This opinion gains weight from the fact that the Jews for thousands of years have predominantly married within their own group. Such a custom may indeed *preserve* a homogeneous race—if it existed originally; it cannot produce uniformity of the race—if there was originally a racial intermixture. The Jews, however, are beyond doubt a mixed race, just as are all other groups of our civilization. Sincere anthropologists are agreed on this point; assertions to the contrary all belong to the field of political propaganda and must be rated accordingly.

Perhaps even more than on its own tradition, the Jewish group has thrived on oppression and on the antagonism it has forever met in the world. Here undoubtedly lies one of the main reasons for its continued existence through so many thousands of years.

The Jewish group, which we have briefly characterized in the foregoing, embraces about sixteen million people— less than one per cent of mankind, or about half as many as the population of present-day Poland. Their significance as a political factor is negligible. They are scattered over almost the entire earth and are in no way organized as a whole—which means that they are incapable of concerted action of any kind.

Were anyone to form a picture of the Jews solely from the utterances of their enemies, he would have to reach the conclusion that they represent a world power. At first sight that seems downright absurd; and yet, in my view, there is a certain meaning behind it. The Jews as a group may be powerless, but the sum of the achievements of their individual members is everywhere considerable and telling, even though these achievements were made in the face of obstacles. The forces dormant in the individual are mobilized, and the individual himself is stimulated to self-sacrificing effort, by the spirit that is alive in the group.

Hence the hatred of the Jews by those who have reason to shun popular enlightenment. More than anything else in the world, they fear the influence of men of intellectual independence. I see in this the essential cause for the savage hatred of Jews raging in present-day Germany. To the Nazi group the Jews are not merely a means for turning the resentment of the people away from themselves, the oppressors; they see the Jews as a nonassimilable element that cannot be driven into uncritical acceptance of dogma, and that, therefore—as long as it exists at all—threatens their authority because of its insistence on popular enlightenment of the masses.

Proof that this conception goes to the heart of the matter is convincingly furnished by the solemn ceremony of the burning of the books staged by the Nazi regime shortly after its seizure of power. This act, senseless from a political point of view, can only be understood as a spontaneous emotional outburst. For that reason it seems to me more revealing than many acts of greater purpose and practical importance.

In the field of politics and social science there has grown up a justified distrust of generalizations pushed too far. When thought is too greatly dominated by such generalizations, misinterpretations of specific sequences of cause and effect readily occur, doing injustice to the actual multiplicity of events. Abandonment of generalization, on the other hand, means to relinquish understanding altogether. For that reason I believe one may and must risk generalization, as long as one remains aware of its uncertainty. It is in this spirit that I wish to present in all modesty my conception of anti-Semitism, considered from a general point of view.

In political life I see two opposed tendencies at work, locked in constant struggle with each other. The first, optimistic trend proceeds from the belief that the free unfolding of the productive forces of individuals and groups essentially leads to a satisfactory state of society. It recognizes the need for a central power, placed above groups and individuals, but concedes to such power only organizational and regulatory functions. The second, pessimistic trend assumes that free interplay of individuals and groups leads to the destruction of society; it thus seeks to base society exclusively upon authority, blind obedience, and coercion. Actually this trend is pessimistic only to a limited extent; for it is optimistic in regard to those who are, and desire to be, the bearers of power and authority. The adherents of this second trend are the enemies of the free groups and of education for independent thought. They are, moreover, the carriers of political anti-Semitism.

Here in America all pay lip service to the first, optimistic, tendency. Nevertheless, the second group is strongly represented. It appears on the scene everywhere, though for the most part it hides its true nature. Its aim is political and spiritual dominion over the people by a minority, by the circuitous route of control over the means of production. Its proponents have already tried to utilize the weapon of anti-Semitism as well as of hostility to various other groups.

They will repeat the attempt in times to come. So far all such tendencies have failed because of the people's sound political instinct.

And so it will remain in the future, if we cling to the rule: Beware of flatterers, especially when they come preaching hatred.

3

THE WAR YEARS

1939–1945

May 1939: The British issue a white paper, declaring:
- Only 75,000 Jews will be allowed into Palestine in the next five years;
- An independent Palestine will be considered in the next ten years.

The white paper enrages Zionists, who step up terror attacks.*

May 1942: The first international conference of Zionists in the United States is held at New York's Biltmore Hotel. The Biltmore Conference advocates—for the first time as a (public) Zionist position—that Palestine become a Jewish Commonwealth; Ben-Gurion calls for a Jewish army.

---

*The Jewish response to the 1939 British White Paper included: "Illegal immigration . . . intensified, new settlements founded, and stronger emphasis placed on military training for young people. . . . Haganah carried out several acts of sabotage . . . including destruction of a patrol boat used to combat illegal immigration" (Laqueur, *A History of Zionism*, 529–30).

November 1944: Zionists assassinate Lord Moyne, British minister of state, while he is visiting Cairo.*

In early 1940, the Arab Union of Railway Workers, which had virtually ceased to exist during the rebellion (1936–1939), resumed activity and met with their Jewish railway union counterparts in Haifa to draw up a joint list of their economic demands. And what was true for the railroad workers also held for workers in many other areas.

Among the many myths that decorate this history is the widely held perception that all Arabs, out of anti-Jewish bias, supported Hitler. There were some who did.** But

---

*Moyne was assassinated by the Stern Group, a Jewish underground paramilitary group that considered him an enemy of the Zionists, although only two days before the assassination, Winston Churchill, in a conversation with Chaim Weizmann, "hinted that Lord Moyne had moved to a position which the Zionists would find acceptable" (Laqueur, *A History of Zionism*, 542). Einstein saw the Stern Group and the Irgun as terrorists. (See Einstein's letter to Shepard Rifkin, April 10, 1948, page 187.)

**Muhammed Amin al-Husseini (there are many spelling variations), the son of the Mufti of Jerusalem and member of one of the richest and most powerful of Arab families, was appointed Grand Mufti by the British in 1922. Prior to his rise to power, there were active Arab factions supporting cooperative development of Palestine involving Arabs and Jews. But al-Husseini denounced them.

Though the Grand Mufti was a Nazi toady—he spent the war years as Hitler's guest in Berlin, advocating the extermination of Jews in radio broadcasts to the Middle East, and was later indicted by Yugoslavia for war crimes—this did not reflect the position of the entire Palestinian leadership. Al-Husseini's cousin Jemal, for example, was in favor of cutting a deal with Britain for Palestine.

There is conflicting evidence about the Grand Mufti's relationship with Adolf Eichmann. Some testimony at the Eichmann trial indicated that Eichmann helped finance al-Husseini's efforts, and Eichmann's deputy Dieter Wisliceny (subsequently

prominent historians also point out that the war years witnessed a new level of cooperation between Arab and Jewish
workers in Palestine.

Historian Zachary Lockman notes that as wartime activity brought industrialization and many more workers to
Palestine, it also brought wartime inflation and a sharp decline in real wages. With Arab and Jewish railroad workers
in Haifa and Lydda leading the way,* militant cross-cultural

---

executed as a war criminal) testified that the Mufti had been a collaborator and adviser of Eichmann and Heinrich Himmler and was one of Eichmann's best friends.

But Hannah Arendt, who attended the complete Eichmann trial, concluded in
her book *Eichmann in Jerusalem: A Report on the Banality of Evil*, that "The
trial revealed only that all rumours about Eichmann's connection with Haj Amin
el Husseini, the former Mufti of Jerusalem, were unfounded." Rafael Medoff concluded that "actually there is no evidence that the Mufti's presence was a factor at
all; the Wisliceny hearsay is not merely uncorroborated, but conflicts with everything else that is known about the origins of the Final Solution" (Rafael Medoff,
"The Mufti's Nazi Years Re-examined," *Journal of Israeli History*, 17, no. 3,
1996). Bernard Lewis also called Wisliceny's testimony into doubt: "There is no
independent documentary confirmation of Wisliceny's statements" (Lewis, *Semites and Anti-Semites*, 156).

"The Mufti's support for Nazi Germany definitely demonstrated the evils of
extremist nationalism," historian Tom Segev points out in a recent *New York
Times* book review, adding: "However, the Arabs were not the only chauvinists in
Palestine looking to make a deal with the Nazis. At the end of 1940 and again at
the end of 1941, a small Zionist terrorist organization known as the Stern Gang
made contact with Nazi representatives in Beirut, seeking support for its struggle
against the British. One of the Sternists, in a British jail at the time, was Yitshak
Shamir, a future Israeli prime minister" (Tom Segev, review of *Icon of Evil*,
"Courting Hitler," *New York Times Book Review*, September 28, 2008).

*Even as this is written, a new or freshly painted sign of Arab-Jewish cross-
cultural trade unionism has emerged: " 'Israeli and Palestinian Trade Unions Reach
Historic Agreement'—Brussels, 6 August 2008: The Israeli national trade union
centre Histadrut and the Palestinian General Federation of Trade Unions (PGFTU),
both of which are affiliated to the International Trade Union Confederation (ITUC),
have reached a landmark agreement to protect the rights of Palestinian workers em-
ployed by Israeli employers, and to base future relations on negotiations, dialogue
and joint initiatives to advance 'fraternity and coexistence between the two peoples' " (International Trade Union Confederation online, August 6, 2008).

trade unionism spread throughout the region: "The war
and immediate postwar years would witness not only an
unprecedented degree of cooperation between Arab and
Jewish railway unions but also unprecedented militancy,
highlighting trends manifested by other segments of the
Arab and Jewish working classes in Palestine, as well."[1]

The majority of Palestinians, including the Palestinian
Communist Party (which supported the Soviet Union), socialists, and antifascist Islamic circles were committed to the
anti-Nazi struggle. On the Jewish side, Hashomer Hatzair,
the left-leaning Zionists, as well as Jewish Communists,
played a key role in forging Jewish-Arab antifascist unity.
For many in Palestine, the war with its common enemy—the
fascists—had put the Arab-Zionist conflict on hold and increased a coordination of activities and planning among
many workers' groups, Jewish and Arab.

But the approach of the Zionist leadership was different:
"During the war, [Zionist leader David] Ben Gurion became
ever more assertive about the Jewish right to political sovereignty, while denying this right to the Arab majority in
Palestine."[2] Indeed, as early as 1942—before the Holocaust
had become a worldwide symbol of horror and genocide—
the Zionists adopted their "Biltmore Program,"[3] which for
the first time publicly called for Palestine to be declared "a
Jewish Commonwealth" after the war.

Einstein, meanwhile, in the midst of the wartime cooperation, reiterated his long-held position that Jews and
Arabs could and should simply agree on a binational
state. "I have no doubt," he declared, "that they [the Jews
in Palestine] will succeed in a good measure of cooperation with the Arab people if only both our people and the

Arabs succeed in conquering that childhood complaint of narrow-minded nationalism imported from Europe and aggravated by professional politicians. . . . [N]o rigid legal formula but only a lively mutual understanding and faithful cooperation in the daily tasks can open the right way."[4]

It may well be that Einstein underestimated the intensity of Arab nationalism and Arab (especially Palestinian) resentment toward the arrival year after year of increasing numbers of Jewish settlers in Palestine. While he criticized both sides for their "childhood complaint of narrow-minded nationalism," his implication that if Jews and Arabs could start to cooperate "in the daily tasks" a binational state was sure to follow was optimistic at best. The Zionist leadership clearly rejected any such partnership. But it also seems unlikely that years of Arab resentment could be so easily overcome.

Laqueur describes Einstein's attitude as "more than a little naive . . . for there were basic clashes between two national movements."[5] Stachel agrees, pointing out that as early as 1923, Einstein "listed debts and malaria as the main difficulties encountered by 'our workers on the land [and] in comparison with these two evils the Arab question becomes as nothing.' "[6]

Einstein, nonetheless, was always sharply critical of the wealthy landowners and politicians who constituted the Arab ruling circles. A two-part article published in *The Princeton Herald* on April 14 and April 28, 1944, and cosigned by Einstein and Eric Kahler, declared: "The rich Arabian landowners did nothing to improve the nature, the civilization, or the living standards of their countries. . . .

[T]he masses of the people are held in a backward and inferior condition."[7]

In fact, the anti-Nazi cooperation during the war among some labor unions and left-wing Zionists, as well as Arab, Jewish, and Islamic antifascist groups, gave rise to postwar activity, as we shall see, both within Palestine and in the United States, calling for the establishment of a binational state in Palestine with equal rights and equal power for Arabs and Jews.

January 12, 1939
Message to the U.S. Zionist Convention,
Washington, D.C.

In this time of difficulty everywhere, it is of particular importance not to forsake, in a mood of despondence, what has been achieved in Palestine so far by unspeakable efforts. Provided we don't let ourselves be disoriented by the hard experience of the last years, we will succeed in achieving a lasting accommodation with the moderate elements of the Arabs in Palestine, and in bringing our construction work for the benefit of the whole population of Palestine to a happy end.

We should desist from trying to inspire the illusion that the whole current problem of enforced Jewish migration could be solved by Palestine. We should, however, also be vividly conscious of the fact that our position in Palestine has made it possible to offer many of our persecuted brothers a sanctuary befitting human beings. Once more, this shows that often actions engendered by true idealism also turn out to be valuable in a practical sense. The greatest achievement of the Zionist work, however, remains that it has animated this idealism to an extent hitherto unknown. It is only such idealism that works of voluntary mutual help grow from, as well as that happy self-assurance of the community which has already in the past enabled us to survive all persecution and oppression.

March 21, 1939
"The Dispersal of European Jewry," CBS Radio Address for the United Jewish Appeal

The history of the persecutions which the Jewish people have had to suffer is almost inconceivably long. Yet the war that is being waged against us in Central Europe today falls into a special category of its own. In the past we were persecuted despite the fact that we were the people of the Bible; today, however, it is just because we are the people of the Book that we are persecuted. The aim is to exterminate not only ourselves but to destroy, together with us, that spirit expressed in the Bible and in Christianity which made possible the rise of civilization in Central and Northern Europe. If this aim is achieved Europe will become a barren waste. For human community life cannot long endure on a basis of crude force, brutality, terror, and hate.

Only understanding for our neighbors, justice in our dealings, and willingness to help our fellow men can give human society permanence and assure security for the individual. Neither intelligence nor inventions nor institutions can serve as substitutes for these most vital parts of education.

Many Jewish communities have been uprooted in the wake of the present upheaval in Europe. Hundreds of thousands of men, women, and children have been driven from their homes and made to wander in despair over the highways of the world. The tragedy of the Jewish people today is a tragedy which reflects a challenge to the fundamental structure of modern civilization.

One of the most tragic aspects of the oppression of Jews and other groups has been the creation of a refugee class. Many distinguished men in science, art, and literature have been driven from the lands which they enriched with their talents. In a period of economic decline these exiles have within them the possibilities for reviving economic and cultural effort; many of these refugees are highly skilled experts in industry and science. They have a valuable contribution to make to the progress of the world. They are in a position to repay hospitality with new economic development and the opening up of new opportunities of employment for native populations. I am told that in England the admission of refugees was directly responsible for giving jobs to 15,000 unemployed.

As one of the former citizens of Germany who have been fortunate enough to leave that country, I know I can speak for my fellow refugees, both here and in other countries, when I give thanks to the democracies of the world for the splendid manner in which they have received us. We, all of us, owe a debt of gratitude to our new countries, and each and every one of us is doing the utmost to show our gratitude by the quality of our contributions to the economic, social, and cultural work of the countries in which we reside.

It is, however, a source of gravest concern that the ranks of the refugees are being constantly increased. The developments of the past week have added several hundred thousand potential refugees from Czechoslovakia. Again we are confronted with a major tragedy for a Jewish community which had a noble tradition of democracy and communal service.

The power of resistance which has enabled the Jewish people to survive for thousands of years is a direct outgrowth of Jewish adherence to the Biblical doctrines on the relationships among men. In these years of affliction our readiness to help one another is being put to an especially severe test. Each of us must personally face this test, that we may stand it as well as our fathers did before us. We have no other means of self-defense than our solidarity and our knowledge that the cause for which we are suffering is a momentous and sacred cause.

May 28, 1939
Address at the Opening of the Palestinian Pavilion at the New York World's Fair

The World's Fair is something akin to an image of humanity and its current knowledge and ambition. But on the other hand in a way it shows the world of human beings like a wishful dream, inasmuch as only the creative powers are on display, but not the dark, destructive powers which today, more than in a long time before, call into question the happiness, and even the very existence, of civilized humanity.

Despite its one-sided character, this account is entirely justified. For anyone who has learned to appreciate and admire the positive ambitions of man will also be willing to act with all his forces for the defense of the achieved, and if necessary to fight for it. It is my beautiful duty here to officially hand over this building, which my Palestinian brethren have dedicated to the World's Fair. What the appreciative observer will notice in this work is probably the elegant, noble calm that emanates from it, a spirit of plain, quiet harmony. There are a tiny people in Palestine that see themselves threatened in their position, conquered by hard work and great sacrifice, by the political intrigues of the powers and by bloody acts of violence committed by an incited mob. They are confronted by constant raids, and everyone living there has to strive for the preservation of his life through a hard economic struggle for existence. Of all this, nothing is revealed here. There is just a house with quiet, noble lines, and in it, a presentation of the nature of a Palestinian new, and at the same time ancient homeland, as well as an exemplification of what productive work is creating there. To express themselves that way, only a people are capable that have found, in a deeply rooted tradition, a sort of inner security which has stood the test of time during the millennia of an extremely grim history.

May the dignified artistic spirit of those who have created this work be appreciated by sympathetic spectators.

April 22, 1941
Address to Friends of Hebrew University
at Columbia University

We Jews are a group of human beings bound together by age-old traditions, but without any organized unity. Perhaps we might long ago have been absorbed among the nations created by geographical or linguistic factors, had it not been that outside pressure isolated our more or less common pattern of suffering, again and again delimited it sharply; and united us, at least locally, for mutual assistance.

The fateful developments of recent years have accentuated this isolation and solidarity to a degree far greater than could have been anticipated, turning our voluntary and devoted cooperation into a simple law of self-preservation. This cooperation has as its first goal the sheer saving of life. But we must also stand together to preserve and foster the spiritual and intellectual values which have given us our peculiar vigour and cultural significance in the frame of human society.

You all know how important a part our constructive work in Palestine has played in this work of consolidation and defense. It has rescued valuable elements from destruction and given new strength to our sorely pressed people all over the world. It has created institutions whose vigorous development is not only vitally significant for the work in Palestine but also of potential importance to the Jewish people as a whole.

In this connection the Hebrew University stands in the first rank. Under difficult material conditions, through the selfless and tireless labor of some excellent scholars it already shows considerable achievement not only as an educational institution but also in some fields of purely scientific research as well.

In the development of the medical-biological department at the University, the organized assistance of Jewish medical men in the United States has played a decisive part. On the other hand, no advantage has been taken of the opportunity to enlist the services of scientists in other fields. It is due to the initiative of certain men to whom the University is already indebted that we have come together today to fill these gaps. It will be possible for us to assist certain promising undertakings which up till now have been restricted in means and connections, and give them a chance for fruitful development.

You will rejoice to put yourselves at the service of this work. Regard it not alone as a kind of charitable activity, but also as a source of strength which will profit in its turn the whole Jewish community.

Do not be intimidated by the perils which seem now to threaten even Palestine itself. For whatever may come, resolute cooperation is our only refuge in these heavy times. Things can only work out for good, if we summon all our strength and pull together.

June 14, 1942
Letter from Kurt Blumenfeld

Dear Professor Einstein—

In the attachment, I'm sending you the draft of a letter to Mr. Lapson for the event of the Jewish Culture Council.

I think that the unexaggerated form of this letter is congenial to your outlook, and that you will do a good service to the work of the Jewish Culture Council by sending it. If you agree with the message, I'd like to ask you to have it typed on your personal stationary and to send it back to me, complete with your signature, in the envelope I am attaching.

With best thanks and affectionate regards—very respectfully

June 1942
Letter to Kurt Blumenfeld

Dear Mr. Blumenfeld,

I thank you for the excellent draft. I wouldn't have been able to work out such a good piece on my own, which is why I feel pretty much like a plagiarist and am ashamed to put my signature beneath it. Out of this feeling, while the remarks are quite good, I have deleted some of them in order to avoid highlighting this actually quite minor affair.*

June 20, 1945
Letter to Joseph Levy

My dear Mr. Levy:

I thank you for your telegram inviting me to join a Jewish Citizens Committee to protest the excommunication of Dr. Mordecai Kaplan by the Union of Orthodox Rabbis. However, I have come to the decision not to join your committee because to take these fools in clerical garb seriously is to show them too much honor.

Yours very sincerely,
Albert Einstein

---

*While a number of Einstein's letters and essays on Zionism were drafted by others, especially Blumenfeld, it was not uncommon for Einstein to revise or reject such drafts.

4

STRUGGLE OVER THE STATE

1945–1948

August 1945: The Twenty-second World Zionist Congress demands immediate admission of one hundred thousand Jewish refugees to Eretz Israel. Britain refuses, prompting violent revolts by the Jewish underground in Palestine. (Einstein attacks the Jewish underground groups.*)

May 13, 1948: Weizmann writes to Truman asking him to "Promptly recognize the provisional government of Israel."

T he war is won but the peace is not," Einstein told the Nobel Prize anniversary dinner in 1945 at New York's

---

*Einstein was sharply and publicly critical of the Jewish underground paramilitary groups, such as the Irgun and the Stern Group. In his words, "I regard it [the Irgun] as a disaster" (interview with I. Z. David). Also: "I am not willing to see anybody associated with those misled and criminal people" (letter to Shepard Rifkin). Also see letter from Einstein and others, criticizing Menachem Begin, pages 213–16.

Irgun — Rahm Emanuel's father belonged to this group!

Astor Hotel. Even as he rejoiced at the defeat of Nazism, he warned against colonial exploitation and the arms race.[1] He argued against leaving Jews indefinitely in displaced persons camps, calling for both the admission of Jewish refugees into the United States and their settlement in Palestine. At the same time, he continued to make it clear that he opposed the idea of a Jewish state.

While the Zionist leadership was negotiating for support from world leaders for the partition of Palestine and the building of an armed force (with financial aid from Jews in the United States and elsewhere), a lesser-known but perhaps historically as significant movement was under way—in the United States and other countries as well as inside Palestine—opposing the establishment of a Jewish state.

The World War II years of cooperation gave rise to new postwar activity, within Palestine and in the United States, by groups calling for the establishment of a binational state in Palestine with complete equality for Arabs and Jews.

"Curiously" is the word Lockman chooses for the fact that even as Arab-Jewish tension and violence were rising throughout Palestine, the same period saw "an unprecedented level of joint struggle among Arab and Jewish workers in pursuit of common economic goals, along with strenuous (if ultimately futile) efforts by Arab and Jewish political forces to seek a peaceful resolution of the . . . crisis."

Among the Arab groups involved in this bipartisan peace effort, the National Liberation League and the Arab Workers' Congress "continued to insist on preserving the long-standing ideological distinction [cited frequently by Arab Communist Parties] between Zionism and the Jewish masses in Palestine." In a 1945 article, a representative of

the Palestine Arab Workers clearly distinguished "between
the Zionist movement as an exploitative movement and
the Jews, the Jewish workers specifically, as a minority [in
Palestine]" and called for "an independent national regime
[to] ensure all just national rights to the Jews and the other
minorities settled in Palestine."[2]

The highlight of this period of united action was a general
strike that Lockman calls "the largest and most dramatic
episode of joint action between Arab and Jewish workers in
the history of Palestine."[3] Begun in April 1946, by Arab and
Jewish postal workers, the strike quickly spread to railway
workers and then white-collar government employees—in
every case, both Arabs and Jews. By mid-April, less than a
week after the first postal workers went out, Lockman reports that the strike had spread to some twenty-three thousand employees of the Palestine government. Although top
Arab and Zionist leaders did their best to limit and dampen
the strike, the workers won significant demands, including
pay and pension increases.[4]

At the same time, the movement among dissident Jews,
including those in the United States, for Arab-Jewish cooperation and for a binational state in Palestine was more active
than ever—even as the Zionist leaders in Palestine continued
to negotiate for a Jewish state.[5] The dissident movement was
led by Judah Magnes, president of the Hebrew University,
and included Henrietta Szold, one of the founders of the
New Women's Zionist Organization, or Hadassah (which
became the world's largest Zionist organization), and Martin Buber (then a professor of Jewish philosophy at Hebrew
University). Magnes and Szold established an organization
called Ihud (Unity), which described itself as "the movement

for Arab-Jewish rapprochement."[6] Ihud called repeatedly for peace and a binational state in Palestine, as several *New York Times* articles reported early in 1948[7]—only weeks before the declaration of the state of Israel in May:

MAGNES IN NEW PLEA FOR
PALESTINE PEACE (March 11)

HOLY LAND TRUCE URGED (March 27)

TRUCE CALL HAILED BY MAGNES
GROUP (March 29)

Other dissidents, including Einstein and Hannah Arendt, while not members of Magnes's organization, were among the more outspoken on this issue. As early as January 1946, Einstein had testified before the Anglo-American Committee of Inquiry on Palestine, arguing against the idea of a Jewish state.[8]

Einstein's testimony disturbed many Zionists, including his friend Rabbi Stephen Wise, who asked Einstein to sign the following statement, clarifying Einstein's views and specifically not advocating a binational state in Palestine:

A National Home I consider a territory in which the Jews have such rights that they can integrate freely within the limits of the economic absorptive possibilities and they can purchase land without undue encroachment upon the Arab population. The Jews should have the right of cultural autonomy, their language should be one of the languages of the country, and a government should exist,

working under strict constitutional rules that guar-
antee to both groups that no "Majoritization" of
one group by the other is possible. There must be
no discriminatory laws against the interest of either
group.

Einstein agreed to sign Wise's draft but was clearly not satisfied and sent Wise the following sentence to be added: "I am firmly convinced that a rigid demand for a 'Jewish State' will have only undesirable results for us."[9]

Like Henrietta Szold, most of these Jewish dissidents advocating a binational state considered themselves Zionists or friends of Zionism. But theirs was a different Zionism. Just as Christianity comes in thirty-nine different flavors, each with its own strains and schisms, so, albeit on a smaller scale, there have been—and still are—many Zionisms: labor Zionism, Revisionist Zionism, political Zionism, socialist Zionism, cultural Zionism, territorial Zionism, and many more.

In this case, the dissidents, including Einstein, were primarily identified with what has been called cultural Zionism,[10] emphasizing the establishment of cultural and educational centers among Jews, not a political nation with borders and therefore armies to protect the borders. The cultural Zionists advocated complete equality for Arabs and Jews, primarily through the establishment of a binational state.

The cultural Zionist movement included some of the most highly respected Jewish leaders in the world. The American gadfly journalist I. F. Stone—himself a cultural

Zionist*—points out that the highly respected German-Jewish philosopher Martin Buber "saw relations with the Arabs as crucial" to "Hebrew humanism": "He set forth the idea of a bi-national state as early as 1921 in a proposal to the Zionist Congress held that year [that] the Congress officially proclaim 'its desire to live in peace and brotherhood with the Arab people and to develop the common homeland into a republic in which both peoples will have the possibility of free development.' "[11] (Today, cultural Zionism is omitted from most histories.)

One of the dissidents' most dramatic—and effective—actions was the December 1948 letter (published in *The New York Times*) that Einstein cosigned with Hannah Arendt, Seymour Melman, Sidney Hook, and a number of others—as Menachem Begin was about to visit the United States. The letter denounced Begin and his party as "closely akin in its organization, methods, political philosophy and social appeal to the Nazi and Fascist parties." (Full text of the letter is on pages 213–16.)

Begin had been the commander of the Irgun, the underground, right-wing Zionist military organization responsible for bombing, among other civilian targets, the King David Hotel in Jerusalem in 1946, killing nearly one hundred

---

*"Although I was very much a Zionist and still am, I was very proud of Einstein," Stone declared after hearing Einstein's testimony before the Anglo-American Commission (Stone covered the hearings for the liberal New York newspaper *PM*), explaining, "To have the greatest Jewish figure of the period oppose a Jewish state as unfair to the Arabs was a very noble thing" (Brian, *Einstein*, 349).

people, and "indiscriminate bomb throwing in Arab markets and at bus stations"[12] Einstein was sharply and publicly critical of the Jewish underground paramilitary groups, such as the Irgun and the Stern Group. In his words, "I regard it [the Irgun] as a disaster."[13]

The letter in the *Times* convinced numerous leaders of American society, including then congressman John F. Kennedy, to cancel their previously scheduled meetings with Begin.

Einstein himself was quite clear on his position, reiterating it in statements, letters, and especially in response to questions. As early as June 1921 he had declared: "The object which the leaders of Zionism have before their eyes is not a political but a social and cultural one."[14]

Despite the scanty attention paid to dissident Zionism in the mainstream media, Einstein was fully aware of its significance. When the Hungarian journalist Bela Kornitzer interviewed Einstein in early 1948, he asked, "What is your opinion about Palestine? Do you think partition is a solution? What would be your plan?" Einstein answered: "Cooperation with Arabs."[15]

Indeed, the centerpieces of Einstein's Zionism, foremost in his vision of the new society, were mutual respect and friendship between Arabs and Jews, and equality—equal rights and equal power. This, in turn, meant that there could not be a Jewish state, as full equal rights would be impossible if one group or the other ran the government. It meant a binational state built along the lines of the Swiss model, which Einstein viewed as "a higher stage of political development than any [other] national state, precisely because of the greater political problems which had to be solved before a stable community could be built up out of groups of different nationality."[16]

In one of his last letters, Einstein wrote (to Zvi Lurie): "The most important aspect of our policy must be our ever-present, manifest desire to institute complete equality for the Arab citizens living in our midst. . . . The attitude we adopt toward the Arab minority will provide the real test of our moral standards as a people."[17]

In today's world, that hardly sounds like Zionism—and even in 1955, it was far from the Zionist mainstream. But those, like Stachel, who have studied Einstein's Judaism have pointed out that his commitment to religion was not mainstream, either. "Einstein's Judaism, his *concept* of Judaism was fundamentally humanitarian: As quoted by Stachel, Einstein believed that "the bond that has united the Jews for thousands of years and that unites them today is, above all, the democratic ideal of social justice, coupled with the ideal of mutual aid and tolerance among all men."[18]

This is a long way from the Chosen People concept of Judaism, and its emphasis on social justice, mutual aid, and tolerance goes a long way toward explaining Einstein on Zionism. Einstein had expanded on this theme in *Jüdische Rundschau,* where he had criticized Jews for their tendency to form their own national groups: "This seems regrettable to Jews like myself who consider membership in the human species as the ideal, possible to attain even though difficult." In quoting this, Einstein biographer Ronald Clark points out that "as practical Zionist aims narrowed to nation-state or nothing, such internationalist and pacifist leanings began to make Einstein's position within the Zionist movement frequently difficult and sometimes anomalous."[19]

November 2, 1945
Letter to Judge Jerome Frank*

Dear Judge Frank:

I thank you for your kind letter of November 8th. Your arguments,** however, do not convince me. Anti-Semitism and Jew-baiting did flourish very well before Zionism was born. The Gentiles had always "reasons" to justify their behavior; in this respect, there may be little difference between the Americans and other people.

The cause for the fact that we Jews are a "separate people" is not only that *we* have the desire to set ourselves apart, but that we are treated and persecuted as a separate people. I believe we have to accept this fact and cherish the solidarity of all Jewry independent of all questions of religion. Zionism has the great merit that it has contributed to make all Jews in all countries conscious of that fact; Zionism has also a very good influence on the Jewish people . . . for our worst spiritual affliction, our inferiority complex which also seems to be one of the pillars of the American Council for Judaism. . . . Jews who have a vivid feeling of Jewish national solidarity are much better equipped to overcome with dignity all the dangers and hardships which we have to face. . . .

---

*Einstein also sent a copy of this letter to Rabbi Louis Wolsey in Philadelphia.
**Frank had argued that Zionism might contribute to the spread of anti-Semitism.

I dislike nationalism very much—even Jewish national-ism. But our own national solidarity is forced upon us by a hostile world and not the aggressive feelings which we con-nect with the word "Nationalism"—at least when we are not speaking about Jewish questions.

Yours very sincerely,

AE

December 10, 1945
Address at the Fifth Annual Nobel Prize Anniversary
Dinner at New York's Hotel Astor

PROF. EINSTEIN INDICTS WORLD'S LEADERS

We shall never forget the heroic efforts of the small coun-tries, of the Scandinavian, the Dutch, the Swiss nations, and of individuals . . . who did all in their power to protect Jew-ish lives. We do not forget the humane attitude of the Soviet Union who was the only one among the big powers to open her doors to hundreds of thousands of Jews when Nazi armies were advancing on Poland.

[But today Jews], one-fifth of the pre-war population, are again denied access to their haven in Palestine and left to hunger and cold and persisting hostility. . . . [A]nd the fact that so many are kept in the degrading conditions of concentration camps by the Allies gives sufficient evidence of the shamefulness and hopelessness of the situation.

The people are forbidden to enter Palestine. . . . [T]he Western powers are yielding to the threats and external pres-sure of five vast and underpopulated Arab states.

December 12, 1945

Response to Einstein's Remarks from His Friend Rabbi Stephen Wise

Dear friend:

You stated our Zionist case in your address . . . with such clarity and wisdom that, instead of speaking last night before a great Zionist gathering, I rose and read your statement published in *PM*. A thousand thanks to you! Your evaluation of the situation as it obtains today is of enormous help to us.

December 10, 1945

Statement on Birobidjan*

We must not forget that in those years of atrocious persecution of the Jewish people, Soviet Russia has been the only great nation who has saved hundreds of thousands of Jewish lives. The enterprise to settle 30,000 Jewish war orphans in Birobidjan and secure for them in this way a satisfying and happy future is new proof for the humane attitude of Russia towards our Jewish people. In helping this cause we will contribute in a very effective way to the salvation of the remnants of European Jewry.

---

*Birobidjan was established within the Soviet Union under Stalin, in the late 1920s, as an autonomous Jewish region, located near the Russian border with China. Into the 1950s, it had the support of a number of committees around the world. Today, Birobidjan still has a small Jewish community of some four thousand. Einstein was honorary president of Ambidjan, the American Committee for Birobidjan.

March 11, 1946
As Reported in *The New York Times*

BIROBIDJAN GROUPS MERGE TO AID JEWS

The American Birobidjan Committee and the ICOR Association for Jewish colonization in Russia have merged into one organization to be known temporarily as the American Birobidjan Committee. . . . Albert Einstein will be honorary president of the new organization.

May 6, 1946
Except from a Letter to Edward G. Robinson
Dear Mr. Robinson:
I know how vitally interested you are in the plight of the Jews and how much you have done for Jewish rehabilitation. I therefore feel that you should interest yourself in the work of the American Birobidjan Committee, of which I am happy to be the Honorary President.

The American Birobidjan Committee is helping settle and support thousands of Jewish war orphans in Birobidjan—the Jewish Autonomous Region in the USSR. The Committee is also supporting 1,000 orphans of the heroes of Stalingrad in the Silver Ponds Home and Sanitarium of that city. Last but not least, the Committee is cooperating in the development of the Jewish Autonomous Region. I do not need to emphasize that these activities help to promote friendship between the Soviet Union and our country, indispensable for a durable peace. . . .

Very sincerely yours,
Albert Einstein
Honorary President—American Birobidjan Commitee

January 2, 1946
Letter to Emery Reves

Dear Mr. Reves,

I am confronted here by a very good fencing master, and your position is by and large the only healthy one. I think that nationalism is always a bad thing, even if it is Jews among whom it is raging. But I also believe that it is unjust of you to simply brandish Zionism as nationalism, and what is more, to do so at a time when the majority of the European Jews have been slain. Perhaps your assessment would have been a bit different if we were talking, for example, about Armenians, instead of Jews. If someone is menaced in such a way as has happened to us, he must shift, physically and morally, into defense alert as effectively as possible, regardless of the intensity of his adherence to the ideal of our old prophets.

Do you know what happened to our cosmopolitan brother Theodor Herzl (he, too, a journalist from Budapest) when his mission thrust itself upon him during the Dreyfus trial in Paris? He didn't turn into a nationalist because of this. But he clearly saw the physical and moral danger we were in and acted accordingly. Anyone who, over his striving for the highest goal, forgets the duty of solidarity with his persecuted and endangered brethren resembles a man who allows his family to starve to death in order to prevent his work as an artist or productive person from being harmed.

Please read through this in calm, and better refrain from answering me at all, lest in the end our cause is hurt by the art of fencing.

Yours with kind regards,
Albert Einstein

January 11, 1946
Testimony* Before the Anglo-American Committee of
Inquiry on Palestine,** Washington, D.C.

DR. EINSTEIN: First, I have to excuse myself for my faulty
English, but it is my best English. Secondly, I have come here
to make a contribution which most of the people here will
not enjoy. But I do so sincerely, and I hope it will be taken in
the same spirit.

JUDGE HUTCHESON: Will you speak a little louder, sir.

DR. EINSTEIN: Yes, I will try.

In 1921 I was happy to be the guest of Lord Haldane,
one time Minister of War, and a very clever man. In the conversation which I had with him there came up the Jewish
Palestine question. He said to me, "You had better not oc-
cupy yourself with this question but keep away from it."

I was very astonished to hear him make that statement.
It was a short time before that the Balfour Declaration was
made and I could not make up my mind what was the motive. It took me many years to understand the meaning of
the declaration. I was greatly disappointed in what Lord
Haldane had said, for I could not see any reason for him to
say this, and I feel that he said it in kindness.

---

*Published here for the first time (see note 8, page 308), this transcript reflects—
besides Einstein's views—the thinly veiled rivalry between Britain and the United
States over future dominance in the Middle East.
**The Anglo-American Committee of Inquiry on Palestine was established in
1945 to review the issue of Jewish immigration to Palestine. U.S. president Truman had called for the British to allow one hundred thousand Jewish refugees into
Palestine. In response, British prime minister Attlee proposed a joint commission
to study means of resolving the crisis. The committee heard testimony from wit-
nesses in Washington, London, Europe, and the Middle East.

Now, I had a very high opinion of our British colonial world; that is, I did at that time. Now I have no more [high] opinion. I want to explain to you how I came to my changed impression.

There are, of course, a lot of things that one hears here and hears there. I wish to explain why I believe that the difficulties in Palestine exist. First, difficulties between the Jews and Arabs are artificially created, and are created by the English. I believe, if there would be a really honest government for the people there, that got the Arabs and the Jews together, there would be nothing to fear. I cannot convince you gentlemen, but I can only say what convinces me.

I may first state what I think about British colonial rule. I find that the British colonial rule is based on a native. Do you know what that means? The native was exploited already before the English came into the land. Of course, the English had two interests. The first was to have raw materials for their industry. Also the oil in those countries. I find that everywhere there are big landowners who are exploiters of that race of people. These big landowners, of course, are in a precarious situation because they are always afraid that they will be gotten rid of. The British are always in a passive alliance with those land-possessing owners which suppress the work of the people in the different trades.

It is my impression that Palestine is a kind of small model of India. There is an attempt, with the help of a few officials, to dominate the people of Palestine, and it seems to me that the English rule it. Palestine is absolutely of this kind. It is difficult to imagine how it could be otherwise. Of course, we must consider there are different nationalities in Palestine.

From time to time, people are saying through the newspapers this and that people who have lived in those countries. I wish to say why I came to this kind of conviction. I regret very much that I had to come to such a conviction because before that I was an admirer of the British system. I am compelled to consider in Palestine the Mufti. Professor Hitti is an authority on that subject. He has given solid facts concerning the election of this Mufti to the position he occupies now.

The electors did not elect him. They refuted him. The separatists used their power to bring [him] to his important position. And why? He was a politician. When war came and the star of the Axis Powers was very shiny and bright, some believed that it was better to work together with the Axis and not with the English, who are little mild[er], but it was better to work with the Germans so they could exterminate the people easily.

Now, of course, the British are not responsible for that. In fact, they were very much opposed to it. I am not sure where the Mufti is now.

JUDGE HUTCHESON: Excuse me, Dr. Einstein. Did you say "the Mufti"?

DR. EINSTEIN: Yes, the Mufti.

Now how can I explain otherwise that national trouble-making is a British enterprise? It is not so easy to get information about all that is going on that cannot be directly proved. For instance, if there were pogroms against the Jews in Palestine, there was a taking away of arms so that the Jews could not defend themselves. It is hard to prove all this, so I will not insist too much on such a thing. But there are certain things which are far more strong arguments.

For instance, there was presented the committee in 1929

a letter from a sheik promising no punishment for anybody participating in this activity. The sheik sent a letter. It was signed by an official of the High Commission. I don't know if he is dead, but a letter from him was presented and in this letter it was stated that this man would not punish them for participating in this activity [pogrom].

DR. EINSTEIN: Give the name of the man who wrote that letter.

DR. EINSTEIN: Mills.

MR. GROSSMAN: Is this letter one which has been filed in the records of this Commission?

DR. EINSTEIN: I do not know.

MR. GROSSMAN: From whom did you get it?

DR. EINSTEIN: This I cannot say. I cannot prove that. I have not the time or the possibility to do it. But I can assure you that the people who told me that are reliable people. So I cannot say that it is true, but I believe it is very suspicious at least.

There is a rather simple police official who was in the disorder of 1929. He was active himself. Apparently out of great conscience, he wrote two books. Of course, they were not masterpieces of literature, but those books were about the duties he had to fulfill in his capacity as a police official and concerning his office in 1929. I can give you the title of the books. I think this is very important. The name of the man is Douglas V. Duff. The title of his first book is "Sword for Hire: The Saga of a Modern Free Companion." That was published in 1934. If what he says is true, it is a very important document. I am convinced that the people who informed me are honest and intelligent people. I have no reason to disbelieve them.

It is very easy to make out the contents of those books. They are little books that are easy to read. It would not be a great achievement to do so. I think it would be possible to find them even in the Library of Congress. I think it is very interesting to read the confession of a man who acted as a British police officer. It is not probable that such a man would write lies. For if he lived there and wrote falsehoods about what happened with him, it would become very bad for him. If it could be shown that what he wrote was lies, it would be very embarrassing for him.

Well, these are some of the things that gave me a very strong impression and supported my convictions. I think there will be no peace between Jews and Arabs, but I know also from people who know many people in Palestine that the pogroms are not half as bad as the conditions brought about by the professional politicians. I believe that people, if they are able to live in a half-way satisfactory condition, will not be so much interested in politics if it is not artificially produced by some interested person.

So I believe it is not good to take more of your patience. When I say certain facts came to me, then I formed my impressions.

I believe that is really a very honest book. You see, if the thing is really so, the British have really very badly violated their obligations. Such kinds of things as I have told you did, it seems to me, really happen.

The most important thing for international relations is confidence in international rule. I believe that complete honesty in the procedure is the most important thing [needed] to create confidence. I may add that to believe that the frame of mind of the colonial people of the British is so rigid that I am absolutely convinced that any councils will not have any effect.

I think commissions like this are like a smoke-screen to show good will. I believe that the Palestine people, under severe influence of the United Nations, will be able to create a better state of affairs. But with the British rule as it is, I believe it is impossible to find a real remedy. I may be wrong, but that is my conviction.

DR. AYDELOTTE: It may be that you will find more people who will agree with you in Britain than anywhere else. (Laughter.)

I should like to ask you for your advice. We are a little discouraged by your notion that whatever we do will not make matters different, but nevertheless we must proceed on the assumption that we must do our best.

DR. EINSTEIN: Yes.

DR. AYDELOTTE: One of the things which we must do is to figure out some kind of report or some kind of advice with reference to what the authority shall be, or who to have authority over Palestine. Now, do you think that the United Nations or some other outside authority should force the Arabs to allow unlimited immigration into Palestine, or do you think they should take the Arab point of view into consideration and close off immigration? Just what do you think should be done with Palestine by whatever power has the trusteeship over it?

DR. EINSTEIN: Of course, it is very difficult to answer such a question in a general way. I believe that such a government should be composed for the people concerned. It should be handled from the human standpoint of the matter. For instance, there is a great difficulty with the refugees. Of course, there should be something done about them. I believe it is natural to bring the bulk of them to Palestine. In Palestine the Jews who are already there will take care of the ones that are brought in. I believe that such kind of action should not be taken from a political stand-point but from a human standpoint. It would be best for the population of Palestine to feed those people and take care of them. I believe it is quite natural that they can take into their homes people who have no place to stay.

DR. AYDELOTTE: What would you do if the Arabs refused to consent to bringing these refugees to Palestine? Suppose the Arab population were prepared to resist it by force; would you compel them by force to receive the refugees?

DR. EINSTEIN: That would never be the case if there were no politics. But there are not only Arab politicians, but Jewish politicians, as well.

MR. MCDONALD: Would you eliminate the Jewish and Arab politicians both?

DR. EINSTEIN: No; you cannot eliminate them. If you elim-inate one, ten others grow up in their place. (Laughter.)

DR. AYDELOTTE: An Arab was talking this afternoon before you came in, and he is a man who has lived in Pales-tine the greater part of his life. He contends that the Arabs are afraid, [and] that they need no instigation to resist Jew-ish immigration. They are afraid that the Zionists are try-ing to develop a majority in Palestine so that they will have political control. Of course, the Arabs are in the majority now, but they fear that the Jews may attain a majority and then they would be in the minority.

DR. EINSTEIN: But who has created that mentality? If the people work together, they will not care anything about the idea of who has the biggest number. The number doesn't count if it is not politically activized. Nobody is interested in how many people in the United States speak French, German, English or Italian. It is all in the minds of the people.

MR. GROSSMAN: Do you believe that what you have complained about has been caused by the British people in Palestine?

DR. EINSTEIN: I do not say that it is the British alone.

MR. GROSSMAN: No, but you feel that the state of mind to which you refer is not there?

DR. EINSTEIN: I do.

MR. GROSSMAN: And do you think the state of mind is currently there to produce people who are willing to accept each other?

DR. EINSTEIN: No.

MR. GROSSMAN: But they are shooting each other.

DR. EINSTEIN: Yes.

MR. GROSSMAN: Shooting is taking place there and has taken place.

DR. EINSTEIN: Yes.

MR. GROSSMAN: Is it a figment of the imagination of newspaper editors or is it a fact?

DR. EINSTEIN: Yes; they are shooting each other over there.

MR. GROSSMAN: Then the state of mind is sufficient for shooting.

DR. EINSTEIN: No; you see, what is happening now in Palestine is that, of course, they see their mother and their father and their brother being sent out of Europe, and the government takes over their country, and [there is] no place left for them to go.

MR. GROSSMAN: But from the point of view of the British, the motive does not affect you. Suppose you were to reverse the situation and allow unrestricted immigration into Palestine, and allowed the Jews to come in, is it just a British imperialistic fiction that suggests to you that the Arabs might shoot?

DR. EINSTEIN: No, it is not a fiction.

MR. GROSSMAN: It is not a fiction, it is a fact. But if you were to recommend sending the Jews there to Palestine despite the danger of the Arabs shooting . . .

DR. EINSTEIN: I believe that danger is not so great as some people think it is.

MR. GROSSMAN: Then, under this terrible British imperialism, this terrible British realism, the people in Palestine will be stimulated to further shooting. . . .

DR. EINSTEIN: Oh, no; it will not be bad.

MR. GROSSMAN: Oh, it is not going to be so wicked from now on?

DR. EINSTEIN: No. There is an enmity between nationalities, but it is not enough to make them shoot each other.

MR. GROSSMAN: But in the past you think that the British have aroused such hatred that the Arabs will now continue to hate the Jewish immigrants but will not shoot them?

DR. EINSTEIN: Yes.

MR. GROSSMAN: You think the British are so clever that they can control to a degree the hatred of the Arabs for the Jews, but that the Arabs will not shoot them.

DR. EINSTEIN: Oh, now— (Laughter.)

MR. GROSSMAN: You are certainly a great admirer of my country.

Another question: Since the British are, according to your point of view, completely incompetent to rule in the various parts of the world where they have ruled—

DR. EINSTEIN: No, oh, no.

MR. GROSSMAN: Well, at least in Palestine—you say they should not rule Palestine. Would you be prepared to advocate publicly that the American people should take over the mandate and assume full military responsibility for unlimited Jewish immigration, and thereby prove—

DR. EINSTEIN: No, I would not do that. I would be King of Palestine if I did that. God forbid! (Laughter.)

MR. GROSSMAN: Your point of view is that you wish to blame the British, and you are not prepared to suggest that the other great democracies, since we have failed, should take responsibility for carrying out the job which we have failed to do. We have failed, according to you. Why shouldn't you take the responsibility and show how wrong we are?

MR. MCDONALD: When he says "you," he means the United States.

MR. GROSSMAN: Yes, the United States.

DR. EINSTEIN: It should be done under an international regime.

MR. GROSSMAN: Well, what soldiers should go there to Palestine to carry out the American policy?

DR. EINSTEIN: There should be a mixed organization.

MR. GROSSMAN: So the officials could be of 54 nations. Or 6 or 5 or 2?

DR. EINSTEIN: I think it should be arranged.

MR. GROSSMAN: But you would not advise the United States of America to do it alone?

DR. EINSTEIN: No.

MR. GROSSMAN: You think it is too much for one nation to do?

DR. EINSTEIN: No, I believe that any enterprise that is not too difficult, if successfully done, could be done by an international organization.

MR. GROSSMAN: In view of the tremendous success of the rule in Austria, and in order to help your Jewish friends introduce the same type of Jewish organizations in Palestine you are prepared—

DR. EINSTEIN: No; I would take only a part of Palestine for governing the land, and do it like other countries do it. I would not take a democratic basis in the American sense, for the circumstances are different.

MR. GROSSMAN: But you would permit, perhaps, a Frenchman, a Russian, an American, an Englishman and an Arab, all to sit in on a council together and formulate the policies to be carried out by the government of Palestine?

DR. EINSTEIN: Yes; but I would not say so many people as that. (Laughter.)

MR. GROSSMAN: Well, we rather thought that inasmuch as we had failed, you Americans should take the executive and perhaps the military responsibility and then prove whether your theory is right.

JUDGE HUTCHESON: I doubt if that is the way you should authorize the Americans to do it. (Laughter.)

DR. EINSTEIN: Of course, the British are not responsible for the things they have had no influence in. That is my feeling about it.

DR. AYDELOTTE: Dr. Einstein, what is your attitude toward the idea of a political Zionism, a political Jewish state, as versus a cultural center? There are two conceptions of Palestine. You understand them.

DR. EINSTEIN: Yes. I was never in favor of a state.

JUDGE HUTCHESON: Dr. Einstein, many years ago I undertook to make a speech on relativity. (Laughter.)

I am not sure that I had a much better scientific and general acquaintance with relativity than perhaps you have with all these general Palestine problems. But I have my view of relativity and you have yours of Palestine. (Laughter.)

But there is a question which, as a citizen of the world, in a way, as I regard you—I have considerable respect for your ability to impress the world as you have done it—I do not know how you have done it, but you have impressed the world (laughter)—I know that you do not live in a small, narrow, bigoted, pestilential, partisan attitude. You do not, do you?

DR. EINSTEIN: No sir; I never have.

JUDGE HUTCHESON: No, you never have.

DR. EINSTEIN: No.

JUDGE HUTCHESON: Now, your views about the British shenanigans are shared by many, not only with reference to Palestine, but Ireland and many other countries, so we need not debate that matter. I have never had much experience with it and know little about it. But those things are personal, as you started out to say. To some extent, you are like an Irishman. The British made a mess.

DR. EINSTEIN: An Irishman?

JUDGE HUTCHESON: Yes. (Prolonged laughter.)

DR. EINSTEIN: The Irishmen have for a long time suffered under your rule. I have not. (Laughter.)

JUDGE HUTCHESON: I am not a Britisher. I am an American.

DR. EINSTEIN: Oh, excuse me. (Laughter.)

JUDGE HUTCHESON: Now we will come to my question. It seems to us who are, as you say, just another committee to come and go—but I am a Texan and I do not take it in that way—we are going to try to do something about it.

DR. EINSTEIN: Good.

JUDGE HUTCHESON: It has been told to our committee by the Zionists that the passionate heart of every Jew will never be satisfied until they have a Jewish state in Palestine. It is contended, I suppose, that they must have a majority over the Arabs. It has been told to us by the Arab representatives that the Arabs are not going to permit any such condition as that, that they will not permit having themselves converted from a majority into a minority.

DR. EINSTEIN: Yes.

JUDGE HUTCHESON: I have asked these various persons if it is essential to the right or the privilege of the Jews to go to Palestine, if it is essential to real Zionism that a setup be fixed so that the Jews may have a Jewish state and a Jewish majority without regard to the Arab view. Do you share that point of view, or do you think the matter can be handled on any other basis?

DR. EINSTEIN: Yes, absolutely. The state idea is not according to my heart. I cannot understand why it is needed. It is connected with many difficulties and a narrow-mindedness. I believe it is bad.

JUDGE HUTCHESON: Isn't it spiritual and ethical—I do not mean this particular Zionist movement, I do not mean the idea of insisting that a Jewish state must be created—isn't it anachronistic?

DR. EINSTEIN: In my opinion, yes. I am against it—but not for the same reasons that Mr. Rosenwald has stated.

JUDGE HUTCHESON: No. Well, I am obliged to you.

MR. BUXTON: Professor, in your general impeachment of British colonial rule, you did not quite explain why it is to the interest of the British to stir up strife over a country where the responsibility of governing the country rests with them. Why should they make their own task more difficult?

DR. EINSTEIN: If people are united with each other and they come to the idea that they do not need the foreign rule, then they want to make themselves independent. Every country with a decent standard of living will have, of course, its idea and will strive forward. So an enduring rule is not impossible if you keep down the burden of the people. That is my thesis.

MR. AYDELOTTE: What you are now saying is not very convincing because the British nation has for a long time specialized in bringing independence to other nations, and has given independence to a large number of colonies which they formerly ruled. Of course, the British do not rule Palestine. They have a Mandate—

DR. EINSTEIN: Unhappily. (Laughter.)

MR. AYDELOTTE: But, after all, they have to make an annual report. I do not quite get your idea of why the situation in Palestine is maintained as an advantage to the British.

DR. EINSTEIN: At the present time the whole situation makes for trouble. A little enmity is good for everybody, but much is not. (Laughter.)

MR. CRUM: Dr. Einstein, you have given us a great deal of information, as you call it, about the British.

DR. EINSTEIN: Yes.

MR. CRUM: I should like to have you accept my statement on the basis of personal experience with this Commission. Our British and American colleagues are doing everything in their power to find a speedy solution of the Palestine problem. I for one think it wrong for you, as a citizen of the world, to say that this committee is a smokescreen because, believe me, sir, it is not.

DR. EINSTEIN: How can you know it is not?

MR. CRUM: I know it from my own activities.

DR. EINSTEIN: Yes, but you estimate it is not a smokescreen. I believe the Colonial Office makes it that.

MR. CRUM: May I suggest, Doctor, that you judge us by the actions following the recommendations of the committee.

DR. EINSTEIN: I would be glad to be wrong. Nobody would be more elated than I.

(Thereupon the Committee adjourned.)

January 13, 1946
Letter from Maurice Dunay

My dear Dr. Einstein,

There can be no greater harm done to any man's life than to be betrayed by one who is supposedly one's friend.

Your statement in opposition to a Jewish homeland in

Palestine at this tragic moment in Jewish history fills me with a certain horror and sincere doubt as to your mental processes.

In view of the overwhelming number of Jews who are for it and for whom there is no other hope, would it not have been better to remain silent? Or is the thinking of the soil of Naziland too deeply ingrained for any logic to be used on the Jewish question?

What terrible damage you have done to the haunted Jews of Europe! And also to your prestige!

January 19, 1946
Letter to Maurice Dunay

Dear Sir:

I have served as a witness before the Anglo-American Inquiry Commission on Palestine for the sole purpose to act in favor of our just cause. But it is, of course, impossible to prevent distortion by the press. I am in favor of Palestine being developed as a Jewish Homeland but not as a separate state. It seems to me a matter of simple common sense that we cannot ask to be given the political rule over Palestine where two thirds of the population are not Jewish. What we can and should ask is a secured bi-national status in Palestine with free immigration. If we ask more we are damaging our own cause, and it is difficult for me to grasp that our own Zionists are taking such an intransigent position which can only impair our common cause.

Sincerely yours,
Albert Einstein

January 29, 1946
Letter to Martin Buber

Dear Mr. Buber,

Unfortunately, I do not have a manuscript of my testimony before the Anglo-American Palestine Commission, but I want to give you a sketch of what was its main content: When I went to London in 1921 for a short visit as a guest of the former Minister of War, Lord Haldane, an unusually benevolent man, he counseled me, without being asked, not to involve myself in the Jewish construction work in Palestine. I was very surprised, and it took me years to find an explanation for the incident. He simply wanted to protect me from disappointments, because he apparently knew, the Balfour Declaration notwithstanding, that our efforts fit badly into the scheme of the British Colonial Office, according to which it treats all colonies: a joint venture with the large-scale landed property, economic and cultural suppression of the bulk of the population. Into this scheme the Jews, who brought with them the lifting of the wages and concomitantly, an aggravation of the position of the landlords, didn't fit. From there the efforts, right from the beginning, to sabotage the realization of the Balfour Declaration, restrictions on immigration, limitations on land acquisition by Jews, and systematic incitement of the Arab masses, in addition to the arrangement of turmoil in whose instigation the Mandate Government took an active part. Under these circumstances, [there is] no hope for an amelioration of the situation as long as Great Britain holds the mandate in its hand. My suggestion [would be] similar to the one by Magnes (bi-national government directly under the UNO [United Nations Organization]), creation of a Jewish state [to be] rejected as practically unfeasible, given the current distribution of the population.

My evidence:

1. Sponsoring of the Mufti (I have called him the "British pet-troublemaker" [English in the original]) who, even though an open traitor during the war and subpoenaed as a war criminal by Yugoslavia, all the same continues to be tolerated and sponsored by the British. This affair is described excellently in a letter written by Professor A. S. Yahuda a couple of months ago to the *New York Times*.

2. The fact-finding commission that met after the turmoil of 1929 was presented by one of the "contributors," a Sheik, with a letter promising impunity, coming from Eric Mills, the second highest officer of the British administration.

3. A police officer, Douglas V. Duff, who was assigned to participate in the dissemination of the unrest, has—apparently in an attempt to relieve his conscience—publicized his experiences in Scotland, in two publications: "Sword for Hire," J. Murray, published in 1929, and "Galilee Galoper," 1935. In addition to this, I also mentioned the gun requisitionings which, conspicuously, always took place "at exactly the right time." As you see, these statements were a bit too tough for the Commission, one half of which consisted of Englishmen. But I submitted all this very calmly and amicably, without getting impulsive in any way.

In the above, I have forgotten to mention that in the course of the debate, I expressed my opinion that from the perspective of the British government, the Commission meant no more than some sort of a "smoke-screen," and that it [the government] did not have the slightest intent to be influenced by the latter's recommendations and suggestions. When I said this, some of the commission members got pretty heated.

With kind regards and wishes

February 15, 1946
Report by *The New York Times*

EINSTEIN URGES UNO RUN PALESTINE REGIME

WASHINGTON, Feb.14—A government in Palestine under the UN's direct control and a constitution assuring Jews' and Arabs' security against being outvoted by each other would solve the Jewish-Arab difficulties, Prof. Albert Einstein believes.

In a letter to the first public meeting of the Washington branch of the Progressive Palestine Association, Professor Einstein said: "I agree whole-heartedly with your program and I am convinced that your work will be of real value for the solution of the hard problems the Palestine situation is presenting."

Adrian B. Schwartz, chairman of the meeting, said that the association proposed to fight for the opening of free Jewish immigration and to support a program of Arab-Jewish cooperation in Palestine. . . .

April 3, 1946
Letter to Hans Mühsam

I see it as impossible that the running of the entire country would be ceded to the Jews, who are but a third of the population, since that would result in intolerable tensions. A division could certainly be possible but in my opinion, not to our advantage. The national problems would, at best, continue for both factions, our options for development would be limited and, added to that, the antagonism of both parties towards each other. . . . Well, no matter what one says or thinks, the facts are primarily affected by the half-brains, i.e. the activists. . . .

With kind regards

April 21, 1946
Letter to Michele Besso

Dear Michele,

The article you sent me is a rather accurate report of my statement before the Palestine Commission in Washington. If you had an idea of the perfidy with which the English act to apply their well-tried principle of "divide et impera," you wouldn't have been as surprised by the brusqueness of my charge as has apparently been the case. My testimony relies on very reliable information and was also much more precise than the article reveals.

If you see my name brought up from time to time in connection with political excursions, you shouldn't think that I spend much time on such matters, since it would be sad to waste much energy for the skimpy soil of politics. From time to time, however, a moment arrives when I cannot help myself, . . . when one can draw public attention to the necessity of a world government, without which all our human grandeur will go to the dogs. . . .

Yours with affectionate regards,

Albert

globalization

August 7, 1946
Letter to the Committee for a Progressive Palestine Association

Dear Mr. [Adrian] Schwartz:

You know well that I completely agree with your program and I am willing any time to support it. However, I cannot accept the Honorary Chairmanship of your organization for the simple reason that I am not able to assume responsibility for activities in which my participation is mostly a formal one.

I am glad that you have decided to support the Institute for Jewish-Arab Relations fostered by the Hashomer Hatzair.*

Sincerely yours,

AE

January 22, 1947
Excerpt from a Letter to Hans Mühsam

With respect to Palestine, we have posed unreasonable and unjustified demands, influenced by demagogues and other loudmouths. Our powerlessness is terrible; if we did have power, it might be even worse. Our imitation of the

---

*Hashomer Hatzair (The Young Guards) was the socialist-oriented Zionist youth movement.

goyim even extends to their imbecilic nationalism and obsession with race, and this after an unprecedented school of suffering.

With kind regards,

AE

March 3, 1947

Questionnaire Returned to I. Z. David of Tel Aviv*

1. What is your opinion about the establishment of a free National Jewish Palestine?

   A: Jewish National Home? Yes. Jewish National Palestine? No.

   I favor a free, bi-national Palestine at a later date after agreement with the Arabs.

2. Opinion about partition of Palestine and Chaim Weizmann's proposals re partition?

   A: I am against partition.

3. Opinion about official Jewish representation at the UN?

   A. This would be good if it could be achieved. It presupposes the [UN's] acceptance of the representation of national groups.

4. Opinion about immediate establishment of a Jewish government in exile?

   A. I am against it. . . . [I]t would be detrimental to the peace of Palestine.

---

*I. Z. David, a member of the Irgun, on a visit to New York, sent Einstein a list of questions. The Irgun was the armed underground group, led by Menachem Begin, denounced by Einstein and others as "closely akin . . . to the Nazi and Fascist parties."

5. Opinion regarding the establishment of a coalition government between Palestinian Arabs and Jews in Palestine?

A. See my answer to question 1.

6. Opinion about the Palestinian [Jewish] underground, especially the Irgun Zwaj Leumi?

A. I regard it as a disaster.

7. What do you propose as a solution to the Palestinian problem?

A. There should be a provisional UN government with a gradually increasing decentralized, bi-national self-government.

April 11, 1947
Excerpt from a Letter to Hans Mühsam

I'm not all that badly informed about Palestine, even more so since my beloved and very talented assistant is a Palestinian.* But I think that the bad times there will soon be over, since after a while everyone will have had enough of the quarrels. If I were appointed commander there, I would leave the people alone and would rather have both the Arab and the Jewish wanna-be politicians sent to Cyprus and have them locked up there together, and have them fight out their quarrels among themselves, without having to resort to these unnecessary detours. . . .

It seems to me that our beloved Americans are now patterning their foreign policy on the model of the Germans,

---

*Einstein's assistant, Bruria Kaufman, was a Jewish Palestinian.

since they appear to have inherited the latter's inflatedness and arrogance. Apparently, they also want to take on the role England has played up to now. They refuse to learn from each other; and learn little even from their own harsh experience. What has been implanted into the heads from early youth is rooted more firmly than experience and reasoning. The English are yet another good example of this. Their old-fashioned methods of suppressing the masses by using indigenous unscrupulous elements from the economic upper class will soon cost them their whole empire, but they are incapable to bring themselves to change their methods; no matter whether it's the Tories or the Socialists. With the Germans, it was exactly the same. All of this would be good and well, except for the fact that it's so sad for the better elements and the oppressed. . . .

With kind regards

August 6, 1947
Excerpt from a Letter to Joseph Brainin of the American Committee of Jewish Writers

Dear Mr. Brainin:

[I have] long held that for Palestine the only fair and suitable form of government is a bi-national arrangement. However, [it] would have to be [run by] the United Nations for the foreseeable future, because the political life of Palestine is thoroughly muddled and, therefore, the land is not ripe for political independence.

September 22, 1947
Excerpt from a Letter to Judge Jerome Frank

Dear Judge Frank:

I was very much pleased to learn that you have resigned from the American Council for Judaism. . . . I have never favored a Jewish State in Palestine but a binational state, held under strict United Nations government as long as national antagonisms are prevailing there.

Yours very sincerely

November 28, 1947
Excerpt from a Message to the Histadrut* Conference in Israel

. . . Our aim is to save the remnants of our people in central and eastern Europe after the terrible catastrophe and to lead them to a future of fruitful work in Palestine. The entire world—with the exception of [British prime minister] Mr. Bevin—seems to have realized that our tortured brethren must be led out of Europe; it is psychologically impossible for them to continue living among the murderers of their brothers. The venom of the German propaganda of lies has also made it objectively impossible for them to continue living among those nations.

In Palestine there awaits them and all of us a great and beautiful task, before which we hope to be placed by decisive action of the UN. It will be the first time since the destruction of Jerusalem by the Romans that we will be able to construct an independent society as a free nation. . . .

---

*Zionist Labor Federation.

March 24, 1948
Excerpt from a Letter to Hans Mühsam

Dear friend,

. . . But at night, I'm thinking of both of you, and of what you have to suffer and to go through from illness and because of the chronic state of war in Palestine. By now, it is not only the English, but also the Americans who have sold and betrayed us politically for a song. And in the rest of the world, too, no ray of light is to be seen. In Washington, they are conspiring for a preventive war against Russia—a fact that, by the way, is also related to the villainy in Palestine. I believe that even in America, we Jews are by no means safe. Anti-Semitism has increased very much, in part because of the dispute over Palestine, and if an economic crisis should be super-added to this, things could really get queasy. . . .

The psychological situation of the Jews over here is quite similar to the one in Germany before Hitler. The rich and the successful try to cloak their Jewish descent and act out as super patriots. The rest rarely get into any contact with the goyim, but rather live among themselves instead. This separation is even sharper than it used to be anywhere in Western Europe, Germany included. Cohesion among the Jews is limited to charity, but in this realm, astonishingly much is done, much more than in Europe. . . .

With kind regards,

AE

April 10, 1948
Response to Shepard Rifkin, Executive Director of the Stern Group,*

Dear Sir:

When a real and final catastrophe should befall us in Palestine the first responsible for it would be the British and the second responsible for it the Terrorist organizations built up from our own ranks.

I am not willing to see anybody associated with those misled and criminal people.

Sincerely yours,
Albert Einstein

April 12, 1948
Letter to the Editor of *The New York Times***

PALESTINE COOPERATION

To the Editor:

Both Arab and Jewish extremists are today recklessly pushing Palestine into a futile war. While believing in the defense of legitimate claims, these extremists on each side play into each other's hands. In this reign of terror the needs and desires of the common man in Palestine are being ignored.

We believe that in such a situation of national conflict it

---

*See Tom Segev's comment cited above (page 137, footnote). Rifkin had requested Einstein meet with the group's deputy commander, who was visiting New York, to discuss "the attitude of the Stern Group towards the Palestine problem."
**Published on April 18, 1948.

is vitally important that each group and particularly its leaders uphold standards of morality and reason in their own ranks rather than confine themselves to accuse their opponents of the violation of these standards. Hence we feel it to be our duty to declare emphatically that we do not condone methods of terrorism and of fanatical nationalism any more if practiced by Jews than if by Arabs. We hope that responsible Arabs will appeal to their people as we do to the Jews.

Were war to occur, the peace would still leave the necessity of the two peoples working together, unless one or the other were exterminated or enslaved. Short of such a calamity, a decisive victory by either would yield a corroding bitterness. Common sense dictates joint efforts to prevent war and to foster cooperation now.

OPPOSITION TO TERROR

Jewish-Arab cooperation has been for many years the aim of far-sighted Jewish groups opposed to any form of terror. Recently a declaration of such a group was published in the American press under the dateline Jerusalem, March 28, 1948, to which we want to draw attention. We quote here some of the key sentences:

"An understanding between the two peoples is possible, despite the constant refrain that Jewish and Arab aspirations are irreconcilable. The claims of their extremists are indeed irreconcilable, but the common Jew and the common Arab are not extremists. They yearn for the opportunity of building up their common country, the Holy Land, through labor and cooperation. "

The signers of the statement represent various groups in Palestine Jewry. Besides Dr. Magnes, the chairman, those who signed were Dr. Martin Buber, Professor of Jewish Philosophy at Hebrew University; Dr. David Senator, administrator of the university; Dr. Kurt Wilhelm, rabbi of Emeth Ve'Emunah liberal congregation in Jerusalem; Simon Shereshevsky, a surgeon, who belongs to the Mizrachi Zionist religious group, and Isaac Molho of the Spanish Jewish community.

Those who signed this declaration represent at the moment only a minority. However, besides the fact that they speak for a much wider circle of inarticulate people, they speak in the name of principles which have been the most significant contribution of the Jewish people to humanity.

We appeal to the Jews in this country and in Palestine not to permit themselves to be driven into a mood of despair or false heroism which eventually results in suicidal measures. While such a mood is undoubtedly understandable as a reaction to the wanton destruction of six million Jewish lives in the last decade, it is nevertheless destructive morally as well as practically.

We believe that any constructive solution is possible only if it is based on the concern for the welfare and cooperation of both Jews and Arabs in Palestine. We believe that it is the unquestionable right of the Jewish community in Palestine to protect its life and work, and that Jewish immigration into Palestine must be permitted to the optimal degree.

The undersigned plead with all Jews to focus on the one

important goal: the survival and permanent development of
the Jewish settlement in Palestine on a peaceful and democratic basis, the single one which secures its future in accordance with the fundamental spiritual and moral principles
inherent in the Jewish tradition and essential for Jewish hope.

Leo Baeck

Albert Einstein

THE FINAL YEARS

1948–1955

November 29, 1947: U.N. General Assembly votes 33 to 13, with 10 abstentions,* to end British Mandate for Palestine, in favor of partition.

May 14, 1948: British Mandate ends; State of Israel is proclaimed.

May 15, 1948: Arab armies from Egypt, Transjordan, Syria, Lebanon, and Iraq attack Israel. They are defeated and the war officially ends in July 1949.

---

*Thirty-three countries (58 percent) voted in favor of partition: Australia, Belgium, Bolivia, Brazil, Byelorussian SSR, Canada, Costa Rica, Czechoslovakia, Denmark, Dominican Republic, Ecuador, France, Guatemala, Haiti, Iceland, Liberia, Luxembourg, Netherlands, New Zealand, Nicaragua, Norway, Panama, Paraguay, Peru, Philippines, Poland, Sweden, South Africa, Ukrainian SSR, United States of America, Union of Soviet Socialist Republics, Uruguay, Venezuela.

Thirteen countries (23 percent) voted against: Afghanistan, Cuba, Egypt, Greece, India, Iran, Iraq, Lebanon, Pakistan, Saudi Arabia, Syria, Turkey, Yemen.

Ten countries (17 percent) abstained: Argentina, Chile, Republic of China, Colombia, El Salvador, Ethiopia, Honduras, Mexico, United Kingdom of Great Britain and Northern Ireland, Yugoslavia.

One country (2 percent) was absent: Thailand.

Einstein was particularly concerned during this period of his life with the rise of the Cold War, Cold War politics, and McCarthyism in America. He opposed the nuclear arms race and the establishment of NATO and supported the third-party candidacy of Henry Wallace in 1948. He urged Americans not to testify before congressional investigating committees such as the McCarthy committee.* In foreign policy, he supported the nonaligned movement led by people like Nehru and countries like India, Indonesia, and Yugoslavia. When Israel came into existence, he made it clear that he wanted the new state to join the nonaligned camp and he was terribly disappointed at its pro-Western stance on every issue.

Several commentators, including two recent Einstein biographers, have claimed that Einstein "embraced" the formation of Israel or became an enthusiastic supporter of Zionism, and an editor of *The New York Times* argued in 1972 that Einstein had changed to become a fan of the Jewish state after Israel was established in 1948.[1] Clearly, Einstein had mixed feelings about the issue and after the Holocaust he saw a need for a refuge for Jews, but his letters and statements—including his 1952 letter to Louis Rabinowitz—make it clear that he continued to be critical of the idea—and policies—of the Jewish state. In September 1948, just after the establishment of Israel, he wrote to his friend Hans Mühsam, "As for the state idea, I have never thought it was a good one, for economic, political, and military reasons. But now there is no turning back anymore, and the matter must be contended with." Clearly,

---

*The Senate Permanent Subcommittee on Investigations.

something less than an embrace. As he said in his last published interview, "We thought [Israel] might be better than other nations, but it was no better."

Had Einstein known what we all now know about the violent eviction of Palestinians from their homes and their land by the Israeli army (IDF), had he been able to read the books by Michael Palumbo (*The Palestinian Catastrophe* and *Imperial Israel*),* Ilan Pappe (*The Ethnic Cleansing of Palestine*), or the classic Hebrew novel *Khirbet Khizeh* by S. Yizhar** what more might he have said? As it was, he made it clear in his 1952 conversation with Mohamed Heikal, described below, the great concern he felt for the hundreds of thousands of Palestinian refugees evicted by Israel.

In December 1952, a thirty-two-year-old Egyptian journalist, Mohamed Heikal, on a visit to the United States, requested an interview with Albert Einstein in Princeton, and—to his astonishment—Einstein agreed. Einstein could not have known, of course, that Heikal would go on to become the Arab world's "most famous journalist,"[2] nor could Heikal have known, as he arrived at Einstein's house

---

*"In the UN Archives in New York, I found reports by neutral observers which clearly indicated that many of the Palestinians had been expelled from their homes in 1948 at the point of a gun" (Palumbo, *Imperial Israel*, 5).

**This poetic and totally unsettling short novel explores the agonized mind of an Israeli soldier in the 1948 war, as his long-held idealism is shattered by the brutality and indifference to suffering of his own actions and those of his fellow IDF members in the course of occupying others' land and exiling innocent people. Einstein would have had to be able to read Hebrew; the novel was not published in English (by Ibis Editions) until 2007, more than half a century after it was written.

on Mercer Street in Princeton, that their discussion would be much more than an interview.

As he rang Einstein's doorbell that winter afternoon, the quiet streets of Princeton must have seemed a world away (as indeed they were) from the revolutionary events Heikal had recently been part of. Only a few months earlier, in Cairo, he had joined a group of young Egyptian army officers and their supporters in taking over the Egyptian government offices and radio station and announcing, "The tyranny of King Farouk is finished." The corpulent king barely escaped with his life on a boat to Italy.[3]

Heikal had allied himself with the group of Egyptian "Free Officers," who—on July 23—had overthrown the corrupt, pro-Western king, renamed themselves the Revolutionary Command Council, immediately begun a process of land-reform redistribution, and set about establishing the new Egyptian Republic.[4]

Heikal was already a rising journalistic star, having won a national press award for a piece he wrote called "Fear in the Holy Land." A year earlier, he had covered the United Nations, and the Korean War, as a reporter for *Akhbar Yom* (*Daily News*), and had gotten to know a number of U.S. journalists.[5] He returned to the United States in November 1952, this time representing the new revolutionary regime.

More than fifty years later— it is October 2006—as we sit in the living room of Heikal's office-apartment on Nile Street in Cairo,* I am amazed at how young and vigorous he is.

---

*Heikal's comments in this chapter are based entirely on my notes, which he subsequently reviewed.

How does he like working on TV, I ask, after so many years in print journalism? His answer floors me: "At *Al-Ahram*, I would receive sometimes twenty to twenty-five letters about one of my columns. The most I think I ever received was forty to fifty letters. Now the weekly commentary I do on Al Jazeera has an audience of 91 million viewers and Al Jazeera receives sixty-five to seventy *thousand* e-mail messages about the program every week."

Now, silver-haired and dapper in his three-piece suit, looking and acting far more like sixty-four than eighty-four, he recalls his 1952 visit to the United States:

> I must admit that meeting Albert Einstein was not something I planned for as I prepared for that trip. My interests focused on two main points. First, I went to the United States to cover the presidential elections [Eisenhower vs. Stevenson] and, assuming Eisenhower would win, to go with him to Korea, as he had promised to bring an end to the war there.
>
> And, of course, I also went to help, in whatever ways I could, the new Egyptian government. Its new diplomatic corps had not yet been assigned. At that point, in October 1952, after Farouk was overthrown, Naguib was still the official government leader, but everyone knew—and some press reports even stated—that Nasser was the real leader.[6] So I went to Washington on October 3, 1952, and met, among others, Henry Byroade, who would later become U.S. ambassador to Egypt.
>
> I also arranged to go to Princeton, New Jersey, in December, to see George Gallup and to visit the

*Gallup Institute there, since the new Egyptian gov-
ernment was interested in whether the polling process was really a way of gauging public opinion.*

*Dr. Mahmood Azmi, who had been sent to
Washington by the new government (he would become head of Egypt's UN delegation), a former professor of international affairs at Cairo University,
and a friend of mine, asked me cheerfully, "So, you
are going to Princeton to meet Einstein?"*

*The truth is, I said, I will have a meeting with Dr.
Gallup and spend the weekend with him because I
want to get to learn his methodology in surveying
public opinion.*

*Dr. Azmi shouted, "Is this possible? You go to
Princeton and you don't meet with Einstein?" Then
he added, "You are wasting your time! If you go to
Princeton and see anyone, it should be Albert Einstein. We will send him a request to let you do an interview." So the Egyptian delegates, including Azmi,
said they would try to arrange it.*

*At first, I never thought he would agree to see
me. One day before I went to Princeton, they told
me that, yes, Einstein had agreed to see me. They
were as amazed as I was. There were two conditions, however. The first was that our meeting must
take place during his daily walk in the woods that
surround the university, since that was the only time
he had available. (It was clear that an interview with
an Egyptian journalist was exceptional. But Einstein
had—as I would learn—his reasons.) The second
condition was that the meeting would last no longer*

than fifteen to thirty minutes, depending on Einstein's mood.

For a moment, I thought of apologizing and declining because the conditions seemed so very, perhaps even arrogantly, restrictive. Then I thought better of it, swallowed my pride, and accepted.

So the next day, I spent the morning with Gallup and then went to visit Einstein. I had no idea where his office was, and I was hardly prepared to interview him. Really, all I knew about Einstein was that he had discovered something called the theory of relativity and he was in some way involved with the atomic bomb.

I arrived at his house on Mercer Street at 3 P.M., and I remember that when he came downstairs, I was really shocked by his shabby clothes: a sweater that was too big for him, old pants, and sandals with no socks. (Some time later, I met the great movie actress Luise Rainer*—I knew her [second] husband [publisher Robert Knittel]—and she explained that I should not be misled by Einstein's sloppy appearance, that it was just his way of being informal and that his mind was not at all sloppy.) Instead of

---

*Luise Rainer was the first person to win an Academy Award two years in a row, in 1936 (*The Great Ziegfeld*) and 1937 (*The Good Earth*). In January 2007, Ms. Rainer, then ninety-seven years old, was kind enough to invite my wife and me to visit her in her London apartment on Eaton Square. We spent more than an hour together, chatting over coffee and cake as she reminisced about Albert Einstein— "He was such a wonderful, gentle human being!"—and showed us several as-clear-as-if-they-had-just-been-taken photos of the two of them together—walking and rowing—in Princeton in the early 1930s. "Everyone talked politics back then," she recalled, "especially about the war in Spain and fighting the fascists."

embarking immediately on his exercise routine, Einstein told me he had only twenty minutes to talk. We spoke mostly about general matters. At one point he mentioned Israel, and I said I had covered the war in Palestine. Twenty minutes later, he said it was time for his daily walk, and he invited me to join him. When I agreed, he said that I would have to do most of the talking and ask questions. Once more, I agreed.

"What did you ask him?" I interjected. Heikal continued:

Silly things—like "Tell me about the atom bomb." He was polite but clearly not amused, perhaps a little annoyed. About the atom bomb, he said it was a pity that so few people were interested in the potential of working for world peace, that most were just concerned about the bomb, but that the bomb was really the least important element of working for peace. He seemed to be getting more enjoyment from the sound of leaves crunching beneath our feet than he was from my questions. Of all the people I've interviewed,[7] he is the only one I wish I could meet again—if only to ask the questions I should have asked. I was simply superficial.

But let me tell you more of our conversation. As we walked, Einstein began to talk about Jews and Arabs, and he discussed the development of his feelings of identification with the Jewish people and with Israel. But he felt that he had shared only the beginnings of their suffering, since he had left for the

United States before the worst of the Nazi anti-Semitism and atrocities.

Einstein said that the first time he had come to America was in 1921, in the company of Chaim Weizmann, who was then president of the Jewish Agency and later became the first president of the state of Israel. Weizmann had solicited Einstein's participation in a campaign to raise funds for the Hebrew University in Jerusalem; Einstein had agreed, he told me, because he felt that the Jews are "like my family." He made very clear his sympathy for the suffering they had endured, and his belief in the common dream of a homeland, a place where no one would wrong the Jews or treat them with prejudice.

He went on, with the same intensity and clarity, to say that he wanted the Jews to treat no one else with prejudice, either. The Arabs, he declared, have the right to their homeland, a place for which they know no substitute, and no one can deny this to them. He talked about the events and upheavals that had taken place in my part of the world in 1948. What saddened him, indeed caused him to have a "crisis of conscience," was that it seemed to him to be "a clash between two rights." He had assumed that the international powers involved would be able to handle this clash. But these powers had failed to do so, perhaps, he said, because it served their own interests to deepen the conflict instead of resolving it.

Einstein asked if I had read the statement to the editor of The New York Times *that he had signed, protesting Menachem Begin's visit to the United*

States at the end of 1948. The statement, he said, described Begin as a slaughterer and a terrorist and asserted that it was improper to allow him to visit America. Begin came anyway, and Einstein boycotted all the events that took place during his visit. Also, although Begin asked to visit Einstein, even making a comment in which he said that he wanted to learn from Einstein, to come to him as a student, Einstein declined to have him as a guest in his house. He apologized but refused, he said, because he believed that it was useless to try to teach those who believe in violence. No one, he said, can cure them.

Characterizing his attitude toward both the Jews and the state of Israel as "humanitarian," Einstein emphasized that he held the very same attitude toward the Arab refugees. Then he asked if I wanted to discuss the subject further with him, and said he was ready to do so when we finished walking and returned to his house. He had at home, he said, some things he thought might interest me. We were still walking. And when he stopped talking, everything became quiet again except for our footsteps on the dry leaves that covered the road with their mixture of different colors.

He took up the subject again without my having to ask him, saying that he didn't want the Jews to fall into the narrow handcuffs of nationalism, but that he feared that this was what was happening. Throughout their history, he explained, the Jews were oppressed because of ignorance and racism and perhaps due to economic and cultural circumstances.

*As a result, they often were confined in little neighbor-
hoods of their own, ghettos that were a necessity for
protection. They felt the need for a home that would
protect them, and to that end, he said, they nurtured
an ancient dream of Palestine, and they went toward it.*

*The ones who went, said Einstein, were a minority
of Jews, those who no longer believed that humanity
could protect them and felt that only a homeland
would do so. He urged me to take note of the many
other Jews who did not want that homeland, not in
Palestine or elsewhere. And while he understood that
there was a certain logic to the wish for a homeland,
he saw this logic as containing a larger problem. The
Jewish homeland in Palestine is surrounded by Arabs
who do not want it in their midst, he said. And the
problem with the logic of a homeland, in Einstein's
view, certainly this homeland, confined and opposed
by all its neighbors, is that it gives rise to a state of
what he termed "narrow nationalism." This nationalism, in turn, brings about what he called "location
suffocation," a hostile tendency to live in violence
that can dampen the spirit of any people and hence
spoil their politics. Having said that, he asked that I
not publish our interview—"for the present at least,
because it might create a fuss that would benefit no
one." His wish for now, he said, was just to make his
position and its framework clear, so that there would
be no misconception in our conversation. "We shall
talk about this later," he said.*

He went on to talk about his own level of identi-

fication as a Jew and Zionist. "Am I Jewish? Definitely, I am Jewish. Zionist? I don't know." He said he agreed that Jews should have a "house and a homeland," a place to which any of them could go at any time to find true peace. But he had his differences with many of the leading Zionists, as well. He said that he used to be fond of Weizmann, and that Ben-Gurion "confuses me sometimes," but Menachem Begin made him the most nervous of all "because he reminds me of [the] Nazis."

So, if he is a Jew and yet is uncertain about being a Zionist, how would Einstein feel about being an Israeli? He said that he did not think he could be an Israeli. Although he sympathized with the idea and its lofty aims, he feared that, in reality, the "narrow nationalism" that he had referred to earlier would lead to a situation of hostility and violence quite at odds with the ideology of a safe and secure homeland. When the foundations of any ideology clash with the process of applying it, he said, this clash in itself must point us to the fact that there is an error somewhere—an error that we must find and try to fix, whether it is in "us" or in "them" or an inherent part of the ideology itself.

"This is my position," Einstein said. "Those are my fears!"

The professor's house had come into view through the trees. The hike was over and so was my interview. I looked at my watch; one hour and five minutes had passed since I met Einstein. I expected that now he would shake my hand and I'd then go back to the train station in Princeton to head to New York. Instead, he invited me into his house for a cup of tea because it was his "turn to ask me what he had wanted to ask about since the beginning of our meeting."

I entered after him, and he asked me with amazing simplicity—as he transformed from a great scientist into a generous host—whether I wanted to go to the rest room while he went to the kitchen to make some tea! I asked if he was going to make the tea himself, and he answered yes. He paid no attention to my surprise and went through a door beneath the stairs. He came back a few minutes later with a tray containing a teapot, two cups, and a little dish with two biscuits. I advanced to pour the tea, but Einstein preceded me and did the honors. Then he sat on a chair in front of me. I was staring at him. I was trying to figure out this mysterious man, who had been described to me by Dr. Azmi and Dr. Lewis Awad* as "the greatest living person of our era" and the "first immortal-to-be of our time."

I remained silent, waiting for him to begin the conversation from any direction he wished. I did not have long to wait before Einstein, speaking in a soft voice, said that he would tell me now what it was he wanted. He went back over some of ground he had covered earlier, reminding me that, as a Jew, he was interested in the fate of the Jews, and of Israel; that

---

*Poet, author, literary critic, and the first Egyptian to head Cairo University's English Department.

he had seen what the Jews had suffered in Germany before the war and with the rise of Nazism; and that, although he had left Germany and the Jews to come to America, the Jews remained his people: He shared with them the dream of a homeland, wanted them to have a place where no one would suffer what they had suffered in Germany. He reiterated that the conflict in the Middle East was a struggle between two rights: the right of Jews to a homeland and the right of Arabs to their land. He had followed the 1948 war with a heavy heart, he said. He felt guilty, and was miserable about the tragedy to which the Arabs in Palestine were subjected.

"My position, my feeling toward my people [the refugees during World War II and since the war], is one of human understanding. And that is exactly my position toward the Arab refugees.

"As I said, I don't want the Jews to be captives of narrow nationalism. Their history is international— subjected to lots of suffering throughout the world. I admire Ben-Gurion, but I am afraid for the soul of Israel."

He wanted me to understand the nature of his concern. He had, he said, told Chaim Weizmann, even before 1948, that while he wanted a homeland for the Jews, he did not want that to happen at the cost of the suffering of the Palestinian Arabs. When Weizmann said to him in reply that "God promised the Jews this land," Einstein told me that he had responded, "We must take God out of this argument—because both sides see God on their side. If God is the one who promised this land to the Jews, then God is also the one who placed the Arabs in it."

When I made no comment in response, Einstein continued. I had told him that I knew General Naguib, and now he wanted to know just how well I knew him. He asked if it was true, as he had read in the newspapers, that I had close ties to the general and his officers. I replied that I knew the general to an extent, and I knew a number of the officers who had made the revolution in Egypt. Einstein then wanted to know if it was true, as he had also read in the papers, that the general was just a front, and that the real authority was in the hands of the young officers. "There is no secret about that," I said, and told him that the general really was a facade, chosen as a cover for the real leader of the revolution, a young colonel named Gamal Abdel Nasser. Einstein said that he had never heard that name, but wanted to know, as he had about Naguib, whether I knew Nasser. I answered as I had before: yes, to an extent.

Einstein then asked me just what it was that Colonel Nasser wanted. I briefly outlined the situation in Egypt, recounted the story of the revolution, explained the role of the young officers among the rebels, and offered some description of the character of Nasser. Einstein replied that, while it seemed I knew the colonel pretty well, I had not yet told him what it was that Nasser wanted from the Jews or Israel.

I said that I didn't think that Colonel Nasser or General Naguib or any other officers had a problem with Jews as Jewish people. Their problem was with Israel, with its aggressive plans against Palestinians, and with its expansionary plans against the rest of the Arab world. "That," I said, "is the problem."

In response, Einstein said that when it comes to people like Menachem Begin and his massacre of Arabs in the village of Deir Yassin, he thought I was completely right. These people are Nazis in their thoughts and their deeds, he said, but I am talking about others. Those like Begin, he maintained, do not embody the Jews or the concept of Israel.

To this, I said what I believed: "Ben-Gurion is no less a Nazi than Menachem Begin." Here, Einstein interrupted me and said, "No, no. Ben-Gurion is different than Begin. Moreover, there are good people in Israel." And again I said what I believed: "Until now, we haven't been able to find these good people!"

"Maybe you can't," Einstein replied, "but I could if given a chance."

Then he moved directly to what seemed now to be his main concern. He asked me if I could send a message on his behalf to General Naguib, or to the colonel I had mentioned, whose name he had forgotten. "Gamal Abdel Nasser," I reminded him. He said, "Yes, yes," and asked again if I could deliver a message from him to both of them. I told him that it would be my honor to personally deliver a message from Albert Einstein, and that I believed the general and the colonel would both be very pleased to receive a message from him. Although I also made clear that *this would depend on the nature of the message and its contents.*

The professor's face was a mix of hope and hesitation. Then he stood up, went to his office, and returned with a large envelope in his hand. As I watched with nervousness and curiosity, he took his seat again, held up the envelope, and said that he assumed I knew that Weizmann, the first president of Israel, had died at the beginning of the prior month. I nodded my head; of course I knew. I kept looking at Einstein while his fingers started fumbling with the envelope and pulling out the papers it contained. He seemed be sorting them at first, then he handed me one, telling me to read this first.

It was a telegram, and I quickly scanned to the bottom of the page and saw that the sender was Abba Eban, the Israeli ambassador to the United States, and the message was basically asking if Einstein would agree to meet on the following day. As I read, Einstein apparently saw the signs of surprise that came over my face. He said with naïve excitement, "Read! Read!" Then he passed over a letter, also signed by Eban, formally proposing that Einstein accept the presidency of Israel, and my astonishment grew. Finally, he showed me another letter, this one in German, in which—he explained to me—he declined the offer. I breathed a sigh of relief.

I put down the three sheets of paper, and I could think of nothing to say except "This is news to me." Still speaking with an excitement that sounded naïve to me, Einstein said that the offer had come as a sur-

*prise to him as well, that it was something he never
expected. Then the tone of excitement faded, and he
went on to tell me that, although he had indeed been
surprised to be asked by the Israeli leaders to succeed
Weizmann as president, he was aware that what they
wanted was "my name, not my person," since they
faced a problem in filling the gap left by the loss of
such a popular and famous character as Weizmann.
He had apologized to those who had offered him this
honor, Einstein continued, but he could not accept it.
He knew himself better than that, he said, and knew
that this kind of position was something well beyond
his knowledge and experience. He was not born to be
a president.*

*I listened to him in silence, feeling that these as-
tounding revelations required some care and caution
on my part lest I find myself in delicate territory, deal-
ing with a forbidden or even a booby-trapped situation. Clearly sensing my hesitation, Einstein told me
that all he wanted from me was to deliver a message
from him to General Naguib and to the colonel I had
mentioned, whose name once again escaped him. ("I
can't easily remember names anymore," Einstein
said.) I smiled, sounded out Nasser's name for him
again, and listened as he repeated "Gamal Abdel
Nasser" several times, attempting to memorize the
parts of the name.*

*Then he asked me again if I could deliver a mes-
sage to them, and told me that he had three specific
questions: First, are they ready to make peace with
Israel? Second, if they are, what conditions would*

be required for both sides to achieve peace? And finally, what method would they suggest for negotiating peace: discussion directly between the two sides or through an intermediary (and, if the latter, which international body)?

"I am not offering myself as a mediator," Einstein said, because he did not think himself capable of that. "I am not good enough for that," he said. "Maybe I could—as they say in chemistry—work as a catalyst." His intention, he went on, was not to play a major part, but simply to establish the connection, then leave the details to those who knew better how to take it from there.

"I couldn't take the message to Cairo, since I was going to Korea to report on Eisenhower's trip there," Heikal explained at the end of our chat in his living room. "So Dr. Azmi sent Einstein's message in code to the foreign minister, Dr. [Mahmud] Fawzi. When I returned to Cairo, after going to Korea, Dr. Fawzi had sent a report to Nasser and Naguib with the message from Einstein, and advising, 'Needs to be treated with great attention.' The report included the three questions and also Einstein's overall attitude.

"They told Dr. Azmi to tell Einstein that they would consider his message and they would reply later. But they didn't.

"Not easily discouraged, and a great believer in stubbornness,[8] Einstein sent a second message to Nasser, this time in writing, through Dr. Azmi. But again, Nasser made no response.

In his 1997 book, *Secret Channels: The Inside Story of*

Arab-Israeli Peace Negotiations, Heikal reports that when Azmi's letter brought no response, Einstein "enlisted the help of Jawaharal Nehru, prime minister of India, whose views carried great weight in the Third World." Nonetheless, according to Heikal, "Nasser continued to feel that it was best not to respond."[9]

Nehru spent almost the entire month of June 1953 in Egypt. But Nasser told him, Heikal said, "Unfortunately, this is not yet the proper time to discuss the problem."

"At the time," Heikal explained more than fifty years later, "in 1953 and 1954, because of what was happening, Israeli sabotage against Egypt and especially the Lavon affair [see following page], I agreed that they could not really respond to Einstein."

Indeed, possible reasons for Nasser's nonresponse are legion—it may be most surprising that he considered responding at all. Even had he trusted Einstein—and it was a time of rapidly evaporating trust on all sides—in those days the Israelis simply would not have met with Nasser and his colleagues.

"Israeli officials were worried," according to historian Kirk Beattie, "about signs of collaboration" between Egypt and the United States, which was beginning to compete with Britain and France for control of the Middle East. The Eisenhower administration "initially displayed no dissatisfaction with Egypt's nationalistic exhortations, retained hopes of some day harnessing Egypt to a Western defense organization and continued to provide [Egypt] CIA training." This clearly did not sit well with the Israeli leadership: "Alarmed by the prospect of broad cooperation between Western powers and their Arab enemies, some Is-

raelis implemented plans designed to sabotage the establishment of warm Western-Arab relations."[10]

If Nasser's reply to Einstein was waiting for a period of
peace, it never came. "Incidents of violence between Israel
and surrounding states, especially Egypt, rose throughout
1954. . . . Meanwhile, Egypt told the Security Council on
March 13 that it would not give up its practice of halting
Israeli bound ships through the Suez Canal [because of] Israeli truce violations."[11]

Perhaps the most flagrant Israeli conspiracy against Egypt
was the misnamed Lavon affair, or what has become known
as "Ben-Gurion's Banana Peel."[12] It merits special mention
here because it is at least one key to understanding why Einstein's message was not answered.

It began in 1954—although high-level planning in Israel
undoubtedly began in 1953—when an Israeli spy ring se-
cretly planted bombs intended to destroy U.S. and British
targets in Egypt. The Israeli government then blamed the
Nasser regime, with the aim of driving a wedge between the
new Egyptian government and the West and, the Israelis
hoped, blocking Egypt's plan to nationalize the Suez Canal.

The first three bombs went off in July 1954 in the Alexandria Post Office and the U.S. Information Service libraries in
Alexandria and Cairo. A fourth bomb exploded prematurely
in the pocket of one of the Israeli agents, nearly killing him,
as he was entering the British-owned Rio movie theater in
Alexandria. The agent, Philip Natanson, was arrested and
subsequently confessed.

With little choice but to admit the conspiracy, the Israelis
blamed it on their foreign minister, Pinhas Lavon, who was
forced to resign. It subsequently emerged that knowledge, if

not planning, of the conspiracy included higher Israeli officials, including Ben-Gurion.

While very few Americans and fewer Israelis whom I
met there (practically no one under the age of sixty) know
anything about the Lavon affair, it is documented in numerous sources.[13]

Beyond explaining Nasser's nonresponse to Einstein, these
events and Israel's anti-Nasser policies[14] make it clear that
Einstein and the Israeli leadership were operating on two
different—even opposing—programs. To Einstein, Nasser
and the new Egyptian leadership represented a hope for rapprochement, a possible door to peace. The Israelis, on the
other hand, felt threatened by his pan-Arabism, his anticolo-
nialism, and by his joining with such figures as Nehru of India, Sukarno of Indonesia, and Tito of Yugoslavia in the
nonaligned coalition of nations.[15]

September 24, 1948
Excerpt from a Letter to Hans Mühsam in Haifa

You are quite correct in what you're saying about the
underhanded posture of England and America toward us.
All the Arabs are only poor hirelings who must risk their
lives for them. . . . I also think that in these last years, an
accommodation between us and the Arabs that could have
led to a binational administration has ceased to be possible.
But earlier on—and actually since 1918—we have neglected
the Arabs and have always put our trust in the English. As for
the state idea, I have never thought it was a good one, for economic, political, and military reasons. But now there is no

turning back anymore, and the matter must be contended with. At the same time, we must be aware that the "big shots" simply play a cat-and-mouse game with us and are able to destroy us anytime they want to. . . .

December 4, 1948
Letter of Protest About Visit by Menachem Begin to the United States, as Published in *The New York Times*

New Palestine Party
Visit of Menachem Begin and Aims of Political
Movement Discussed

To the Editors of *The New York Times*:

Among the most disturbing political phenomena of our time is the emergence in the newly created state of Israel of the "Freedom Party" (Tnuat Haherut), a political party closely akin in its organization, methods, political philosophy and social appeal to the Nazi and Fascist parties. It was formed out of the membership and following of the former Irgun Zvai Leumi, a terrorist, right-wing, chauvinist organization in Palestine.

The current visit of Menachem Begin, leader of this party, to the United States is obviously calculated to give the impression of American support for his party in the coming Israeli elections, and to cement political ties with conservative Zionist elements in the United States. Several Americans of national repute have lent their names to welcome his visit. It is inconceivable that those who oppose fascism throughout the world, if correctly informed as to Mr. Begin's political record and perspectives, could add their names and support to the movement he represents.

Before irreparable damage is done by way of financial contributions, public manifestations in Begin's behalf, and the creation in Palestine of the impression that a large segment of America supports Fascist elements in Israel, the American public must be informed as to the record and objectives of Mr. Begin and his movement.

The public avowals of Begin's party are no guide whatever to its actual character. Today they speak of freedom, democracy and anti-imperialism, whereas until recently they openly preached the doctrine of the Fascist state. It is in its actions that the terrorist party betrays its real character; from its past actions we can judge what it may be expected to do in the future.

ATTACK ON ARAB VILLAGE

A shocking example was their behavior in the Arab village of Deir Yassin. This village, off the main roads and surrounded by Jewish lands, had taken no part in the war, and had even fought off Arab bands who wanted to use the village as their base. On April 9, terrorist bands attacked this peaceful village, which was not a military objective in the fighting, killed most of its inhabitants—240 men, women, and children—and kept a few of them alive to parade as captives through the streets of Jerusalem. Most of the Jewish community was horrified at the deed, and the Jewish Agency sent a telegram of apology to King Abdullah of Trans-Jordan. But the terrorists, far from being ashamed of their act, were proud of this massacre, publicized it widely, and invited all the foreign correspondents present in the country to view the heaped corpses and the general havoc at Deir Yassin.

The Deir Yassin incident exemplifies the character and actions of the Freedom Party.

Within the Jewish community they have preached an admixture of ultranationalism, religious mysticism, and racial superiority. Like other Fascist parties they have been used to break strikes, and have themselves pressed for the destruction of free trade unions. In their stead they have proposed corporate unions on the Italian Fascist model.

During the last years of sporadic anti-British violence, the IZL and Stern groups inaugurated a reign of terror in the Palestine Jewish community. Teachers were beaten up for speaking against them, adults were shot for not letting their children join them. By gangster methods, beatings, window-smashing, and wide-spread robberies, the terrorists intimidated the population and exacted a heavy tribute.

The people of the Freedom Party have had no part in the constructive achievements in Palestine. They have reclaimed no land, built no settlements, and only detracted from the Jewish defense activity. Their much-publicized immigration endeavors were minute, and devoted mainly to bringing in Fascist compatriots.

DISCREPANCIES SEEN

The discrepancies between the bold claims now being made by Begin and his party, and their record of past performance in Palestine bear the imprint of no ordinary political party.

This is the unmistakable stamp of a Fascist party for whom terrorism (against Jews, Arabs, and British alike), and misrepresentation are means, and a "Leader State" is the goal.

In the light of the foregoing considerations, it is imperative that the truth about Mr. Begin and his movement be made known in this country. It is all the more tragic that the top leadership of American Zionism has refused to campaign against Begin's efforts, or even to expose to its own constituents the dangers to Israel from support to Begin.

The undersigned therefore take this means of publicly presenting a few salient facts concerning Begin and his party; and of urging all concerned not to support this latest manifestation of fascism.

Isidore Abramowitz, Hannah Arendt, Abraham Brick, Rabbi Jessurun Cardozo, Albert Einstein, Herman Eisen, M.D., Hayim Fineman, M. Gallen, M.D., H. H. Harris, Zelig S. Harris, Sidney Hook, Fred Karush, Bruria Kaufman, Irma L. Lindheim, Nachman Majsel, Seymour Melman, Myer D. Mendelson, M.D., Harry M. Orlinsky, Samuel Pitlick, Fritz Rohrlich, Louis P. Rocker, Ruth Saget, Itzhak Sankowsky, I. J. Shoenberg, Samuel Shuman, M. Singer, Irma Wolpe, Stefan Wolpe.

March 15, 1949
Excerpt from a Statement to the Hebrew University of Jerusalem upon Being Presented with an Honorary Doctorate, as Reported in *The New York Times* the Following Day

The wisdom and moderation the leaders of the new State have shown gives me confidence that gradually relations will be established with the Arab people which are based on fruitful cooperation and mutual trust. For this is the only means through which both parties can obtain true independence from the outside world.

April and May 1949
Excerpt from Alfred Werner Interview with Einstein in
Liberal Judaism
Q:"You began to appear publicly as a supporter of Zionism as far back as 1921 when a Jewish state was still a remote dream. Are you in favor of the present state of Israel?"

A: "Zionism in 1921 strove for the establishment of a national homeland, not the foundation of a state in a political sense. However, this latter aim has been realized due to the pressure of necessity, or rather emergency. To discuss this development retrospectively seems to be academic."

September 19, 1949
Excerpt from a Letter to Hans Mühsam
Dear Mühsam,

It is not right for me to come to Palestine, despite the fact that the things happening there are close to my heart. Quite generally, I just remain sitting here for the rest of my days, segregating myself as completely as possible. Whatever I try to do in the human sphere invariably tends to deteriorate into a foolish comedy.

I totally agree with your description of the Palestinian situation as well as your opinion about Bevin's bad designs. But unfortunately, Bevin is not the only one who wants to destroy us, or wants to forestall our development. It is the power struggle between West and East. Each party works to prevent any autonomous development in its own sphere. They want to tolerate only vassals and blind subordination. All the idle talk about democracy and social justice is dishonest and hypocritical. Even so, people in England (and America) are beginning to feel that Jewish Palestine can't be suppressed, but has instead to be reckoned with as a permanent factor.

I do not doubt that the clever folks in Palestine will be able to cope with the horrendous difficulties in directing the mass immigration to the proper places, just as well as they were able to cope with the foreign policy problem. A more serious difficulty will probably arise from orthodox narrowness, based on an intensified nationalism—and if I can read our folks correctly, also supported by the hypocrisy of the non-"believers." Weizmann's autobiography, I have of course also read. In addition to everything else, he is a talented writer. On the other hand, he is not generous in his acknowledgment of the merits of others (e.g., Herzl!), but rather small-minded and egocentric instead. . . .

November 27, 1949
Excerpt from "The Jews of Israel," NBC Radio Broadcast

One of [our people's] ideals is peace, based on understanding and self restraint, and not on violence. . . . Our relations with the Arabs are far from this ideal at the present time. . . . It was much less our fault or that of our neighbors [the Arabs] than that of the Mandatory Power [Britain] that we did not achieve an undivided Palestine in which Jews and Arabs would live as equals, in peace. [Britain has been] following the notorious device of Divide et Impera. In plain language, this means: create discord among the governed people so they will not unite in order to shake off the yoke imposed upon them. Well, the yoke has been removed but the seed of dissension has borne fruit and may still do harm for some time to come—let us hope not for too long.

1950
Message from Einstein on the Visit of the Israeli Philharmonic Orchestra to the United States*

[Einstein received a statement drafted by a Zionist official as the proposed words for Einstein to deliver on the occasion of the orchestra's visit. That draft included the following.]

Not only is [the orchestra] the cultural center of a country sincerely devoted to freedom of the creative artist in every field, but also it is the concrete manifestation of the spiritual and moral stamina of the people of Israel.

The people of America will welcome this great Orchestra because it is sent to us in a spirit of gratitude for the part we have played in helping to establish a democratic state of Israel. Israel's contribution to the beauty of living, like all artistic creations, will help not only Israel, but the entire Middle East.

[Einstein crossed out the words written by someone else and substituted his own words.]

---

*Einstein's conflicted feelings about Israel were also reflected in his purchase of the two hundred thousandth $500 State of Israel Bond, as reported in *The New York Times*, November 30, 1951, as well as in the letters on the following pages.

I extend my heartiest congratulations and best wishes to the American Fund for Israeli Institutions and to the Israel Philharmonic Orchestra upon the occasion of the first American tour of the Orchestra. The fond hopes that all of us have for Israel are beautifully symbolized in the Israeli Philharmonic Orchestra. Israel's tradition has always been to create and embody intellectual and spiritual values. The new State should be regarded only as a means to serve these goals effectively and not as a means in itself, still less as an instrument of political ambitions.

In this sense, every Jew may look upon Israel as his country in whose efforts and achievements he takes part. And in this sense I am greeting the Orchestra as *our* Orchestra. May it prosper and find the response it so well deserves.

Princeton, N.J.

March 17, 1952
Letter to Louis Rabinowitz*

Dear Mr. Rabinowitz:

My assistant, Bruria Kaufman, who is an Israeli citizen, translated your letter of March 12th to me. I have also read your statement in English with great interest. Both documents impressed me as utterances of a really benevolent person and a good son of our people.

I was astonished that an old son of such an old people can be so young in his ideals and expectations. Did it not come to your mind that the "Pilgrims" who came from England to

---

*Rabinowitz, a Revisionist (right-wing) Zionist, had written (in Hebrew) to Einstein, praising the continued Israeli colonization of Palestine.

colonize this country came to realize a plan very similar to your own? Do you also know how tyrannical, intolerant and aggressive these people became after a short while? Being baptized in Jewish water is no protection either. God Almighty has so created the human species and there is no help against it. I sympathize with your attempt although I do not share your lofty expectations about the result.

With kind regards and wishes,

Sincerely yours,

Albert Einstein

March 31, 1952
Excerpt from a Message to the "Children of Palestine" Dinner, as Reported in *The New York Times* the Following Day

The unparalleled persecution which the Jewish people have suffered, particularly during the last decades, [has] produced a kind of nationalism that ought to be curbed if only to permit a friendly and fruitful co-existence with the Arabs. Apart from that, it is evident that a humane and generous attitude with respect to social relations is altogether indispensable for the survival of mankind.

November 18, 1952
Excerpt from a Letter to Abba Eban

My relationship with the Jewish people has become my strongest human bond, ever since I became fully aware of our precarious situation among the nations of the world.

November 21, 1952
Excerpt from a Letter to Azriel Carlebach, Editor of
the Israeli Paper *Ma'ariv*, Who Had Cabled Urging
Einstein to Accept the Presidency of Israel

I also gave thought to the difficult situation that could create a conflict with my conscience; for the fact that one has no actual influence on the course of history does not relieve one of moral responsibility.

January 4, 1955
Letter to Zvi Lurie

Dear Mr. Lurie:

In your December 29, 1954, letter, you asked me to give a written summary of the views I stated during our meeting on December 22 [1954]. In a nutshell, it is this:

First: Neutrality with regard to the international East-West antagonism. Not only would taking such a stance enable us [the State of Israel] to make a modest contribution to alleviating the antagonism on a large scale, but we will also facilitate the achievement of good neighborly relations with the Arab nation and its governments.

Second, and most importantly: We must incessantly strive to treat the citizens of Arab descent living in our midst as our equals in every respect, and we must develop the necessary understanding for the difficulties of their situation naturally accompanying it. By such a stance, we will both win loyal fellow citizens and improve, slowly but steadily, our relations with the Arab world. In this regard, the Kibbutz movement takes an exemplary stance. Our stance toward the Arab minority is the true touchstone of our moral standard.

Yours with kind regards

March 8, 1955
Excerpt from a Letter to an Indian Friend*

Of course I regret the constant state of tension existing between Israel and the Arab states. Such tension could hardly have been avoided in view of the nationalistic attitude of both sides. . . . Worst of all has been the policy of the new Administration in the United States [Eisenhower] which, due to its own imperialist and military interests, seeks to win the sympathy of the Arab nations by sacrificing Israel. As a consequence, the very existence of Israel has become seriously imperiled. . . . This man Dulles is a real misfortune.

March 13, 1955
Excerpt from Einstein's Last Media Statement, published in the "Dear Reader" column of the *New York Post*

We had great hopes for Israel at first. We thought it might be better than other nations, but it is no better.

March 25, 1955
Letter to Kurt Blumenfeld

Dear Mr. Blumenfeld,

I am glad that the objectionable article a hussy wrote about me in abuse of a private visit has contributed to the fact that we received such an interesting letter from you.

The politics of the Western powers towards the Arabs

---

*This was "an Indian friend with whom Einstein frequently discussed world affairs and who enjoyed access to high political quarters in his homeland" (Nathan, *Einstein on Peace*, 578).

and Israel really worries me. In addition, the methodic deception of our domestic audience by press and radio was and is impossible to overlook.

Moreover, I must say that I had a quite favorable impression of the official government people who came from Israel, in particular of Ben-Gurion and Dinur—[they are] incomparably better than the officials here. Small wonder, since the powerful can afford more stupidity and narrow-mindedness than those who are unable to rely on naked force. As far as I am concerned, if I were in Israel, of the "old Jewish fool" only the "Jewish" bit would be omitted for the obvious reasons. Otherwise, it would be exactly the same. Anyone who isn't a professional follower will be inconvenient anywhere in the long run. I think in Israel there is as of yet no hypocrisy, apart from the extremely pious, who regard and behave themselves as the legitimate representatives of an invisible majesty. I still want to thank you after the fact for helping me to bring the Jewish soul to consciousness and remain

Yours with affectionate regards and wishes,
Albert Einstein

EPILOGUE: MAKING A MYTH

The myth of Einstein the advocate for Israel was born in the U.S. mass media just one day after Einstein died. An obituary published by *The New York Times* on April 19, 1955, included the phrase "Israel, whose establishment as a state [Einstein] had championed. . . ." It was a description of Einstein the media had never used while he was alive. Then, as now, the *Times* was the media agenda-setter, and other newspapers and major magazines carried similar statements. The *Chicago Tribune* obituary, for example, declared that Einstein had "urged the . . . establishment of a democratic Jewish commonwealth [in Palestine]," and the *New York World Telegram and Sun* called him "a staunch supporter of the young state of Israel."

Since it is common practice for news media to prepare obituaries of famous people well before they die, it is quite likely that the Einstein-builds-Israel description was prepared by *Times* editors months or more in advance.

Had the obituary writers simply gone to the paper's

morgue and looked through their own past stories about Einstein, what they would have found is quite different, indeed. Here is just a small sampling of *New York Times* items published during the last quarter century of Einstein's life:

EINSTEIN ATTACKS BRITISH ZION POLICY
[Einstein declared that] . . . Palestine offers ample room for Jews and Arabs [to] live side by side in peace and harmony in a common country. (December 3, 1930)

3,000 HEAR EINSTEIN AT SEDER SERVICE
Against Palestine State
Division Might Give Rise
to "Narrow Nationalism" That Is Being Fought
I should rather see reasonable agreement with the Arabs on the basis of living together in peace than the creation of a Jewish state. (April 18, 1938)

EINSTEIN CONDEMNS RULE IN PALESTINE
Calls British Unfit but Bars
Jewish State and Favors UNO (January 12, 1946)

Besides reviewing their own clipping files, if the *Times* editors had sent a reporter to his home in Princeton on a fact-checking visit during the months before Einstein died, the scientist could have set the record straight. No, he might well have explained, he had never advocated a Jewish state, and he would perhaps have added, as he had stated in the past, that "the essential nature of Judaism resists the idea of a Jewish state with borders, an army, and a measure of temporal power. . . . I am afraid of the inner damage Judaism will sustain—especially from the development of a narrow nationalism within our own ranks."

But more likely, Einstein being Einstein, he would have told the *Times* reporter, with a twinkle in his eyes, "I give you my solemn promise not to say anything to contradict whatever is published in my obituary."

Such a visit did not actually take place, of course, but the thought may well have occurred to the *Times* obit writer that whatever he wrote in Einstein's obituary would be safe from Einstein's criticism.

That obituary was not the end but only the beginning of the myth. Only two weeks later, on May 1, 1955, the *Times* published this "follow-up" story on its front page, based on an interview with Reuven Dafni, the Israeli consul general in New York, who had visited Einstein shortly before he died:

PLEA BY EINSTEIN FOR ISRAEL BARED
In Last Illness, He Worked on TV Address to Review
Nation's Achievements

One of the last things Dr. Albert Einstein did was to prepare a speech reviewing the achievements in Israel in its seven years as a nation.

. . . [He] left notes of the proposed address. These, with the exception of a single missing page, were expanded into literary form by the Israeli Consulate [Dafni] here, it was learned yesterday.

The *Times* article includes the following: "As put together from the notes . . . edited by Dr. Einstein, the consulate

quoted the scientist as saying: 'The establishment of the State
of Israel was internationally approved and recognized . . .
[and] is an event which actively engages the conscience of this
generation.' " The article also quotes Dafni as saying that
Einstein's draft refers to "Arab hostility" as "the root cause
of the tension."

For an Israeli official to claim Einstein's endorsement was
then, as now, understandable—even without evidence to
support the claim.* Not so understandable is why the *Times*
didn't check on the story simply by calling Einstein's longtime friend and assistant, Helen Dukas.

Had they checked, the editors would have found that
Helen Dukas had Einstein's original handwritten notes on
the conversation with Dafni, and Einstein's notes—reprinted
in Nathan and Heinz Norden's book *Einstein on Peace*—
contain no mention of any of the points Reuven Dafni "put
together," allegedly from those notes. Indeed, Einstein's
notes say nothing at all about "the establishment of the State
of Israel," let alone about Israel having been "internationally
approved," and make no mention of "Arab hostility."**

The same *Times* article reports on a letter that Einstein

---

*Einstein envisioned the Hebrew University "as part of the foundation for the
Jewish State to come," according to a a fundraising brochure mailed out in 2005
by Friends of the Hebrew University of Jerusalem. The brochure also asked for
funds to subsidize the Hebrew University's "student soldiers"—members of the
Israeli army. No source is cited for the alleged Einstein quote.
**Nathan and Norden, *Einstein on Peace*, 640–41, and (Einstein's handwritten
notes) 642–43. See also Rowe and Schulmann, eds., *Einstein on Politics*, 506–7.
The notes begin, "I speak to you today not as an American citizen and not as a
Jew, but as a human being. . . ." There is also nothing in Dafni's story of what is in
Gerald Tauber's report—in the Einstein Archives at the Hebrew University of
Jerusalem—of Einstein's "Last Address" in 1955 (Tauber, *Einstein on Zionism*,
59–60).

wrote to Dafni, agreeing to meet with Israeli officials to discuss drafting an article about Israel. In the letter, Einstein says, "It seems to me that an evaluation of the political situation is necessary to make any impression on public opinion. . . . To do this well it has to be carefully prepared in cooperation with responsible Israelis. I am, of course, not able to know in advance whether such attempt would result in agreement between them and myself."[1] The last sentence is the only sentence omitted from the *Times*'s version of Einstein's letter—with no elipses.

The next piece about what we might call the alternate Einstein appeared on the front page of the *Times* on March 29, 1972—an article about letters and documents newly released by Einstein's estate, headed "The Einstein Papers: A Man of Many Parts." (Significantly, the *Times* article was reprinted one day later in a number of other newspapers around the country, most notably the *Chicago Tribune* and its affiliates.*) Under a photo of Einstein with Israeli prime minister David Ben-Gurion (who visited the scientist in Princeton in 1951), the caption declares, "Einstein papers tell of scientist's efforts toward the creation of Israel." The article claims that "the papers tell of his long

---

Not surprisingly, Nathan and Norden report (640) that Einstein's last notes focused primarily on the need for world peace and his advocacy of world government: "Not one statesman in a position of responsibility has dared to pursue the only course that holds any promise of peace, the course of supranational security."

*Several other mainstream-media publications ran articles in the decades following Einstein's death, claiming his support for Israel: To cite just two examples from the *Los Angeles Times*: February 8, 1972 ("Albert Einstein would have been honored by Israel putting his face on its new five-shekel bill"), and December 13, 1982 ("Strong Links to the State of Israel").

efforts on behalf of the creation of a Jewish national state."

No excerpt or example from the Einstein papers is cited by the *Times*—nor has any been cited at any time since—to support the claim about the scientist's "efforts."

Why the *Times* would create an Einstein who exerted "long efforts on behalf of the creation of a Jewish national state" is a question readers (and conspiracy theorists) may discuss at great length.

We don't, however, have to wonder what would have happened if a knowledgeable reader had questioned the *Times* about its Einstein articles. In 1972 Alfred M. Lilienthal, who was the first to write about the newspaper's questionable coverage of Einstein,* telephoned the newspaper's then op-ed-page editor, Harrison Salisbury, to "suggest that it would be appropriate for him to run a piece presenting the true views of the learned scientist" on Israel. Lilienthal, who has written two books sharply critical of Zionism, then wrote such an article and sent it to Salisbury, only to have it rejected because, in Salisbury's opinion, "Dr. Einstein's views . . . underwent a series of changes over the years."

The argument that Einstein changed his views after the

---

*Among Lilienthal's criticisms of the *Times*: *Times* book editors arrange for books about the Middle East to be reviewed by pro-Zionist critics in the Sunday Book Review. For example, he points out, Israeli prime minister Begin's *The Revolt* and Joseph Charles's *America's Decline in the Middle East* were both reviewed by Wolf Blitzer, Washington correspondent for the *Jerusalem Post* and editor of *Near-East Report*, which Lilienthal describes as "the Zionist lobby's official publication" (Lilienthal, *The Zionist Connection*, 343).

establishment of Israel in 1948 and became an enthusiast of
the new state has been put forward by others besides Salisbury, including a number of Zionist leaders.* But it is simply not supported by the evidence. He may have resigned
himself to the fact—"As for the state idea, I have never
thought it was a good one, for economic, political, and military reasons. But now there is no turning back, and the
matter must be contended with. . . ."[2]—but that is hardly
enthusiasm. As Barbara Wolff has pointed out, "This statement, out of context, is usually quoted as Einstein's enthusiastic support for the Jewish state. Yet it actually expresses
bitter resignation in the face of a *fait accompli*. . . ."[3] We
have already noted Einstein's concern, expressed to Mohamed Heikal, about the Palestinian refugees evicted by the
Israelis.

Totally different from, if not diametrically opposed to,
the description in the obituaries in the *Times* and other
major newspapers, Einstein's position on Israel was expressed in articles, letters, interviews, and speeches *over a
period of more than thirty-five years*. Here is a representative example: "The state idea is not according to my heart.
I cannot understand why it is needed. It is connected with
many difficulties and a narrow-mindedness. I believe it is
bad. . . . [4]

---

*In "Einstein the Jew," Blumenfeld takes credit for Einstein's Zionism. He concedes
that "there were times when Einstein rejected the idea of a Jewish State and favored
the idea of a bi-national state in Palestine." At one time, Blumenfeld acknowledges,
Einstein "found himself in sympathy with the late Dr. [Judah] Magnes," but he
claims that Einstein "was later disappointed in Magnes." *B'nai B'rith Messenger*,
September 16, 1955, 39. In fact, Einstein's differences with Magnes were about the
Hebrew University, not about the binational state.

While a number of Einstein's letters have never been previously published, or even translated from the German, most of his speeches and interviews, in fact, were reported—often, as we have seen, by the same *New York Times* that created the new, mythological Einstein in his obituary.

FINAL NOTE

"If history were past, history wouldn't matter," James Baldwin wrote. "But history is the present. . . . You and I are history. We carry our history. We act our history."[1]

When the mainstream media (including "the newspaper of record") publish the obituary of a historical figure as important as Albert Einstein and don't even read (or, worse, ignore) their own extensive files on him, to give him a pro-Israel bias he had rejected in life, it is a clear indication of history that matters.

It is perhaps too much to expect that one small volume, simply by presenting the facts, can set the historical record straight when it has taken so much time and effort to tangle it. Let us rather hope simply for a reopening of minds, and that, discovering that Einstein advocated a binational state in Palestine with equal rights and equal power for Arabs and Jews, readers will ask what Gore Vidal has called "the only question that really matters: Why?" Why have we not known? And that at least some readers will choose discussion and debate—and struggle—over silence.

APPENDIX:
TEXTS ATTRIBUTED TO EINSTEIN

Author's Note: The following pieces were not written by Einstein (although he agreed to put his name to them). Since they run counter to the general trend of his writings and were written by others, they are presented here separately.

October 12, 1929
Letter to *The Manchester Guardian*

It was with a wonderful enthusiasm and a deep sense of gratitude that the Jews, afflicted more than any other people by the chaos and horror of the war, obtained from Great Britain a pledge to support the reestablishment of the Jewish national home in Palestine. The Jewish people, beset with a thousand physical wrongs and moral degradations, saw in the British promise the sure rock on which it could re-create a Jewish national life in Palestine, which, by its very existence as well as by its material and intellectual achievements, would give the Jewish masses, dispersed all over the world, a new sense of hope, dignity, and pride. Jews of all lands gave of their best in manpower and in material wealth in order to fulfill the inspiration that had kept the race alive through a martyrdom of centuries.

Within a brief decade some £10,000,000 were raised by voluntary contributions, and 100,000 picked Jews entered Palestine to redeem by their physical labour the almost derelict land. Deserts were irrigated, forests planted, swamps drained, and their crippling diseases subdued. A work of peace was created which, although still perhaps small in size, compelled the admiration of every observer.

Has the rock on which we have built begun to shake? A considerable section of the British press now meets our aspirations with lack of understanding, with coldness, and with disfavour. What has happened?

Arab mobs, organized and fanaticized by political intriguers working on the religious fury of the ignorant, attacked scattered Jewish settlements and murdered and plundered wherever no resistance was offered. In Hebron, the inmates of a rabbinical college, innocent youths who had never handled weapons in their lives, were butchered in cold blood; in Safed the same fate befell aged rabbis and their wives and children. Recently some Arabs raided a Jewish orphan settlement where the pathetic remnants of the great Russian pogroms had found a haven of refuge. Is it not then amazing that an orgy of such primitive brutality upon a peaceful population has been utilised by a certain section of the British press for a campaign of propaganda directed, not against the authors and instigators of these brutalities, but against their victims?

No less disappointing is the amazing degree of ignorance of the character and the achievement of Jewish reconstruction in Palestine displayed in many organs of the press. A decade has elapsed since the policy of the establishment of a Jewish national home in Palestine was officially endorsed by the British Government with the almost unanimous support of the entire British press and of the leaders of all political parties. On the basis of that official recognition, which was approved by almost every civilised Government, and which found its legal embodiment in the Palestine Mandate, Jews have sent their sons and daughters and have given their voluntary offerings for this great work of peaceful reconstruction. I think it may be stated without fear of exaggeration that, except for the war efforts of the European nations, our generation has seen no national effort of such spiritual intensity and such heroic devotion as that which the Jews have shown during the last ten years in favour of a work of peace in Palestine. When one travels through the country, as I had the good fortune to do a few years ago, and sees young pioneers, men and women of magnificent intellectual and moral calibre, breaking stones and building roads under the blazing rays of the Palestinian sun; when one sees flourishing agricultural settlements shooting up from the long-deserted soil under the intensive efforts of the Jewish settlers; when one sees the development of water power and the beginnings of an industry adapted to the needs and possibilities of the country, and, above all, the growth of an educational system ranging from the kindergarten to the university, in the language of the Bible—what observer, whatever his origin or faith, can fail to be seized by the magic of such amazing achievement and of such almost superhuman devotion? Is it not bewildering that, after all this, brutal massacres by a fanaticized mob can destroy all appreciation of the Jewish effort in Palestine and lead to a demand for the repeal of the solemn pledges of official support and protection?

Zionism has a two-fold basis. It arose on the one hand from the fact of Jewish suffering. It is not my intention to paint here a picture of the Jewish martyrdom throughout the ages, which has arisen from the homelessness of the Jew. Even today there is an intensity of Jewish suffering throughout the world of which the public opinion of the civilised West never obtains a comprehensive view. In the whole of Eastern Europe the danger of physical attack against the individual Jew is constantly present. The degrading disabilities of old have been transformed into restrictions of an economic character, while restrictive measures in the educational sphere, such as the "numerus clausus" at the universities, seek to suppress the Jew in the world of intellectual life. There is, I am sure, no need to stress at this time of day that there is a Jewish problem in the Western world also. How many non-Jews have any insight into the spiritual suffering and distortion, the degradation and moral disintegration engendered by the mere fact of the homelessness of a gifted and sensitive people? What underlies all these phenomena is the basic fact, which the first Zionists recognised with profound intuition, that the Jewish problem cannot be solved by the assimilation of the individual Jew to his environment. Jewish individuality is too strong to be effaced by such assimilation, and too conscious to be ready for such self-effacement. It is, of course, clear that it will never be possible to transplant to Palestine anything more than a minority of the Jewish people, but it has for a long time been the deep conviction of enlightened students of the problem, Jews and non-Jews alike, that the establishment of a National Home for the Jewish people in Palestine would raise the status and the dignity of those who would remain in their native countries, and would thereby materially assist in improving the relations between non-Jews and Jews in general.

But Zionism springs from an even deeper motive than Jewish suffering. It is rooted in a Jewish spiritual tradition, whose maintenance and development are for Jews the raison d'être of their continued existence as a community. In the re-establishment of the Jewish nation in the ancient home of the race, where Jewish spiritual values could again be developed in a Jewish atmosphere, the most enlightened representatives of Jewish individuality see the essential preliminary to the regeneration of the race and the setting free of its spiritual creativeness.

It is by these tendencies and aspirations that the Jewish reconstruction in Palestine is informed. Zionism is not a movement inspired by chauvinism or by a sacro egoismo. I am convinced that the great majority of the Jews would refuse to support a movement of that kind. Nor does Zionism aspire to divest anyone in Palestine of any rights or possessions he may enjoy. On the contrary, we are convinced that we shall be able to establish a friendly and constructive co-operation with the kindred Arab race which will be a blessing to both sections of the population materially and spiritually. During the whole of the work of Jewish colonization not a single Arab has been dispossessed; every acre of land acquired by the Jews has been bought at a price fixed by buyer and seller. Indeed every visitor has testified to the enormous improvement in the economic and sanitary standard of the Arab population resulting from the Jewish colonization. Friendly personal relations between the Jewish settlements and the neighbouring Arab villages have been formed throughout the country. Jewish and Arab workers have associated in the trade unions of the Palestine railways, and the standard of living of the Arabs has been raised. Arab scholars can be found working in the great library of the Hebrew University, while the study of the Arabic language and civilisation forms one of the chief subjects of study at this University. Arab workmen have participated in the evening courses conducted at the Jewish Technical Institute at Haifa. The native population has come to realise in an ever-growing measure the benefits, economic, sanitary and intellectual, which the Jewish work of construction has bestowed on the whole country and all its inhabitants. Indeed, one of the most comforting features in the present crisis has been the reports of personal protection afforded by Arabs to their Jewish fellow-citizens against the attacks of the fanaticised mob.

I submit, therefore, that the Zionist movement is entitled,

in the name of its higher objectives and on the strength of the support which has been promised to it most solemnly by the civilised world, to demand that its unprecedented reconstructive effort—carried out in a country which still largely lies fallow, and in which, by methods of intensive cultivation such as the Jews have applied, room can be found for hundreds of thousands of new settlers without detriment to the native population—shall not be defeated by a small clique of agitators, even if they wear the garb of ministers of the Islamic religion. Does public opinion in Great Britain realise that the Grand Mufti of Jerusalem, who is the centre of all the trouble, and speaks so loudly in the name of all the Moslems, is a young political adventurer of not much more, I understand, than thirty years of age, who in 1920 was sentenced to several years' imprisonment for his complicity in the riots of that year, but was pardoned under the terms of an amnesty? The mentality of this man may be gauged from a recent statement he gave to an interviewer accusing me, of all men, of having demanded the rebuilding of the Temple on the site of the Mosque of Omar. Is it tolerable that, in a country where ignorant fanaticism can so easily be incited to rapine and murder by interested agitators, so utterly irresponsible and unscrupulous a politician should be enabled to continue to exercise his evil influence, garbed in all the spiritual sanctity of religion, and invested with all the temporal powers that this involves in an Eastern country?

The realization of the great aims embodied in the Mandate for Palestine depends to a very large degree on the public opinion of Great Britain, on its press, and on its statesmen. The Jewish people is entitled to expect that its work of peace shall receive the active and benevolent support of the Mandatory Power. It is entitled to demand that those found guilty in the recent riots shall be adequately punished, and that the men in whose hands is laid the responsible task of the administration of a country of such a unique past and such unique potentialities for the future shall be so instructed as to ensure that this great trust, bestowed by the civilised world on the Mandatory Power, is carried out with vision and courage in the daily tasks of routine administration. Jews do not wish to live in the land of their fathers under the protection of British bayonets: they come as friends of the kindred Arab nation. What they expect of Great Britain is that it shall promote the growth of friendly relations between Jews and Arabs, that it shall not tolerate poisonous propaganda, and that it shall create such organs of security in the country as will afford adequate protection to life and peaceful labour.

The Jews will never abandon the work of reconstruction which they have undertaken. The reaction of all Jews, Zionist and non-Zionist alike, to the events of the last few weeks has shown this clearly enough. But it lies in the hands of the Mandatory Power materially to further or materially to hamper the progress of the work. It is of fundamental importance that British public opinion and the Governments of Great Britain and of Palestine shall feel themselves responsible for this great trust, not because Great Britain once undertook this responsibility in legal form, but because they are deeply convinced of the significance and importance of the task, and believe that its realization will tend to promote the progress and the peace of mankind, and to right a great historic wrong. I cannot believe that the greatest colonial Power in the world will fail when it is faced with the task of placing its unique colonising experience at the service of the reconstruction of the ancient home of the People of the Bible. The task may not be an easy one for the Mandatory Power, but for the success it will attain it is assured of the undying gratitude not only of the Jews but of all that is noblest in mankind.

If every nation that once was great, Persia, Greece, Italy, Turkey etc. would demand to return to the past and be great again, what would happen? laughter, perhaps?

DID EINSTEIN WRITE "EINSTEIN'S LETTER
TO *THE MANCHESTER GUARDIAN*"?

A thorough search of the Einstein Archives at the Hebrew University in Jerusalem—including a check by archivist Barbara Wolff of every item that might hide any reference to the letter—found no evidence that Einstein was the author. The search included a review of Einstein's correspondence with people in England (and others) who might have requested such an article. No such request was found. Also not found was any draft or part of a draft or any cover letter that might have gone with a draft from Einstein to the newspaper or any such correspondence with the *Jüdische Rundschau* (*Jewish Guardian*), where the *Manchester Guardian* letter was also published on October 18.

As Barbara Wolff points out, an article or letter of that size is not a spontaneous product of one afternoon, so Einstein's correspondence during the week(s) prior to the date this letter was sent (October 7, according to the *Jewish Guardian* of October 18) should in some way reflect the writing of the letter. But the archives search found no such references or discussion in Einstein's correspondence in the weeks and months prior to the article's publication.

Although Leon Simon included the "Letter to the Manchester Guardian" in his collection of Einstein's writings on Zionism, *About Zionism*, Barbara Wolff explains that Simon chose the papers to be included in that volume mainly from published sources and from writings available through the Zionist office(s). Einstein himself, from all available evidence, was not involved with Simon's publication.

Moreover, if Einstein had been the author of the *Manchester Guardian* letter, it would be likely that some parts of that letter would match the wording of other essays or speeches that Einstein composed during the same period (for example, his comments to a large Zionist meeting in Berlin on August 31, 1929, where the main issue was the events in Palestine). But attempts to compare excerpts of that August 1929 text and other Einstein texts written during that period with the *Manchester Guardian* letter suggest different writers.

In our discussion following that thorough archives search, Barbara Wolff stated that Einstein's authorship of the *Manchester Guardian* letter "can seriously be challenged."[1]

June 13, 1947
Letter to Jawaharal Nehru, Prime Minister of the Indian Government, New Delhi, India*

My dear Mr. Nehru:

May I tell you of the deep emotion with which I read recently that the Indian Constituent Assembly has abolished untouchability? I know how large a part you have played in the various phases of India's struggle for emancipation, and how grateful lovers of freedom must be to you, as well as to your great teacher, Mahatma Gandhi. Men everywhere felt freer and stronger because of the act of liberation which has taken place in India.

---

*In 1975 Helen Dukas, who had been Einstein's chief assistant and housekeeper for decades, sent a note to Einstein's close friend (and the executor of Einstein's estate) Otto Nathan, explaining that "Chaim Greenberg of the 'Jewish Chronicle' authored the letter" to Nehru, "after consultation with E."

The note to Otto Nathan, sent from the School of Natural Science at the Institute for Advanced Study (where Dukas still worked), is dated November 25, 1975. For a copy of the original note from Dukas to Nathan, and for its translation into English, we are indebted to Barbara Wolff, archivist at the Einstein Archives in the Hebrew University of Jerusalem. For the reply from Nehru, special thanks to AnnaLee Pauls, photoduplication coordinator for Rare Books and Special Collections at the Princeton University Library.

I read that the curse of the pariah was about to be lifted from millions of Hindus in the very days when the attention of the world was fixed on the problem of another group of human beings who, like the untouchables, have been the victims of persecution and discrimination for centuries.

Those with a sense of history—and I know how eloquently you have written on this theme—could not fail to be aware of the dramatic coincidence by which the plea of the Jewish people for equality was being heard by the United Nations at the very time when a revolutionary measure of redemption was being passed in your country. And because you have been the consistent champion of the forces of political and economic enlightenment in the Orient, I address myself to you in regard to the rights of an ancient people whose roots are in the East.

I should like to discuss only one problem with you—the ethical issues involved in the Zionist effort to recreate a Jewish homeland in Palestine. The legal aspects of the question, the precise commitments contained in the Balfour Declaration and the Mandate, are not the elements I propose to stress, though I appreciate their significance. I shall therefore not review a chapter of contemporary history with which you are familiar. But as a person to whom considerations of morality in international relations are not indifferent, I should like to dwell on the factors of justice and equity which are involved, and whose violation I would protest equally with you.

Long before the emergence of Hitler I made the cause of Zionism mine because through it I saw a means of correcting a flagrant wrong. I refer to the peculiar disability suffered by the Jewish people by which they were deprived of the opportunity to live on the same basis as other peoples. The bigotry of the chauvinists and racists, whose doctrines have brought so much evil to mankind, has always been alien to me. Were the vision of an international society, a true parliament of man, ever to be realized, I venture to say I should be among its most sympathetic supporters. But even in the interests of this ultimate ideal, the preliminary steps are surely the removal of the stigma of inferiority from every group and people in the world. The Jewish people alone has for centuries been in the anamolous position of being victimized and hounded as a people, though bereft of all the rights and protections which even the smallest people normally has. Jews have been persecuted as individuals; the Jewish people has been unable to develop fruitfully as a cultural and ethnic group. The spirit of the people as well as the bodies of its members have been assailed. Zionism offered the means of ending this discrimination. Through the return to the land to which they were bound by close historic ties, and, since the dispersion, hallowed in their daily prayers, Jews sought to abolish their pariah status among peoples.

The advent of Hitler underscored with a savage logic all the disastrous implications contained in the abnormal situation in which Jews found themselves. Millions of Jews perished not only because they were caught in the Nazi murder machine but also because there was no spot on the globe where they could find sanctuary. I need not remind you what the Nazi extermination program cost my people, nor of the tragic plight of the survivors. India, I am sure, mourned not only for six million men, women and children killed in gas-chambers and crematoriums, but also for a civilization which permitted this horror to take place. And I believe that wherever men dream of justice, and struggle for its presence, the cry of those who escaped from the Nazi charnel-house must be heard.

The Jewish survivors demand the right to dwell amid brothers, on the soil of their fathers. Their need is so desperate, their longing so natural that it is superfluous to elaborate this point. There is, however, a legitimate and relevant question which must be answered. Can Jewish need, no matter how acute, be met without the infringement of the vital rights of others? My answer is in the affirmative. One of the most extraordinary features of the Jewish rebuilding of Palestine is that the influx of Jewish pioneers has resulted not in the displacement and impoverishment of the local Arab population, but in its phenomenal increase and greater prosperity.

There has been much lately of a Zionist "invasion." Surely, a consideration of the facts must reveal how irresponsible and dishonest is such an accusation. Jews settled in Palestine on the basis of international agreements entered into by Arabs as well as the nations of the world. They bought every inch of the land on which they settled. Furthermore, and most important for this phase of the argument, the Arab population of Palestine doubled in size since the Balfour Declaration, whereas in the adjoining independent Arab states, the population remained static. Jewish colonization has not only raised the standard of life and the wage level of the Palestinian Arab, it has created conditions by virtue of which the Palestinian Arab has the highest rate of natural [population] increase in the world. This hardly constitutes "invasion."

However, I shall not pretend to misunderstand the nature of Arab opposition. Though the Arab of Palestine has benefited physically and economically, he wants exclusive national sovereignty, such as enjoyed by the Arabs of Saudi Arabia, Iraq, Lebanon or Syria. It is a legitimate and natural desire, and justice would seem to call for its satisfaction. At the close of World War I, 99% of the vast, underpopulated territories liberated from the Turks by the Allies were set aside for the national aspirations of the Arabs. Five independent Arab states have since been established in these territories. Only 1% was reserved for the Jewish people in the land of their origin. The decision which led to the proclamation of the Balfour Declaration was not arbitrary, nor the choice of territory capricious. It took into account the needs and aspirations of both Arab and Jew, and certainly, the lion's share did not fall to the Jews. In the august scale of justice, which weighs need against need, there is no doubt as to whose is more heavy. The "small notch" in the land of their fathers, granted the Jewish people, somewhat redresses the balance.

I believe there is still another factor which must weigh heavily in any consideration of the Zionist case, namely, what Jews have actually accomplished in Palestine, and the fashion of their accomplishment. I find profoundly gratifying the fact that the reconstruction of Palestine has taken place not through the exploitation of native workers—the usual pattern of imperialism—but through the heroic toil of Jewish pioneers. The once malaria-ridden swamps, the stony mountain slopes, the salt shores of the Dead Sea, now fertile and blooming, are evidence of a creative impulse whose thwarting would make mankind, as well as Jew and Arab, the poorer. Jewish labor has created living space; it has made Palestine bigger, and the world richer. Nor can I ignore the new concepts of economic equality which Jewish workers have brought to the Middle East. Their network of flourishing cooperatives, their vigorous trade-union movement, are tokens of a social idealism which is an organic part of their striving for national regeneration. Through the force of this social vision both Arab and Jew will go forward.

I know that the rivalries of power politics and the egotism of petty nationalist appetites seek to stifle the glorious renaissance which has begun in Palestine. May I appeal to you, as the leader of a movement of social and national enfranchisement, to recognize in Zionism a similar movement whose realization will add to the peace and progress of the Orient. Free Jewish immigration to Palestine, and the right of the Jews to continue the upbuilding of their ancient homeland without artificial restrictions, will increase the sum of well-being in the world. It is time to make an end to the ghetto status of Jews in Palestine, and to the pariah status of Jews among peoples. I trust that you, who so boldly have struggled for freedom and justice, will place your great influence on behalf of the claim for justice made by the people who so long and so dreadfully have suffered from its denial.

Yours very sincerely,
Albert Einstein

July 11, 1947
Nehru's response to Einstein

My dear Professor Einstein,

I received your letter of June 13th . . . and read it with the care and attention which it deserved. It is a privilege and an honour to be addressed by you and I was happy to receive your letter, though the subject . . . is a sad one.

I appreciate very much what you say about the recent decision of India's Constituent Assembly to abolish untouchability. This indeed has been our policy for many years past and it is a matter of deep satisfaction to us that what we have been trying to do in many ways will soon have the sanction of law, as embodied in the constitution, behind it. You say very rightly that the degradation of any group of human beings is a degradation of the civilization that has produced it. Ever since Mahatma Gandhi began to play a role in Indian politics and social affairs, he laid the greatest stress on the complete liquidation of untouchability and all that goes with it. He made it part of our freedom struggle and emphasized that it was folly to talk of political freedom when social freedom was denied or restricted for a large number of persons.

You know that in India there has been the deepest sympathy for the great sufferings of the Jewish people. We have rejected completely the racial doctrine which the Nazis and the Fascists proclaimed. Unfortunately, however, that doctrine is still believed in and acted upon by other people. You are no doubt aware of the treatment accorded by the Union of South Africa to Indians there on racial grounds. We made this an issue in the United Nations General Assembly last year and achieved a measure of success there. In raising this question before the United Nations we did not emphasize the limited aspect of it, but stood on the broader plane of human rights for all, in accordance with the Charter of the United Nations.

What has happened in recent years, more especially since the rise to power of Hitler in Germany, was followed by us with deep pain and anxiety. You are quite right in thinking that India has mourned the horrors which resulted in the death of millions of Jews in the murder machines which were set up in Germany and elsewhere. That was terrible enough, but it was still more terrible to contemplate a civilization which, in spite of its proud achievements, could produce this horror.

I need not assure you, therefore, of our deepest sympathy for the Jews and for all they have undergone during these past years. If we can help them in any way I hope and trust that India will not merely stand by and look on. As you know, national policies are unfortunately essentially selfish policies. Each country thinks of its own interest first and then of other interests. If it so happens that some international policy fits in with the national policy of the country, then that nation uses brave language about international betterment. But as soon as that international policy seems to run counter to national interests or selfishness, then a host of reasons are found not to follow that international policy.

We in India, engrossed as we have been in our struggle for freedom and in our domestic difficulties, have been unable to play any effective part in world affairs. The coming months, and possibly years, will not free us from these grave problems of our own country; but I have no doubt that we shall play a progressively more important part in international affairs. What that part will be in the future I can only guess. I earnestly hope that we shall continue to adhere to the idealism which has guided our struggle for freedom. But we have seen often enough idealism followed by something far less noble, and so it would be folly for me to prophesy what the future holds for us. All we can do is try our utmost to keep up standards of moral conduct both in our domestic affairs and in the international sphere.

The problem of Palestine, you will no doubt agree with me, is extraordinarily difficult and intricate. Where rights come into conflict it is not an easy matter to decide. With all our sympathy for the Jews we must and do feel that the rights and future of the Arabs are involved in this question. You have yourself framed the question: "Can Jewish need, no matter how acute, be met without the infringement of the vital rights of others?" Your answer to this question is in the affirmative. Broadly put, many may agree with you in that answer, but when we come to the specific application of this answer, the matter is not at all simple.

But legalities apart, and even apart from the many other issues involved, we have to face a certain existing situation. I do not myself see how this problem can be resolved by violence and conflict on one side or the other. Even if such violence and conflict achieves certain ends for the moment, they must necessarily be temporary. I do earnestly hope that some kind of agreement might be arrived at between the Arabs and the Jews. I do not think even an outside power can impose its will for long or enforce some new arrangement against the will of the parties concerned.

I confess that while I have a very great deal of sympathy for the Jews I feel sympathy for the Arabs also in their predicament. In any event, the whole issue has become one of high emotion and deep passion on both sides. Unless men are big enough on either side to find a solution which is just and generally agreeable to the parties concerned, I see no effective solution for the present.

I have paid a good deal of attention to this problem of Palestine and have read books and pamphlets on the subject issued on either side; yet I cannot say that I know all about it, or that I am competent to pass a final opinion as to what should be done. I know that the Jews have done a wonderful piece of work in Palestine and have raised the standards of the people there, but one question troubles me. After all these remarkable achievements, why have they failed to gain the goodwill of the Arabs? Why do they want to compel the Arabs to submit against their will to certain demands? That way of approach has been one which does not lead to a settlement, but rather to the continuation of the conflict. I have no doubt that the fault is not confined to one party but that all have erred. I think also that the chief difficulty has been the continuation of British rule in Palestine. We know, to our cost, that when a third party dominates, it is exceedingly difficult for the others to settle their differences, even when that third party has good intentions—and third parties seldom have such intentions!

It is difficult for me to argue this question with you who know so much more than I do. I have only indicated to you some of my own difficulties in the matter. But whatever those difficulties might be, I would assure you, with all earnestness, that I would like to do all in my power to help the Jewish people in their distress, insofar as I can do so, without injuring other people.

The world is in a very sorry mess and the appetite for war and destruction has not been satisfied yet. Here in India we stand on the verge of independence for which we have struggled for so long. Yet there is no joy in this country at this turning point in our long history and there will be no celebrations of this historic event next month, for we are all full of sorrow for

Pakistan

what has happened in our country during the past year and for the cutting away of a part from the parent country. This was not how we had envisioned our freedom. What is most distressing is the backgound of all these events, the bitterness, the hatred and violence that have disfigured the face of India in recent months. We have a terribly hard task before us, but we shall face it, of course, with the confidence that we shall overcome these difficulties as we have overcome others in the past.

I have shared your letter with Mahatma Gandhi and some other friends.

With regards,
Yours very sincerely,
Jawaharlal Nehru

After Einstein received Nehru's answer rejecting a vote for partition, one knowledgeable observer reports, "Zionist officials prepared a draft response. The draft letter stressed themes touched on by Nehru . . . and pleaded with Nehru" to reconsider his vote against partition. "It is unclear whether this draft was sent to Einstein and it appears unlikely that Einstein signed it or sent it to Nehru."[2]

It must have been a great help to have 71 billion from Germany after WWII! What could the Palestinians do with money like that?

EINSTEIN'S
CORRESPONDENTS

Norman Bentwich (1887–1971), author of numerous books on Judaism, Israel, and related subjects, was a barrister who served from 1922 to 1929 as the first attorney general in the British Mandate for Palestine. He was president of the Jewish Historical Society from 1960 to 1962.

Schmuel Hugo Bergmann (1883–1975) was a founder—along with Martin Buber, Judah Magnes, and others—of Brit Shalom, an organization created in the mid-1920s to advocate reconciliation and cooperation between Jews and Arabs. Bergmann was born in Czechoslovakia and studied in Prague, where he was part of a Jewish cultural group that included Buber, Franz Kafka, and Max Brod, and where he met Einstein. In 1920 Bergmann emigrated to Palestine, where he was a founder of the Histadrut Labor Federation and the Hebrew University, at which he went on to be a professor of philosophy, rector from 1936 to 1938, and director of the university library. He was a leading Israeli philosopher whose works include writings on the nature of quantum mechanics and causality, and he was twice a recipient of the Israel Prize: in 1954 for his writings in philosophy and in 1974 for his contributions to Israeli society.

Michele Besso (1873–1955), a Swiss/Italian Jewish engineer, became one of Einstein's closest friends and confidants during his years at the Federal Polytechnic Institute in Zurich, and then at the patent office in Bern where they both worked. Besso, whom Einstein regarded as "the best sounding board in Europe" for scientific ideas, is credited with introducing him to the works of physicist Ernst Mach, which influenced Einstein's own approach to the discipline. Besso often offered critical comments on Einstein's formulations, and when Einstein published his theory of special relativity in 1905, he acknowledged Besso's help: "My friend and colleague M. Besso steadfastly stood by me in my work on the problem here discussed, and [I am] indebted to him for many a valuable suggestion."[1]

Kurt Blumenfeld (1884–1963) was director of propaganda for the German Zionists and a proponent of the view that every Jew should emigrate to Palestine. He was secretary general of the World Zionist Organization from 1910 to 1914, president of the Union of German Zionists from 1924 to 1933, editor of the Zionist weekly *Die Welt,* and highly influential in recruiting key intellectuals to the cause. (Hannah Arendt, for one, spent a week in jail in the early 1930s for her efforts to collect materials in the Prussian State Library on anti-Semitic activities, a task she had been asked to do by Blumenfeld, who wished to present the materials to the Eighteenth Zionist Congress.) In 1919, before Einstein became world famous, Blumenfeld attracted Einstein's interest to some of the Zionists' activities. Two years later, Blumenfeld convinced an initially reluctant Einstein to accompany Chaim Weizmann on a 1921 tour (April 2 to May 30) of the United States to raise funds for the Hebrew University— although Blumenfeld cautioned Weizmann to be careful about letting Einstein have free reign in his speechmaking, since "Einstein . . . is no Zionist, and . . . often says things out of naïveté which are unwelcome by us."[2] Blumenfeld emigrated to Palestine in 1933.

Selig Brodetsky (1888–1954), a British mathematician born of a Russian émigré family, won a scholarship to Cambridge University in 1906, received a doctorate in mathematics from Leipzig University in 1913, and was a professor at the University of Leeds from 1924 to 1948. He was active throughout his career as a member and executive of the British Zionist Federation and president of the World Maccabi Federation. He became president of Hebrew University in Jerusalem in 1949, but illness led to his return to London in 1951.

Martin Buber (1878–1965), a prominent philosopher and theologian and a major advocate of cultural Zionism, was born in Vienna, and studied there before moving on to study and teach in Leipzig, Berlin, Zurich, and Frankfurt. In 1938 he emigrated to Palestine and began teaching at the Hebrew University. He campaigned for a binational state founded on Arab-Jewish equality, asserting that the partition of Palestine and creation of a Jewish state could be achieved only by violence, and that maintaining such a state in a hostile region was a recipe for permanent warfare.

Asis Domet (1890–1943), a German Arab poet who was a Zionist.

Paul Ehrenfest (1880–1933) was an Austrian theoretical physicist who was a friend and research collaborator of Einstein. The two met in Prague in 1912, and Ehrenfest was one of Einstein's closest friends for the next twenty years. The two men enjoyed talking and arguing in person and by mail, and they coauthored two papers. Ehrenfest shared Einstein's internationalist outlook. Ehrenfest helped clarify the foundations of the quantum theory and statistical mechanics, and "Einstein described [him] as the best teacher of physics he had ever met, a brilliant but unconventional lecturer who was passionately committed to the welfare and development of his students."[3] Born in Vienna to a Jewish family, Ehrenfest spent most of his career as a professor at the University of Leiden, where he first lectured in 1912. Ehrenfest was long afflicted with insecurities and low self-esteem, and his depression culminated in the fatal shooting first of his younger son, who had Down's syndrome, and then of himself.

Abraham A. Fraenkel (1891–1965) was a German-born mathematician who left his professorship at the University of Marburg in 1928, spent the next year at the University of Kiel, and then emigrated to Jerusalem, where he was the first dean of the Faculty of Mathematics at the Hebrew University and served for a time as rector of the university. Fraenkel was one of the faculty leaders who worked to establish the university's Einstein Institute of Mathematics as a department of pure mathematics, to the exclusion of the several disciplines of applied math. To that end, and via his involvement in the university's efforts to create a first-rate physics department, he was part of a small group that consulted with Einstein on a regular basis. Fraenkel was a committed Zionist, a member of Vaad Leumi (the representative body of the Palestine Jewish National Assembly under the British Mandate), and a member of the Mizrachi Party. After retiring from the Hebrew University in 1959, he continued his writings on mathematics and philosophy and lectured at Bar Ilan University, near Tel Aviv.

Jerome Frank (1889–1957) had a distinguished career as a judge but won perhaps even more renown as a legal philosopher and author. Frank was born September 10, 1889, in New York City. He received a Ph.D. from the University of Chicago in

1909 and a law degree from the University of Chicago Law School in 1912. His next twenty years were spent in private practice, where he specialized in the reorganization of corporations. During the 1930s, Frank became involved in several of the agencies established as part of President Franklin D. Roosevelt's New Deal. In 1933 Felix Frankfurter, then a law professor at Harvard, recommended Frank for the position of general counsel to the Agricultural Adjustment Administration (AAA) and the Federal Surplus Relief Corporation. In 1935, however, Frank and several of his staff were fired because they insisted that benefits provided to cotton growers under AAA contracts should be shared with sharecroppers. Roosevelt then appointed Frank as special counsel to the Reconstruction Finance Corporation. From there Frank went to the Public Works Administration (PWA), where he took an active part in the litigation that surrounded Roosevelt's public power program. After William O. Douglas's appointment to the Supreme Court in 1939, Frank succeeded him as chairman of the Securities and Exchange Commission (SEC). Two years later, in 1941, Frank was appointed to the U.S. Court of Appeals for the Second Circuit, a position that he held until his death.

Chaim Greenberg (1889–1953) was a prominent American labor Zionist thinker and writer. He was a leader of Poalei Zion (Workers of Zion) in the United States, and he was editor (with Marie Syrkin) of *Jewish Frontiers,* a Zionist journal that published David Ben-Gurion, Moshe Shertok, Sholom Asch, and Maurice Samuel, among others. His writings (e.g., "Patriotism and Plural Loyalties") sought to resolve the issue of dual loyalty among American Zionists and provide a distinctly American framework for the Zionist cause. He also did outreach to other countries in support of Israel. There are centers named after him in Argentina, the United States, and Israel.

Fritz Haber (1868–1934), a German chemist and a friend of Einstein in Berlin, was director from 1911 to 1933 of the Kaiser Wilhelm Institute for Physical Chemistry and Electro-chemistry (later renamed the Fritz Haber Institute). He received the 1918 Nobel Prize in Chemistry for his work on synthetic fertilizer, a milestone in the development and production of explosives. As chief of Germany's Chemical Warfare Service in World War I, Haber advocated the use of chlorine gas in warfare, a stance that brought him considerable criticism in the war's aftermath and, more immediately, may have been a precipitating factor in the 1915 suicide of his wife (also a chemist), who disapproved of his involvement in the program. Born a Jew, Haber saw himself as a German patriot and responded to the rise of German anti-Semitism by converting to Christianity. Nonetheless, he remained a Jew in the eyes of the Nazis, and he fled Germany in 1933, fell ill in exile, and died of a heart attack the following year. The arc of Haber's life, as reflected in his long friendship with Einstein, became the subject of a 2003 play, *Einstein's Gift*, by Vern Thiessen.

Willi Hellpach (1877–1955) was a noted social and medical psychologist and an anti-Zionist and liberal politician during the Weimar years. He was the German Democratic Party's unsuccessful candidate for president of the Weimar Republic in 1925, and was a member of the Reichstag from 1928 to 1930, after which time he withdrew from politics and devoted himself to his clinical and academic pursuits.

Maurice B. Hexter (1891–1990) was a leader in Jewish philanthropic and social agencies in the United States; a key figure in the establishment of schools of social work at Hunter College, Brandeis University, and Yeshiva University; and, in later life, a sculptor of note. His work for the Joint Palestine Survey Committee in the late 1920s led to his appointment in 1929 as a non-Zionist member of the Jewish Agency for Palestine and to his moving to Jerusalem, where he directed efforts to raise funds to rebuild homes destroyed during rioting earlier that year between Arabs and Jews, and where he was active in negotiations with the British cabinet. Upon his return to the United States in 1938, he joined the Federation of Jewish Philanthropies, where he held executive positions until his retirement in 1967 and served as a consultant thereafter.

Bernard Lecache (1895–1968), a French journalist, founded the League Against Pogroms following the 1926 assassination in Paris of the leader of the government-in-exile of the Ukrainian People's Republic by a Jewish anarchist seeking to avenge the deaths of his family members in the 1919 pogroms in the Ukraine. Lecache's organization generated media support for the assassin, who was acquitted in 1927 by a French jury. Subsequently, the League Against Pogroms, which received the endorsement and involvement of a number of prominent personalities, including Albert Einstein, evolved into the International League Against Racism and Anti-Semitism (LICRA), which remains an active civil rights group and has extended its interests in recent years to a broad range of civil liberties and social justice issues around the world. Lecache also wrote for *l'Humanité* and was known to be a member of the French Communist Party.

Samuel David Leidesdorf (1881–1968), the head of one of the largest accounting firms in the United States, was a founding trustee of the Institute for Advanced Study and became Albert Einstein's accountant when Einstein joined the institute faculty. Leidesdorf was active in numerous civic and charitable causes: He served on the executive committee of the American Jewish

Committee and the foundation committee of the United Negro College Fund, was chairman of the board of NYU Medical Center from 1956 until his death, and was said to have supported the birth of the state of Israel by personally guaranteeing $500 million to Chase Manhattan Bank to institute the creation of Israel bonds.

Isaac Don Levine (1892–1981), born in Russia, came to the United States in 1911 and began his career as a journalist with the *Kansas City Star*. He went on to cover the Russian revolution and its aftermath for the *New York Herald Tribune* and, later, the *Chicago Daily News*. He was a columnist for Hearst newspapers in the 1930s, editor of the anti-Communist magazine *Plain Talk* in the late 1940s, and was a witness against Alger Hiss before hearings of the House Un-American Activities Committee.

Zvi Lurie (1906–1968) was an American-born Jew who became a major political figure in the Palestine Mandate. He was a member of the Vaad Leumi (the Jewish People's Council within the British Mandate), one of the thirty-seven signers of the Israeli declaration of independence, a founder of Kol Yisrael (which broadcast the declaration), and a representative of the Mapam Party in the Provisional State Council following the declaration. Subsequently he worked with the Jewish Agency for Israel to cement ties with the diaspora and aid Jewish emigration to Israel.

Judah Magnes (1877–1948) was a Reform rabbi in New York and, later, an educator in Palestine. He was a founder of the American Jewish Committee in 1906, and became the first chancellor of the Hebrew University in 1925. While Magnes, who was born and educated in the United States, was doing postgraduate work in Europe, he visited Jewish villages of Galician and Russian Poland, an experience that led to his active involvement in Zionism. In New York, he became a prominent advocate of American liberal causes and of Jewish cultural, social, and labor issues, and he sought to unify American Zionists and their Eastern European counterparts. He was a pacifist and a strong advocate of a binational state, envisioning a Palestine that would be neither Jewish nor Arab but would extend equal rights to all.

Erich Mendelsohn (1887–1953) was a German Jewish architect, known for his expressionist buildings in the 1920s, and for developing a dynamic functionalism in his projects for department stores and cinemas. In 1917 he was offered the opportunity to design the Einsteinturm (Einstein Tower), an astrophysical observatory in the Albert Einstein Science Park in Potsdam, built to support astronomer Erwin Finlay-Freundlich's experiments and observations aimed at confirming Einstein's relativity theory. A highly successful commercial architect in Weimar Germany, Mendelsohn was the first foreign architect invited to plan a building for the USSR, where he designed the Red Flag Textile Factory in 1925. With Nazism taking hold in Germany, Mendelsohn emigrated to England in 1933. His fortune was later seized by the Nazis, and he was ousted from the German Architects' Union and the Prussian Academy of Arts. At the behest of Chaim Weizmann, an old acquaintance, he undertook a series of projects in Palestine and in 1935 opened a bureau in Jerusalem.

Hans Mühsam (1876–1957) was a physician and lifelong friend of Einstein. They wrote jointly when Einstein lived in Berlin (1914–1932), publishing a 1923 research paper on the experimental determination of the permeability of filters. It was most probably in 1917 that the two men first met and became friends. Although they emigrated to different parts of the world in the early 1930s—Einstein to the United States and Mühsam and his wife to Palestine, where they settled in Haifa—their friendship survived the emigration, and they continued their dense correspondence until Einstein's death in 1955.

Otto Nathan (1893–1987) was Einstein's trusted friend, financial adviser, executor of his will, and cotrustee of his estate. He was an economic adviser to the Weimar Republic from 1920 to 1933, when he left Nazi Germany for the United States and took a post in the Economics Department of Princeton University, where he met Einstein. He also taught at New York University, Howard University, and Vassar College, was a consultant on economic literature to the Library of Congress, and worked extensively on development of the Einstein Archives. He lost his teaching job in the McCarthy era of the early fifties and, hoping to find work overseas, was initially denied a passport because "the State Department continued asserting that I was a Communist [and] also held against me my friendship with Einstein. . . ."[4] Nathan was the author of two books on the Nazi economic system, published in the 1940s, and was coeditor (with Heinz Norden) of *Einstein on Peace,* published in 1960.

Louis Isaac Rabinowitz (1906–1984), born in Edinburgh, Scotland, was an Orthodox rabbi, historian, and philologist who held rabbinical appointments in several London synagogues before becoming senior Jewish chaplain of the British Army in World War II. He occupied that post during the Normandy invasion and with the Allied forces in the Middle East. In 1945 he became chief rabbi of the United Hebrew Congregation of Johannesburg. In 1947, as a follower of Zeev Jabotinsky and his brand of Revisionist Zionism, Rabinowitz protested British policies in Palestine, which he viewed as a violation of the Palestine Mandate, by publicly discarding his British war decorations.

Emery Reves (1904–1981) was a Hungarian-born writer, publisher, and proponent of world federalism who was instrumental in disseminating the writings and ideas of Winston Churchill and advocating on behalf of Churchill's call for the nations of the West, notably the United States, to enlist in the fight against fascism in the run-up to World War II. In 1933 Reves operated a publishing company in Berlin that distributed news articles upholding democracy and opposing Nazism. When his office was raided by storm troopers in April of that year, he fled to Paris, where he renewed his efforts to promote the views of leading pro-democracy and anti-Nazi European statesmen. This led him into contact with Churchill, and to his being dispatched to New York to support British propaganda efforts in North and South America. Reves's own 1945 book, *The Anatomy of Peace*, which argued that world peace required world law (and dismissed the fledgling United Nations as an instrument not of law but of power), was cited by Einstein as the "political answer to the atomic bomb."

F. I. Shatara, M.D. (dates unavailable), a Christian Palestinian American born in Jaffa, was a surgeon and instructor of anatomy at Long Island College Hospital. He was a member of the Syrian Educational Society and president of the Arab National League, a lobbying organization founded in the United States in 1936. While president of the league, Shatara met with Einstein to discuss matters that included a possible agreement between Arabs and Jews aimed at avoiding the partition of Palestine.

Leon Simon (1881–1965), after receiving his degree from Oxford, rose through the British civil service ranks to become a director of the postal service. He worked on the Balfour Declaration, and he was for many years chairman of the executive committee of the Hebrew University. "But his main interest has been in the cultural aspect of Jewish nationalism," explains the biographical note from his publisher (the Jewish Publication Society). As a cultural Zionist, Simon sympathized with Einstein more than with Weizmann and the other Zionist leaders. Indeed, his biographical note declares: "A disciple of Ahad Ha-am [often called the founder of cultural Zionism] since his student days, and a personal friend from 1908 onwards, he has published three volumes of translations of Ahad Ha-am's writings and is joint author of [his] Hebrew biography."

Chaim Tchernowitz (1871–1949) was a Russian-born Talmudic student, author, and ordained rabbi. He received his doctorate from the University of Würzburg and moved to the United States in 1923, where he taught the Talmud at the Jewish Institute of Religion in New York. His pseudonym—Rav Tsaïr (Young Rabbi)—reflected his goal of combining traditional Torah study with modern scientific research in order to revitalize Jewish learning. He developed methods for modernizing the teaching of the Talmud and wrote several books detailing the historical development of Jewish laws. A supporter of the Zionist movement, he wrote numerous essays on the struggle for Jewish independence. He and Einstein had met in Berlin and maintained contact over the years. In 1939 Einstein provided a written endorsement for a Hebrew-language literary journal being launched by Tchernowitz, the aims of which Einstein commended as "reviving Jewish tradition and spreading new light."

Max M. Warburg (1867–1946), from 1910 until 1938, was director of M. M. Warburg & Company in Hamburg, a family banking firm that had been established in the late eighteenth century. By the time of the First World War, it was the leading commercial bank in Germany, with Warburg family members strongly represented on Wall Street as well. Although Jewish, Warburg felt that he was as good a German as anyone else, and when the Nazis came to power in the 1930s, he initially believed he could and should wait out the Nazi crisis. The Warburg family worked actively to maintain German American trade and to defeat efforts in the United States to boycott German goods, enlisting the American Jewish Committee and the B'nai B'rith in this effort. Warburg was a member of the board of I. G. Farben from its inception in 1925 until finally being removed because he was a Jew. He joined the board of the German Reichsbank in 1933, a post he maintained until he and his family left for the United States in 1938. Warburg and his clan were at odds with the Zionists; although they supported Jewish settlements in Palestine, they funded agricultural settlements for Jews in Russia and the Ukraine in the 1920s and they opposed a Jewish state, believing that it would lead inevitably to conflict and war between Jews and Arabs.

Chaim Weizmann (1874–1952) was a chemist who became president of the World Zionist Organization (1920–1931 and 1935–1946) and then the first president of Israel (1949–1952). Born in Russia, he became a British subject in 1910 and played a key role during World War I in helping the British Admiralty develop weapons. He was a friend of British foreign secretary Balfour and helped persuade him to issue the Balfour Declaration.

Stephen S. Wise (1874–1949) was born in Budapest and, while still an infant, was brought by his family to New York, where his father was a Conservative rabbi. Wise was ordained at the Jewish Theological Seminary and went on to become a Reform rabbi and, unlike most Reform Jews of the time, a Zionist. He was honorary secretary of the Zionist Organization of America at its founding in 1897 and the next year was elected to the General Action Committee of the Second Zionist Congress in Basel. He graduated from the City College of New York in 1892. In 1914 he worked with Louis Brandeis and the American Zionist movement to obtain Woodrow Wilson's support for the Balfour Declaration, which committed Great Britain to facilitate the establishment of a Jewish national home in Palestine. He took a leading role in a broad range of civic and social justice causes in the United States, and became a confidant of Franklin Delano Roosevelt, who sought his advice on issues pertaining to the Jewish community. In this regard, there is considerable controversy over his role during the rise of the Nazis in Germany and the Holocaust. Some credit him with rallying public opinion against Nazism, organizing groups such as the World Jewish Congress to further that end, and urging Roosevelt to facilitate Jewish emigration to Palestine and to admit Jewish refugees into the United States. Others view him as having been ineffective, overly cautious, and too concerned with muting Jewish criticism of the Roosevelt administration and Jewish activism against the Holocaust. Ultimately, both camps agree, his efforts were ineffective and the Roosevelt administration unresponsive, and Wise found himself isolated in the Jewish hierachy and then replaced as the leader of American Zionism by Rabbi Abba Hillel Silver. But Einstein never wavered in his friendship for Wise. In his eulogy for Wise, Einstein wrote, "Among all those whom I have personally met who have labored in the cause of justice and in the interest of the hardpressed Jewish people, only a few were at all times selfless—but there was no one who gave his love and energy with such consuming devotion as Stephen Wise."[5]

Heinrich York-Steiner (1859–1934) was an Austrian politician, diplomat, and author who began his career as a merchant in Vienna and went on to become an editor at a publishing house there in 1896. He was an early Zionist and a strong supporter of Theodor Herzl. In 1897 he served as chairman of the organizing committee of the First Zionist Congress, in Basel, and he took over technical preparation of the Zionist central organ, *Die Welt*. In 1899, following the Third Zionist Congress, he developed a program for opening subsidiaries of the Jewish Colonial Bank around the world, and in 1903 he became head of the bank's New York branch. He emigrated to Palestine in 1933. In 1929, following the Arab-Jewish riots, Einstein wrote to York-Steiner that the Zionist movement must "avoid the danger of degenerating into blind nationalism [although] the attitude of our [Zionist] officialdom [and] the majority of public expressions in this connection [appear] to leave much to be desired."[6]

BIBLIOGRAPHY

GENERAL WORKS

Books

Abunimah, Ali. *One Country*. New York: Metropolitan Books, Henry Holt, 2006.

Ahad Ha'Am. *Selected Essays*. Translated and edited by Leon Simon. Philadelphia: Jewish Publication Society of America, 1936. Reprint of 1912 edition.

Antonius, George. *The Arab Awakening*. Beirut: Khayat's College Book Co-op, 1938.

Arendt, Hannah. *The Jewish Writings*. New York: Schocken Books, 2007.

Atiyah, Edward. *The Arabs*. London: Penguin Books, 1955.

Avineri, Shlomo. *The Making of Modern Zionism*. New York: Basic Books, 1981.

Avishai, Bernard. *The Tragedy of Zionism*. New York: Helios Press, 2002.

Beattie, Kirk. *Egypt During the Nasser Years*. Boulder, CO: Westview Press, 1994.

Ben-Arieh, Yehoshua. *Jerusalem in the 19th Century*. Vol. 2. New York: Palgrave-MacMillan, 1986.

Ben-Eliezer, Uri. *The Emergence of Israeli Militarism, 1936–1956.* Tel Aviv: Dvir, 1995.

———. *The Making of Israeli Militarism.* Bloomington: Indiana University Press, 1998.

Bennis, Phyllis. *Challenging Empire.* Northampton, MA: Olive Branch Press, 2006.

———. *Understanding the Palestinian-Israeli Conflict.* Foreword by Danny Glover. Northampton, MA: Olive Branch Press, 2007.

Bentwich, Norman. *Fulfillment in the Promised Land.* London: Soncino Press, 1938.

Blumenfeld, Kurt. *Im Kampf um den Zionismus: Briefe aus 5 Jahrzehnten (The War About Zionism: Letters from 5 Decades).* Excerpts translated by Michael Schiffmann. Stuttgart: Deutsche Verlagsanstalt, 1976.

British Ministry of Foreign Affairs. *From Mandate to Independence.* London: British Ministry of Foreign Affairs, 1998.

Buber, Martin. *A Land of Two Peoples.* Chicago: University of Chicago Press, 1948.

Carter, Jimmy. *Palestine: Peace Not Apartheid.* New York: Simon & Schuster, 2006.

Chomsky, Noam. *The Fateful Triangle.* Cambridge, MA: South End Press, 1999.

———. *Middle East Illusions.* Lanham, MD: Rowman & Littlefield, 2003.

Cramer, Richard Ben. *How Israel Lost: The Four Questions.* New York: Simon & Schuster, 2005.

David, Ron. *Arabs and Israel for Beginners.* Danbury, CT: Writers and Readers Publishing, 2001.

Davis, Uri. *Apartheid Israel.* London: Zed Books, 2003.

Eisenberg, Laura Zittrain, Neil Caplan, Naomi B. Sokoloff, and Mohammed Abu-Nimer, eds. *Traditions and Transition in Israel Studies.* Vol. VI. Albany: State University of New York Press, 2003.

Elon, Amos. *Herzl*. New York: Holt, Rinehart and Winston, 1975.

———. *Israelis: Founders and Sons*. New York: Holt, Rinehart and Winston, 1971.

———. *The Pity of It All: A History of Jews in Germany, 1743–1933*. New York: Henry Holt, 2002.

Esco Foundation. *Palestine*. New Haven, CT: Yale University Press, 1947.

Farber, Seth. *Radicals, Rabbis and Peacemakers: Conversations with Jewish Critics of Israel*. Monroe, ME: Common Courage Press, 2005.

Findley, Paul. *They Dare to Speak Out*. Westport, CT: Lawrence Hill, 1985.

Finkelstein, Norman. *Beyond Chutzpah*. Berkeley: University of California Press, 2005.

———. *Image and Reality of the Israel Palestine Conflict*. London: Verso, 1995.

Fisk, Robert. *The Great War for Civilization*. New York: Vintage Books, 2007.

Flapan, Simha. *The Birth of Israel: Myths and Realities*. New York: Pantheon Books, 1987.

———. *Zionism and the Palestinians*. London: Crom Helm, 1979.

Gettleman, Marvin E., and Stuart Schaar, eds. *The Middle East and Islamic World Reader*. New York: Grove Press, 2003.

Gilbert, Martin. *Israel: A History*. New York: William. Morrow, 1998.

Goldmann, Nahum. *The Ben Gurion-Goldmann Debate*. New York: Netzivut Betar, 1967.

———. *The Jewish Paradox*. New York: Weidenfeld and Nicolson, 1978.

Gorenberg, Gershom. *The Accidental Empire*. New York: Times Books, 2006.

Gorny, Yosef. *Zionism and the Arabs, 1882–1948: A Study of Ideology.* New York: Oxford University Press, 1987.

Halper, Jeff. *Obstacles to Peace: A Reframing of the Palestinian-Israeli Conflict.* 3rd ed. Jerusalem: Israeli Committee Against House Demolitions, 2005.

Halpern, Ben. *A Clash of Heroes.* New York: Oxford University Press, 1987.

Heikal, Mohammed. *Autumn of Fury: The Assassination of Sadat.* London: Andre Deutsch, 1983.

———. *Cutting the Lion's Tail.* London: Andre Deutsch, 1986.

———. *Revisiting History.* Published in Arabic, translated by Raed and Majed Jarrar, edited by Niki Akhaven.

———. *The Road to Ramadan.* London: William Collins Sons, 1975.

———. *Secret Channels: The Inside Story of Arab-Israeli Peace Negotiations.* London: HarperCollins, 1997.

———. *Sphinx and Commissar.* London: William Collins Sons, 1978.

Hertzberg, Arthur. *The Fate of Zionism.* San Francisco: Harper, 2003.

———, ed. *The Zionist Idea.* New York: Atheneum and Jewish Publishing Society of America, 1969.

Herzl, Theodor. *The Complete Diaries of Theodor Herzl.* Edited by Rafael Patai. New York: Herzl Press and Thomas Yoseloff, 1960.

Hess, Moses. *Rome and Jerusalem.* New York: Bloch Publishing, 1918.

Higham, Charles. *Trading with the Enemy.* New York: Delacorte Press, 1983.

Hirst, David. *The Gun and the Olive Branch.* New York: Thunder's Mouth Press / Nation Books, 2003.

Hofstadter, Dan, ed. *Egypt and Nasser.* Vol. 1, 1952–1956. New York: Facts on File, 1973.

Howard, Harry N. *The King-Crane Commission*. Beirut: Khayats, 1963.

Hurani, Albert. *A History of the Arab Peoples*. New York: Warner Books, 1992.

Hurewitz, J. C. *The Struggle for Palestine*. New York: Schocken Books, 1976.

Indinopulos, Thomas A. *Weathered by Miracles*. Chicago: Ivan R. Dee, 1998.

Karpf, Anne, Brian Klug, Jacqueline Rose, and Barbara Rosenbaum, eds. *A Time to Speak Out: Independent Jewish Voices on Israel, Zionism and Identity*. London: Verso Books, 2008.

Khalidi, Rashid. *The Iron Cage*. Boston: Beacon Press, 2006.

———. *Palestinian Identity*. New York Columbia University Press, 1998.

———. *Resurrecting Empire*. Boston: Beacon Press, 2005.

Khalidi, Walid. *From Haven to Conquest*. Beirut: Institute for Palestine Studies, 1971.

———. *Palestine Reborn*. London: I. B. Tauris, 1992.

Kiernan, Thomas. *The Arabs*. London: Sphere Books / Abacus, 1978.

Kimmerling, Baruch, and Joel S. Migdal. *The Palestinian People: A History*. Cambridge, MA: Harvard University Press, 2003.

Krämer, Gudrun. *A History of Palestine*. Princeton, NJ: Princeton University Press, 2008.

Kushner, Tony, and Alisa Solomon, eds. *Wrestling with Zion: Progressive Jewish-American Responses to the Israeli-Palestinian Conflict*. New York: Grove Press, 2003.

Laqueur, Walter. *Dying for Jerusalem*. Naperville, IL: Sourcebooks, 2006.

———. *A History of Zionism*. New York: Schocken Books, 1972.

———. *Israel Arab Reader*. New York: Bantam Books, 1976.

LeBor, Adam. *City of Oranges*. New York: W. W. Norton, 2007.

Lerner, Rabbi Michael. *Healing Israel/Palestine*. San Francisco: Tikkun Books, 2003.

Lewis, Bernard. *Semites and Anti-Semites: An Inquiry into Conflict and Prejudice*. New York: W. W. Norton, 1999.

Lewisohn, Ludwig. *Theodor Herzl*. Cleveland: World Publishing, 1955.

Lilienthal, Alfred M. *What Price Israel?* Haverford, CN: Infinity Publishing, 2003.

———. *The Zionist Connection: What Price Peace?* New York: Dodd Mead, 1978.

Lockman, Zachary. *Comrades and Enemies: Arab and Jewish Workers in Palestine, 1906–1948*. Berkeley: University of California Press, 1996.

Lustick, Ian S., ed. *From War to War*. Vol. 3. New York: Garland Publishing, 1994.

Lynch, Marc. *Voices of the New Arab Public*. New York: Columbia University Press, 2006.

Magnes, Judah L. *Like All the Nations?* Jerusalem: Weiss Press, 1930.

Mandel, Neville J. *The Arabs and Zionism*. Berkeley: University of California Press, 1976.

Mansfield, Peter. *A History of the Middle East*. Edited by Nicolas Pelham. New York: Penguin, 2004.

Menuhin, Moshe. *The Decadence of Judaism*. New York: Exposition Press, 1965.

Meyer, Hajo G. *The End of Judaism: An Ethical Tradition Betrayed*. Marathon, FL: G. Meyer Books, 2007.

Morris, Benny. *The Birth of the Palestinian Refugee Problem, 1947–1949*. Cambridge: Cambridge University Press, 1987.

———. *1948: A History of the First Arab-Israeli War*. New Haven, CT: Yale University Press, 2008.

————. *Righteous Victims: A History of Zionist-Arab Conflict, 1881–2001*. New York: Vintage Books, 1999.

Muslih, Muhammad Y. *The Origins of Palestinian Nationalism*. New York: Columbia University Press, 1988.

Neumann, Michael. *The Case Against Israel*. Petrolia, CA: Counterpunch and AK Press, 2005.

Palumbo, Michael. *Imperial Israel: The History of the Occupation of the West Bank and Gaza*. London: Bloomsbury, 1990.

————. *The Palestinian Catastrophe: The 1948 Expulsion of a People from Their Homeland*. London: Faber & Faber, 1987.

Pappe, Ilan, ed. *The Ethnic Cleansing of Palestine*. Oxford: One World Press, 2006.

———. *Israel/Palestine Question: Rewriting Histories*. London: Routledge, 1999.

———. *The Making of the Arab-Israeli Conflict, 1947–1951*. London: I B Tauris, 1992.

Parkes, James. *Whose Land?* New York: Taplinger Publishing, 1949.

Peretz, Don. *The Middle East Today*. Westport, CN: Praeger, 1994.

Petras, James. *The Power of Israel in the United States*. Atlanta: Clarity Press, 2006.

Porath, Yehoshoa. *The Palestinian-Arab National Movement*. Vol. 2, *From Riots to Rebellion, 1929–1939*. London: F. Cass, 1977.

Reinharz, Jehuda. *Chaim Weizmann: The Making of a Statesman*. New York: Oxford University Press, 1993.

Rodinson, Maxime. *Israel: A Colonial Settler State?* New York: Monad Press, 1973.

————. *Israel and the Arabs*. London: Penguin, 1969.

Rogan, Eugene L., and Avi Shlaim, eds. *The War for Palestine: Rewriting the History of 1948*, with an afterword by Edward Said. Cambridge: Cambridge University Press, 2001.

Rokach, Livia. *Israel's Sacred Terrorism: A Study Based on Moshe Sharett's Personal Diary and Other Documents.* Belmont, MA: Association of Arab American University Graduates, 1986.

Sa'di, Ahmad H., and Lila Abu-Lughod, eds. *Nakba: Palestine, 1948, and the Claims of Memory.* New York: Columbia University Press, 2007.

Said, Edward. *The Edward Said Reader.* New York: Vintage Books, 2000.

———. *The Question of Palestine.* New York: Vintage Books, 1992.

Schwartz, Stephen. *Is It Good for the Jews? The Crisis of America's Israel Lobby.* New York: Doubleday, 2006.

Segev, Tom. *The First Israelis.* Jerusalem: Domino Press, 1984.

———. *1967: Israel, the War and the Year That Transformed the Middle East.* New York: Henry Holt, 2007.

———. *One Palestine, Complete: Jews and Arabs Under the British Mandate.* New York: Henry Holt, 2000.

Selfa, Lance, ed. *The Struggle for Palestine.* Chicago: Haymarket Books, 2002.

Selzer, Michael. *The Aryanization of the Jewish State.* New York: Black Star, 1967.

Shahak, Israel. *Racism et l'etat d'Israel.* Paris: Athier, 1975.

Shatz, Adam. *Prophets Outcast: A Century of Dissident Jewish Writing about Zionism and Israel.* New York: Nation Books, 2004.

Shipley, David K. *Arab and Jew.* New York: Times Books, 1986.

Shlaim, Avi. *Collusion Across the Jordan.* New York: Columbia University Press, 1988.

———. *The Iron Wall.* New York: W. W. Norton, 2001.

———. *The Politics of Partition: King Abdullah, The Zionists, and Palestine, 1921–1951.* New York: Oxford University Press, 1990.

Simon, Leon. *Ahad Ha-Am: A Biography*. Philadelphia: Jewish Publication Society, 1960.

Smith, Charles D. *Palestine and the Arab-Israeli Conflict*. New York: St. Martin's Press, 2004.

Stone, I. F. *Underground to Palestine*. New York: Pantheon Books, 1978. (Includes Stone's introductory essays, "Confessions of a Jewish Dissident" and "The Other Zionism," not in the original 1948 edition.)

Swedenburg, Ted. *Memories of Revolt*. Minneapolis: University of Minnesota Press, 1995.

Tessler, Mark. *A History of the Israeli-Palestinian Conflict*. Bloomington: Indiana University Press, 1994.

Teveth, Shabtai. *Ben-Gurion and the Palestinian Arabs*. New York: Oxford University Press, 1985.

———. *Ben-Gurion's Spy: The Story of the Political Scandal That Shaped Modern Israel*. New York: Columbia University Press, 1996.

Thomas, Baylis. *How Israel Was Won: A Concise History of the Arab-Israeli Conflict*. Lanham. MD: Lexington Books, 1999.

Tolan, Sandy. *The Lemon Tree*. New York: Bloomsbury Publishing, 2006.

Tuchman, Barbara W. *Bible and Sword: England and Palestine from the Bronze Age to Balfour*. New York: Funk & Wagnalls, 1956.

Turki, Dr. Benyan Saud. *The King-Crane Commission*. Kuwait City: Kuwait University, 1999.

U.S. Library of Congress, Political and Cultural Zionism, "Dubnow, Herzl, and Ahad Ha-aw," http://lccn.loc.gov/67005834.

Waines, David. *The Unholy War, 1897–1971,* with a foreword by Maxime Rodinson. Montreal: Chateau Books, 1971.

Warschawski, Michel. *On the Border*. London: Pluto Press, 2005.

Weisgal, Meyer W., and Joel Carmichael, eds., *Chaim Weizmann: A Biography by Several Hands*. New York: Athenium, 1953.

Weizmann, Chaim. *Trial and Error*. New York: Harper & Bros., 1949.

Articles

Atiyah, Edward. "What Was Promised in Palestine." Pamphlets on Arab Affairs, United Kingdom Arab Office, London, 1946.

Caplan, Neil. "Ben-Gurion's Banana Peel." *Journal of Palestine Studies* 26, no. 2 (Winter 1997): 106–107.

Chuckman, John. "Israels's Bloody Excesses." *Counterpunch,* April 2003.

Economist, "Israel's Wasted Victory," May 26, 2007.

Goldmann, Nahum. "Zionist Ideology and the Reality of Israel." *Foreign Affairs* (Fall 1978): 70–82.

Halbrook, Stephen. "The Class Origins of Zionist Ideology." *Journal of Palestine Studies* 2, no. 1 (Fall 1972): 86–110.

Kohn, Hans. "Zion and the Jewish National Idea." *Menorah Journal,* Autumn and Winter 1958.

Machover, Moshe. "Israelis and Palestinians: Conflict and Resolution." Barry Amiel and Norman Melburn Trust 2006 Annual Lecture, London University School of Oriental and African Studies, November 30, 2006.

Mallison, W. T., Jr. Review of "Theodor Herzl, Complete Diaries," *George Washington Law Review,* June 1964.

Medoff, Rafael. "The Mufti's Nazi Years Re-examined." *Journal of Israeli History* 17, no. 3, 1966.

Nasser, Gamal Abdel. "Memoirs of the First Palestine War," translated and annotated by Walid Khalidi. *Journal of Palestine Studies* 2, no. 2 (Winter 1972): 3–32.

Oren, Michael B. "Escalation to Suez: The Egypt-Israel Border War, 1949–56." *Journal of Contemporary History* 24, no. 2 (April 1989): 347–74.

Palumbo, Michael. "What Happened to Palestine? The Revisionists Revisited." Americans for Middle East Understanding online, *Link* 23, no. 4 (September–October 1990).

Segev, Tom. "Courting Hitler." *New York Times,* Sunday Book Review, September 28, 2008, 34.

Shavit, Ari. "Waiting for the Barbarians." Interview with Benny Morris. *Ha'aretz,* January 6, 2004, www.haaretz.com.

Sicherman, Harvey. "The Sacred and the Profane: Judaism and International Relations." Foreign Policy Research Institute, *FPRI Wire* 10, no. 1 (January 2002).

BIOGRAPHICAL AND AUTOBIOGRAPHICAL WORKS
Books

Balibar, Francoise. *Einstein: Decoding the Universe.* Translated by David J. Baker and Dorie B. Baker. New York: Harry N. Abrams, 2001.

Berlin, Isaiah. "Einstein and Israel," in *Albert Einstein: Historical and Cultural Perspectives,* Gerald Holton and Yehuda Elkana, eds., Princeton, NJ: Princeton University Press, 1982 (from the Einstein Centennial Symposium, Jerusalem, 1979).

Boni, Nell, Monique Russ, and Dan H. Lawrence, comps. *Bibliographical Checklist and Index to the Published Writing of Albert Einstein.* Paterson, NJ: Pageant Books, 1960.

Brian, Denis. *Einstein: A Life.* New York: John Wiley & Sons, 1996.

———. *The Unexpected Einstein: The Real Man Behind the Icon.* New York: John Wiley & Sons, 2005.

Buchwald, Diana Kormos, gen. ed. *The Collected Papers of Albert Einstein.* 12 vols. Princeton, NJ: Princeton University Press, 1987–2006.

Calaprice, Alice. *The Expanded Quotable Einstein.* Princeton, NJ: Princeton University Press, 2000.

———. *The Quotable Einstein.* Princeton, NJ: Princeton University Press, 1996.

Calder, Nigel. *Einstein's Universe.* New York: Viking Press, 1979.

Clark, Ronald W. *Einstein: The Life and Times.* New York: Avon Books, 1972.

Dukas, Helen, and Banesh Hoffman, eds. *Albert Einstein: The Human Side.* Princeton, NJ: Princeton University Press, 1979.

Einstein, Albert. *The Fight Against War.* New York: John Day, 1933.

———. *Ideas and Opinions* (based on *Mein Weltbild*). Introduction by Alan Lichtman. New York: Modern Library, 1994.

———. *Lettres a Maurice Solovine.* Paris: Gauthier-Villars, 1956.

———. *Out of My Later Years.* New York: Philosophical Library, 1950.

———. *The World As I See It* (*Mein Weltbild*), revised and edited by Carl Seelig. Zurich: Europa-Verlag 1953.

Feldman, Burton. *112 Mercer Street.* New York: Arcade Publishing, 2007.

Feuer, Lewis S. *Einstein and the Generations of Science.* New Brunswick, NJ: Transaction, 1982.

Fölsing, Albrecht. *Albert Einstein: A Biography.* New York: Viking, 1997.

Frank, Philipp. *Einstein: His Life and Times.* New York: Knopf, 1947.

French, A. P., ed. *Einstein: A Centenary Volume.* Cambridge, MA: Harvard University Press, 1979.

Galison, Peter, Gerald Holton, and Silvan S. Schweber, eds. *Einstein for the 21st Century.* Princeton, NJ: Princeton University Press, 2008.

Goldsmith, Donald, and Marcia Bartusiak, eds. *E=Einstein.* New York: Sterling Publishing, 2006. (See esp. chapter by A. Pais, "Einstein and the Jews.")

Grundmann, Siegfried. *Einsteins Akte.* Berlin: Springer-Verlag, 1998.

Hoffmann, Banesh, with Helen Dukas. *Albert Einstein: Creator and Rebel.* London: Hart-Davis MacGibbon, 1973.

Holton, Gerald. *Einstein, History and Other Passions.* New York: Addison Wesley, 1996.

———. *Einstein and Humanism.* New York: Aspen Institute for Humanistic Studies, 1986.

Illy, József, ed. *Albert Meets America: How Journalists Treated Genius During Einstein's 1921 Travel.* Baltimore, MD: Johns Hopkins University Press, 2006.

Infeld, Leopold. *Albert Einstein.* New York: Scribner's, 1950.

Isaacson, Walter. *Einstein: His Life and Universe.* New York: Simon & Schuster, 2007.

Jerome, Fred. *The Einstein File: J. Edgar Hoover's Secret War Against the World's Most Famous Scientist.* New York: St. Martin's Press, 2002.

Jerome, Fred, and Rodger Taylor. *Einstein on Race and Racism.* Piscataway, NJ: Rutgers University Press, 2005.

Jewish Publication and Research Committee. *Einstein: The Man, the Jew.* New York: Jewish Publication and Research Committee, 1955.

Kantha, Sachi Sri. *An Einstein Dictionary.* Westport, CN: Greenwood Press, 1996.

Kramer, Rabbi William. *The Lone Traveler: Einstein in California.* Los Angeles: Skirball Cultural Center, 2004.

Nathan, Otto, and Heinz Norden, eds. *Einstein on Peace.* New York: Simon & Schuster, 1960.

Neffe, Juergen. *Einstein.* Translated by Shelley Frisch. New York: Farrar, Straus and Giroux, 2007.

Pais, Abraham. *Einstein Lived Here*. New York: Oxford University Press, 1994.

————. *Subtle Is the Lord*. New York: Oxford University Press, 1982.

Reichenstein, David. *Albert Einstein: A Picture of His Life and His Conception of the World*. Prague: Edward Goldston, 1934.

Reiser, Anton. *Albert Einstein: A Biographical Portrait*. New York: A. & C. Boni, 1930.

Rosenkranz, Ze'ev, and Barbara Wolff. *Albert Einstein: The Persistent Illusion of Transience*. Jerusalem: Magnes Press, Hebrew University, 2007.

Rowe, David E., and Robert Schulmann, eds. *Einstein on Politics*. Princeton, NJ: Princeton University Press, 2007.

Sayen, Jamie. *Einstein in America*. New York: Crown, 1985.

Schilpp, Paul Arthur, ed. *Albert Einstein: Philosopher-Scientist*. Includes Einstein's "Autobiographical Notes" in English and German. 3rd ed. Peru, IL: Open Court Publishing; Carbondale, IL: Library of Living Philosophers, 1995.

Schweber, Silvan S. *Einstein and Oppenheimer*. Cambridge, MA: Harvard University Press, 2008.

Seelig, Carl. *In Memoriam: Albert Einstein*. Zurich: Europa-Verlag, 1956.

Simon, Leon, ed. and transl. *About Zionism*. Speeches and letters by Einstein. London: Soncino Press, 1930, and New York: Macmillan, 1931.

Stachel, John. *Einstein from B to Z*. Boston: Birkhauser, 2002.

Stern, Fritz. *Einstein's German World*. Princeton, NJ: Princeton University Press, 1999.

Tauber, Gerald E. *Einstein on Zionism, Arabs and Palestine*. Tel Aviv: Tel Aviv University, 1979.

Whitrow, G. J., ed. *Einstein, the Man and His Achievement*.

New York: Dover Publications, 1975, original BBC publication in 1967 (based on three BBC radio broadcasts in 1966).

Articles

Aronowitz, Stanley. "Setting the Record Straight." *Logos* (Summer 2004), http://www.logosjournal.com/issue_3.3/aronowitz .htm.

Berlin, Isaiah. "Einstein and Israel." *New York Review of Books*. November 8, 1979. (Also in Holton and Elkana above.)

Blumenfeld, Kurt. "Einstein and Zionism." *Jewish Frontier*, June 1939.

Castagnetti, Giuseppe, and Hubert Goenner. "Albert Einstein as Pacifist and Democrat during World War I." *Science in Context* 9, no. 4 (1996): 325–86.

Eban, Abba. "Albert Einstein and Israel." *Jewish Chronicle*, October 2, 1959.

Einstein, Albert, and Erich Kahler. "The Arabs and Palestine." *Princeton Herald*, April 14 and 28, 1944 (see note 7, page 306).

Einstein, Albert. "Why Do They Hate the Jews?" *Colliers*, November 26, 1938, 9, 10, 38.

———. "Why Socialism?" *Monthly Review* 1, no. 1 (May 1949).

Farooq, Dr. Mohammad Omar. "Einstein, Zionism and Israel: Setting the Record Straight," http://globalwebpost.com/ farooqm/writings/other/einstein.htm, updated July 2006.

Heckman, Jessica. "Action at a Distance: Einstein as Activist." Vassar College Library for Special Collections, Einstein letters, Poughkeepsie, NY. Online: specialcollections.vassar.edu/ exhibits/einstein/essay3.html.

Hoffmann, Banesh. "Einstein and Zionism." In *General Relativity and Gravitation* by G. Shaviv and J. Rosen. New York: Halsted Press / John Wiley & Sons, 1975.

Kornitzer, Bela. "Einstein Answers 32 Questions." *York (PA) Gazette and Daily,* September 20, 1948.

Peterson, Kim. "Exposed: Albert Einstein Was Not a Zionist," http:www.dissidentvoice.org, May 1, 2003.

Veille, Simon. "Comment Einstein a failli etre president d'Israel." *Historia,* April 2004.

Werner, Alfred. "Passionate Apostle of Peace." *Liberal Judaism* April–May 1949, 9–10.

SOURCES FOR
EINSTEIN'S ARTICLES,
LETTERS, AND INTERVIEWS

The following list includes all the Einstein documents that appear in this volume (except for articles published in newspapers—all of which are clearly identified in the text) and the sources of those documents. Most were obtained from the Einstein Archives at the Hebrew University of Jerusalem. A smaller number came from the archives at Princeton University.

The vast majority of Einstein's papers, letters, and articles are housed in the archives in Jerusalem. Einstein bequeathed his private papers to the Hebrew University as it was an institute he helped to found, and it represented the kind of Jewish cultural center he supported (in contrast to a Jewish political state, with borders and an army, which he opposed).

Copies of many—but far from all—of Einstein's papers and documents are located in the libraries of Princeton University and Boston University in the United States. When copies of a document are in several locations, all copies have the same archive number.

A smaller collection of Einstein letters (mostly between Einstein and his friend and executor, Otto Nathan) and additional documents and photographs are housed in the Vassar College Library in Poughkeepsie, New York. Copies of most of these are also in the Jerusalem Archives.

Most of Einstein's documents were originally written in German. Where this book includes new translations and documents never previously translated, the translators are identified by their initials, as follows:

MS: Michael Schiffmann (who did most of the new translations)

NL: Natalie Lipsett

BW: Barbara Wolff

RJ: Rebecka Jerome

1. FIGHTING ANTI-SEMITISM 1919–1929

March 22, 1919: Excerpt from a letter to Paul Ehrenfest, CPAE 9, Doc. 10.

December 30, 1919: On Jewish immigration to Germany, in *Berliner Tageblatt*. CPAE 7, Doc. 29.

April 3, 1920: From Simon, ed. and trans., *About Zionism: Speeches and Lectures by Professor Albert Einstein* (New York: Macmillan, 1931), 17. (See also Rowe and Schulmann, 142.) Einstein Archives, Hebrew University of Jerusalem, archive #36-625; CPAE 7, Doc. 34.

April 3, 1920: Excerpt from a response to an invitation to a meeting of the Central Association of German Citizens of the Jewish Faith. Simon, *About Zionism*, 23, 24. Einstein Archives, Hebrew University, archive #43-443 and #35-060; CPAE 7, Doc. 37.

March 8, 1921: Excerpt from a letter to Maurice Solovine. Ronald W. Clark, *Einstein: The Life and Times* (New York: Avon Books, 1972), 466, citing Einstein, *Lettres a Solovine*, 27. Paris: Gauthier-Villars, 1956, 27.

March 9, 1921: Letter to Fritz Haber. Archive #12-332; trans. MS.

June 18, 1921: Letter to Paul Ehrenfest. Archive #10-256 (1–2), trans. MS.

June 21, 1921: "How I Became a Zionist," in *Jüdische Rundschau* 26, no. 49 (June 21, 1921): 351–52. CPAE 7, Doc. 57.

June 27, 1921: Address to a Zionist meeting in Berlin. Archive #28-008, #28-009 (1 and 2), and #28-010; CPAE 7, Doc. 59. Also in *Ideas and Opinions* (New York: Modern Library, 1994), 195–97. Also published as "On a Jewish Palestine."

July 1, 1921: "On a Jewish Palestine," in *Jüdische Rundschau* 26, no. 52 (June 21, 1921): 371. CPAE 7, Doc. 60.

May 1, 1923: "My Impression of Palestine," in *New Palestine* 4, no. 18 (May 1, 1923): 341.

February 8, 1924: Letter to Erich Mendelsohn. Archive #43-296, trans. MS.

February 17, 1925: Excerpts from "Mission," in *Jüdische Rundschau* 30, no. 14 (February 17, 1925): 129.

March 20, 1926: Letter to Kurt Blumenfeld in Berlin. Einstein Archives, Hebrew University, archive #43-300.

April 9, 1926: Excerpt from Einstein's response to Don Levine, which also appeared in *The New Palestine*. Levine's letter and Einstein's response, archive #44-289 and #44-289–90. Einstein's response also appeared as "Settlement in Russia," *New Palestine* 11 (1926): 334.

1927: "The Jews and Palestine," in *About Zionism*. Simon, 57–60.

2. YEARS OF CRISIS 1929–1939

1929: Address to Sixteenth Zionist Congress (July 28–August 14, 1929). Gerald Tauber,* *Einstein on Zionism, Arabs and Palestine* (Tel Aviv: Tel Aviv University, 1979), 9–10.

---

*When he died in 1977, Gerald Tauber was still collecting and editing *Einstein on Zionism, Arabs and Palestine*, manuscripts he compiled in three languages (English, Hebrew, and Arabic), available only at the Einstein Archives at the Hebrew University of Jerusalem.

(Courtesy Einstein Archives, Hebrew University of Jerusalem.)

August 1929: "Jew and Arab," in *About Zionism*. Simon, 69–71.

Two letters to Asis Domet. September 27 and December 5, 1929: Einstein Archives, Hebrew University, archive #46-056 and #46-057, trans. MS.

September 27, 1929: Excerpt from a letter to Hugo Bergmann. Einstein Archives, Hebrew University, archive #45-553, trans. MS.

October 8, 1929: Letter to Willy Hellpach. Archive #46-657 (1, 2, and 3). Also *The World As I See It* (*Mein Weltbild*) (Amsterdam: Querido, 1934). and *Ideas and Opinions* (based on *Mein Weltbild*) (New York: Modern Library, 1994), 187–88.

November 19, 1929: Letter to Heinrich York-Steiner. Einstein Archives, Hebrew University, archive #48-836, trans. MS.

Einstein-Weizmann letters of 1929. November 25 and November 30, 1929: Archive #33-411. December 1929: Archive #33-414.

December 4, 1929: Letter to Einstein from Selig Brodetsky, executive of the Zionist Organization, London. Archive #45-663 (1, 2, and 3).

December 14, 1929: Response to Brodetsky. Einstein Archives, Hebew University, trans. BW/RJ.

Two letters to the editors of *Falastin*. February 1, 1930: Simon, *About Zionism*, 85–86. Archive #46-150. March 15, 1930: Einstein, *Ideas and Opinions*, 188–90. Einstein Archives, Hebrew University, archive #46-154.

Exchange of letters about Peru with Max Warburg. April 24, 1930: Archive #47-834. August 5, 1930: Archive #47-849.

November 21, 1930: Excerpt from letter to Einstein in Berlin from the Jewish Colonization Association in Paris. Archive #47-851.

November 28, 1930: Excerpt from Einstein's response. Archive #47-853.

May 16, 1930: Letter to Bernard Lecache. Archive #47-384, trans. MS.

June 19, 1930: Letter to Hugo Bergmann. Archive #45-572. Earlier letter from Bergmann to Einstein, October 8, 1929, Archive #45-555.

December 13, 1930: Excerpt from "The Jewish Mission in Palestine," NBC radio address. Archive #28-121.

December 24, 1930: Letter to Rabbi Louis J. Newman, Congregation Rodeph Sholom, New York City. Archive #47-740.

1931: Excerpt from "Address on the Reconstruction of Palestine." Einstein, *Ideas and Opinions,* 192–93.

February 16, 1931: Excerpt from address at the Ambassador Hotel in Los Angeles. This was a banquet organized by the Jewish National Fund Council of Los Angeles. Archive #28-137. Also see Einstein, *Ideas and Opinions,* 177–78, 194.

July 11, 1932: Letter to Edward M. Freed, New York City. Einstein Archives, Hebrew University, archive #65-490, trans. BW.

May 30, 1932: Letter to Samuel David Leidesdorf. Archive #28-224.

February 13, 1934: Letter about China to Dr. Maurice William. Archive #52-256, trans. RJ. Einstein's exchanges with Dr. William courtesy of the UCLA Library, Rare Books Division.

May 21, 1934: Excerpt from a message to the United Jewish Appeal meeting at the Hotel Commodore, New York City. Archive #28-276, trans. MS.

April 20, 1935: "The Goal of Jewish-Arab Amity," address at

the Manhattan Opera House to the National Labor Committee for Palestine, as reported in *The New York Times* the following day. Archive #28-305. Excerpts in *The New York
Times,* April 21, 1935.

April 23, 1935: Excerpt from a letter to Beinish Epstein, leader
of the Revisionist Zionist Party. Einstein Archives, Hebrew
University, trans. BW.

April 28, 1935: Letter from Elias Ginsburg of the Zionist-
Revisionist Organization of America. Archive #51-461.

April 29, 1935: Letter to Salman Rubaschow of the League
for Labor Palestine in New York City. Archive #51-462,
trans. MS.

May 7, 1935: Letter from Elias Ginsburg. Archive #51-463.

May 10, 1935: Letter from Salman Rubaschow. Archive #51-
464, trans. MS.

May 12, 1935: Letter to Salman Rubaschow. Archive #51-465,
trans. MS.

March 10, 1936: Statement to the Keren Kajemeth (Jewish National Fund) celebration in Philadelphia. Archive #28-347,
trans. MS.

April 17 and April 29, 1938: Address for the Third Seder, Na-
tional Labor Committee for Palestine, as reported in *The New
York Times*. Archive #28-381–28-384/2. Excerpts in *The
New York Times,* April 18, 1938. Entire address published in
New Palestine, April 28, 1938, as "Our Debt to Zionism."
Also in Einstein, *Out of My Later Years* (New York: Philo-
sophical Library, 1950), and *Ideas and Opinions,* 206–208.

April 21, 1938: Letter from F. I. Shatara, president of the Arab
National League. Einstein Archives, Hebrew University,
archive #54-360.

May 16, 1938: Reply from Einstein. Archive #54-365, trans. RJ.

May 24, 1938: Letter to F. I. Shatara. Archive #54-368.

May 30, 1938: Excerpt from a letter to Samuel Leidesdorf. Archive #53-770, trans. MS.

May 31, 1938: Excerpt from a note to Otto Nathan. Einstein Letters, Vassar College Library for Special Collections, Poughkeepsie, NY.

July 1, 1938: Letter from Maurice Hexter at the Federation for the Support of Jewish Philanthropic Societies, New York City. Princeton Archives, archive #53-430.

July 5, 1938: Excerpt from a letter to Maurice B. Hexter. Archive # 53-431.

July 7, 1938: Letter from Maurice B. Hexter. Princeton Archives, archive #53-432.

July 12, 1938: Letter to Chaim Greenberg at *Jewish Frontier*. Archive #53-434, trans. MS.

July 12, 1938: Letter to Maurice Hexter. Archive #53-433, trans. MS.

August 2, 1938: Letter from F. I. Shatara to Einstein at Peconic, Long Island. Einstein Archives, Hebrew University, archive #54-369.

October 30, 1938: Address at the opening of Congress House for Refugees. Archive #28-442 (1, 2, and 3), trans. MS.

November 11, 1938: "Why Do They Hate the Jews?" in *Collier's* magazine. November 26, 1938, 9, 10, 38. Also in Einstein, *Ideas and Opinions*, 208–16.

3. THE WAR YEARS 1939–1945

January 12, 1939: Message to the U.S. Zionist Convention, Washington, D.C. Einstein Archives, Hebrew University, archive #28-462, trans. MS.

March 21, 1939: "The Dispersal of European Jewry," CBS Radio address for the United Jewish Appeal. Archive #28-476. See also Einstein, *Out of My Later Years* (New York: Philosophical Library, 1950), 254ff, and excerpt in Abraham Pais, *Einstein Lived Here* (New York: Oxford University Press, 1994), 247.

May 28, 1939: Address at the opening of the Palestinian Pavilion at the New York World's Fair. Archive #28-491 (2), trans. MS.

April 22, 1941: Address to Friends of Hebrew University at Columbia University. Archive #28-551 (1 and 2).

June 14, 1942: Letter from Kurt Blumenfeld. Archive #54-840.

June 1942: Letter to Kurt Blumenfeld. Archive #54-841, trans. RJ.

June 20, 1945: Letter to Joseph Levy. Einstein Archives, Hebrew University, archive #56-940.

4. STRUGGLE OVER THE STATE 1945–1948

November 2, 1945: Letter to Judge Jerome Frank. Archive #35-075.

December 10, 1945: Address at the fifth annual Nobel Prize anniversary dinner at the Hotel Astor, as reported in the New York afternoon newspaper *PM*.

December 12, 1945: Response to Einstein's remarks from his friend Rabbi Stephen Wise. Archives #35-257.

December 10, 1945: Statement on Birobidjan. Archive #56-517.

May 6, 1946: Letter to Edward G. Robinson. Archive #56-518.

January 2, 1946: Letter to Emery Reves. Archive #57-307, trans. MS.

January 11, 1946: Testimony before the Anglo-American Committee of Inquiry on Palestine, Washington, D.C. Complete transcript of Einstein's testimony courtesy of Einstein Archives, Hebrew University of Jerusalem. Excerpts in *The New York Times,* January 12, 1946. Einstein Archives, Hebrew University, archive #73-335, 1–18.

January 13, 1946: Letter from Maurice Dunay. Archive #56-634.

January 19, 1946: Letter to Maurice Dunay. Archive #56-635.

January 29, 1946: Letter to Martin Buber. Archive #35-053 (1, 2, and 3).

April 3, 1946: Letter to Hans Mühsam. Archive #38-352, trans. NL.

April 21, 1946: Letter to Michele Besso. Archive #7-381, trans. MS.

August 7, 1946: Letter to the Committee for a Progressive Palestine Association. Einstein Archives, Hebrew University, archive #57-236.

January 22, 1947: Letter to Hans Mühsam. Archive #38-360, trans. MS.

March 3, 1947: Questionnaire returned to I. Z. David of Tel Aviv. Archive #28 742 (4).

April 11, 1947: Excerpt from a letter to Hans Mühsam. Archive #38-365–38-366, trans. MS.

August 6, 1947: Excerpt from a letter to Joseph Brainin of the American Committee of Jewish Writers. Archive #57-685.

September 22, 1947: Excerpt from a letter to Judge Jerome Frank. Archive #80-433.

November 28, 1947: Excerpt from a message to the Histadrut Conference in Israel. Courtesy Einstein Archives, Hebrew University, archive #28-792.

March 24, 1948: Excerpt from letter to Hans Mühsam. Archive #38-372 (1 and 2), trans. MS.

April 10, 1948: Response to Shepard Rifkin, executive director of the Stern Group. Einstein Archives, Hebrew University, archive #58-858.

5. THE FINAL YEARS 1948–1955

September 24, 1948: Excerpt from a letter to Hans Mühsam in Haifa. Archive #38-372-38-374, trans. MS. Also see Sayen, *Einstein in America,* 239.

September 19, 1949: Excerpt from a letter to Hans Mühsam. Archive #38-394 and #38-395, trans. MS.

November 27, 1949: Excerpt from "The Jews of Israel," NBC radio broadcast. Published in Einstein's *Out of My Later Years* (New York: Philosophical Library, 1950), 274–76. See also Gerald E. Tauber, *Einstein on Zionism, Arabs and Palestine* (Tel Aviv: Tel Aviv University, 1979), 14–16, and Abraham Pais, *Einstein Lived Here* (New York: Oxford University Press, 1994) 250–51.

1950: Message from Einstein on the visit of the Israeli Philharmonic Orchestra to the United States. Einstein Archives, Hebrew University, archive #28-867. Statement Einstein rewrote and delivered on the orchestra's visit: Einstein Archives, Hebrew University, archive #28-869.

March 17, 1952: Letter to Louis Rabinowitz. Archive #61-066.

November 18, 1952: Excerpt from a letter to Abba Eban. Tauber, *Einstein on Zionism,* 56–58.

November 21, 1952: Excerpt from a letter to Azriel Carlebach, editor of the Israeli paper *Ma'ariv,* who had cabled urging Einstein to accept the presidency of Israel. Otto Nathan and Heinz Norden, eds., *Einstein on Peace* (New York: Simon & Schuster, 1960), 573.

January 4, 1955: Letter to Zvi Lurie. Archive #60-388, trans. MS. Also see Nathan and Norden, eds., *Einstein on Peace,* 637–38.

March 8, 1955: Excerpt from a letter to an Indian friend. Nathan and Norden, eds., *Einstein on Peace,* 638.

March 25, 1955: Letter to Kurt Blumenfeld. Archive #59-274, trans. MS.

APPENDIX: TEXTS ATTRIBUTED TO EINSTEIN

October 12, 1929: Letter to *The Manchester Guardian.* From Simon, *About Zionism,* 71–85.

June 13, 1947: Letter to Jawaharlal Nehru, prime minister of the Indian government, New Delhi, India. Archive #32-725.

July 11, 1947: Nehru's response to Einstein. Archive #32-726.

NOTES

PROLOGUE

1. Dennis Overbye, "From a Companion's Diary: A Portrait of Einstein in Old Age," *New York Times,* April 24, 2004. A description of notes kept by Johanna Fantova.
2. "My life is divided between equations and politics": Jerome, *The Einstein File,* xxii. A list of 135 political articles and 150 *New York Times* citations written before 1951, prepared by Margaret C. Shields, appears in *Albert Einstein Philosopher-Scientist,* edited by Paul Arthur Schilpp, 691–95. (This collection also includes an autobiographical article by Einstein and "Einstein's Reply to His Critics.") The *Bibliographical Checklist and Index to the Collected Writings of Albert Einstein* lists additional Einstein articles published after 1950. The total number of Einstein's nonscience ("general") essays and articles listed in the *Checklist* as published between 1920 and 1955 is 307.
3. Einstein to his stepdaughter Margot, quoted by Sayen, 247.
4. Yitzhak Navon, who was with Ben-Gurion at the time, quoted in Holton and Elkana, eds. *Albert Einstein,* 295.
5. The meeting is described briefly in Heikal's *Secret Channels,*

94–97, and mentioned in a footnote in Sandy Tolan's compelling book *The Lemon Tree,* 319. Heikal's book *Revisiting History* has an entire chapter (chapter 4, "Relativity, the Bomb and Israel," 136–89) on his interview with Einstein, but has not been translated into English. Raed and Majed Jarrar translated the Einstein chapter to help me prepare for this book.

6. "I received your E-mail," read Heikal's prompt reply. "I am familiar with your previous work on Einstein and am at your disposal if I can be of help." A week later, we were chatting in the living room of his apartment/office in Cairo.

7. Simon, introduction to *About Zionism,* 18–19.

THE BACKSTORY

1. Schilpp, *Albert Einstein,* 3.

2. Einstein's father and uncle were in the electrotechnical business, making and selling electric dynamos, at a time when Western Europe was rushing to switch from gaslight to electricity. This family environment undoubtedly helped Einstein, at an early age, to value innovation and creativity. (It also introduced him to electromagnetism, which was to be so central to his future theories.)

3. Schilpp, *Albert Einstein,* 3 and 5.

4. Stachel, *Einstein from B to Z,* 61. The most thorough and nuanced discussion of Einstein's Judaism is Stachel's "Einstein's Jewish Identity," in *Einstein from B to Z,* 57–83.

5. Under the German offer, Einstein would be hired first and foremost as a member of the Prussian Academy of Sciences (Akademie der Wissenschaften). Since being a member of the Academy was not a full-time job and did not pay enough (there were only two paid positions at the Academy, and Einstein got one), he was also offered the directorship of the future Kaiser Wilhelm Institute for Physics,

which was created only a couple of years later and never really "existed" as an institute. In addition he was offered a position as a professor at the University of Berlin, with no classes or administrative duties, free to devote his time purely to research. Clark, *Einstein*, 213–14.

6. Einstein (in 1929) to Willy Hellpach, an anti-Zionist social psychologist who ran for president of the Weimar Republic in 1925 as a member of the German Democratic Party. (Einstein, *Ideas and Opinions*, 187–88.)

7. The Nazis signed an agreement with the Zionist authorities in the 1930s, called the Haavara Agreement. This agreement allowed those Jews who were leaving for Palestine to take with them some goods they would have lost otherwise; in exchange, the Jews agreed not to impose an economic boycott on Nazi Germany; the agreement also provided the Jewish community in Palestine with German products. Another agreement was the one regarding the Hachshara, which allowed the Zionists to give Jewish youth in Germany a training in farming and some crafts that were needed in Palestine, with the promise they would be able to leave for Palestine later.

"The relationship between Nazi Germany and the Palestine Question of the 1930s is widely misunderstood. We tend to read the Nazi policies of World War II back into the 1930s. The Nazis' 'Final Solution of the Jewish Question,' their pro-Arab attitudes, and their battle against Great Britain makes it difficult for most of us to imagine that before the war the Nazis, even the SS, aided the illegal immigration of Jews into Palestine, and that Hitler so feared British displeasure that he absolutely prohibited German support for the Arabs of the Palestine mandate." (Simon Wiesenthal Center online, search for "transfer agreement" in the library catalog search.)

8. Einstein to Paul Ehrenfest in Leyden, December 4, 1919.

9. "How I Became a Zionist" *Jüdische Rundschau*, June 21, 1921, 351–52. Translation from Simon, *About Zionism*, 39–41. Despite Einstein's byline on this article, the editors later explained that he did not actually write it, but it was based on an interview with him while he was in New York.

10. Albert Einstein, "Why Do They Hate the Jews?" *Colliers*, November 26, 1938, 195.

11. See Jerome, *The Einstein File*, and Jerome and Taylor, *Einstein on Race and Racism*.

12. Samuel's notes on Einstein's visit are reported, along with the description of Einstein as "pink rather than red," by Clark in *Einstein*, 514.

13. The leader (president) of the group was Paul Weyland, a charlatan with a record of anti-Semitic activity, among other things. For more on Weyland and "Anti-Relativity, Inc.," see Jerome, *The Einstein File*.

14. "Science . . . is racial. . . .": Clark, *Einstein*, 639, citing Lenard in *Deutsche Physik*, vol. 1 (1934); "The . . . dangerous influence . . .": Clark, *Einstein*, 573, citing Lenard in *Völkischer Beobachter*.

15. "Perhaps we owe it to anti-Semitism that we can maintain ourselves as a race. I at least believe so." Einstein to the Central Association of German Citizens of Jewish Faith, April 3, 1920.

16. Clark, 465.

17. Simon, *About Zionism*, 41.

18. Petah Tikvah (Gate of Hope) was founded in 1878 as an agricultural colony by Orthodox Jews. It is regarded as the first Zionist settlement. Although it was abandoned in 1881 after Arab attacks, it was reestablished in 1883 during the first Aliyah.

19. Jewish immigration to the United States increased dramatically in the early 1880s as a result of persecution in parts of Eastern Europe, with a distinct wave of Yiddish-speaking Ashkenazi Jews arriving from the poor rural Jewish populations of the Russian Empire. More than two million Jews arrived between the late nineteenth century and 1924, when immigration restrictions increased due to the National Origins Quota of 1924 and Immigration Act of 1924. Most of these immigrants, Yiddish-speaking Jews from Eastern Europe, settled in New York City and its immediate environs, establishing what became one of the world's major concentrations of Jewish population.

20. Herzl was born in Budapest, lived in Vienna, and died in 1904 at the age of forty-four.

21. Golda Meir, Israel's former prime minister, reportedly told the London *Times* (June 15, 1969), "There is no such thing as a Palestinian people. . . . It is not as if we came and threw them out and took their country. They didn't exist."

22. Numerous sources cite the Arab population of Palestine as around six hundred thousand at the turn of the twentieth century (1900) and well over a million by midcentury. *The Encyclopedia Britannica* reports: "In the last years of the 19th century and the early years of the 20th, the Palestinian Arabs shared in a general Arab renaissance. Palestinians found opportunities in the service of the Ottoman Empire, and Palestinian deputies sat in the Ottoman parliaments of 1877, 1908, 1912, and 1914. Several Arabic newspapers appeared in the country before 1914. Their pages reveal that Arab nationalism and opposition to Zionism were strong among some sections of the intelligentsia even before World War I. The population of Palestine, predominantly agricultural, was about 690,000 in 1914 (535,000 Muslims; 70,000 Christians, most of whom were Arabs; and 85,000

Jews)." Another report states: "A Zionist estimate claimed there were over 600,000 Arabs in Palestine in the 1890s. At this time, the number of Jewish immigrants to Palestine was still negligible by all accounts." (http://www.mideastweb .org/palpop.htm)

23. David Hirst, one of many historians to report this story, adds his own comment: "But it did not seem to disconcert the Zionists for long." (*The Gun and the Olive Branch*, 139.)

24. Patai, ed., *The Complete Diaries of Theodor Herzl*, vol. 3, 1194.

25. Hess, *Rome and Jerusalem*, 129–30; "sweeping away . . . ," 68.

26. Hess is quoted in Hertzberg, *Zionist Idea*, 621–22.

27. Ibid., 203; see also Lewisohn, *Theodor Herzl*, 55.

28. Lewisohn, 252, 274, 284.

29. Hirst, 137–38, citing Patai, *Complete Diaries*, vol. 1, 343. See also Walid Khalidi, *From Haven to Conquest*, 115.

30. Machover, citing Herzl (*The Jewish State*, 1896), "Israelis and Palestinians," 10.

31. Both the kaiser meeting and the Russian meeting: Palumbo, *The Palestinian Catastrophe*, 6.

32. The Basel Program, adopted by the congress, states: "Zionism seeks to establish a home for the Jewish people in Eretz-Israel secured under public law"—that is, to seek legal permission from the rulers for Jewish migration. Among the key activities advocated to attain this end was: "*Preparatory steps toward obtaining the consent of governments, where necessary, in order to reach the goals of Zionism*" (emphasis added). See also Thomas, *How Israel Was Won*, 1.

33. Thomas, *How Israel Was Won*, v.

34. Ibid., 5–6.

35. Weizmann, *Excerpts from His Historic Statements, Writings and Addresses*, 48.

36. Hirst, *The Gun and the Olive Branch*, 161.
37. Machover, 7. Machover's piece also details the transfer from British sponsorship to American sponsorship, in the late 1940s and 1950s, of the Iron Wall protecting the Zionists.
38. Clark, *Einstein*, 458–59.
39. Ibid., 460.
40. Ibid., 466.
41. Ussishkin, quoted by Clark, *Einstein*, 479.
42. Blumenfeld, cited by Clark, *Einstein*, 462.
43. Blumenfeld, *The War About Zionism*, 65–66.

1. FIGHTING ANTI-SEMITISM 1919–1929

1. Mansfield, *A History of the Middle East*, 181. See also David, *Arabs and Israel for Beginners*, 92–93; Thomas, *How Israel Was Won*, 15; Laqueur, *A History of Zionism*, 451.
2. The *Rotterdam* actually docked at Pier 7 in Hoboken, New Jersey, then one of the major piers in New York Harbor. This meant that the four thousand people had to get to Hoboken to greet Einstein, somewhat more difficult than if the ship had docked in New York City. For more details on the arrival, see *New York Times*, April 2 and April 3, 1921.
3. Brian, *Einstein*, 120.
4. Part of Weizmann's goal was to counter the influence of Supreme Court Justice Louis Brandeis, leader of the American Zionist movement. At least one account (Halpern, *A Clash of Heroes*, 226) describes the struggle with Brandeis as the main purpose of Weizmann's visit. Einstein avoided any involvement in their rivalry.
5. To Solovine (3/8/21): Einstein, *Lettres a Maurice Solovine*, 27; also Clark, *Einstein*, 466. To Haber (3/9/21): Einstein Archive #12-332.
6. Isaiah Berlin says that Weizmann's relationship with Einstein remained "ambivalent" (Weisgal and Carmichael, eds.,

Chaim Weizmann, 42). But there are instances where more antagonistic feelings surfaced. To cite but one example, in a 1933 letter relating to a dispute about the Hebrew University in Jerusalem, Einstein wrote, "Weizmann got ready to discredit me in America and in the world press in an untruthful way" (Einstein to Professor A. Fraenkel, July 3, 1933: archive #37-094).

7. CPAE 9, Doc. 10.

8. Tens of thousands of Eastern European Jews came to Germany during World War I. Some had been POWs, some had deserted during the war, some had been recruited for contract work, and still others were deported from Russia, Romania, and other countries. After the war, anti-Semitic and anti-immigrant campaigns grew inside Germany, partly as a result of military defeat, partly from fear of Bolshevism and the revolution that had taken power in Russia in 1917, and partly because returning German soldiers needed jobs.

9. The original letter was first (and so far has only been) published, as a facsimile, in Christian Dirks and Hermann Simon, *Albert Einstein: Jude, Zionist, Nonkonformist* (Berlin: Textpunkt Verlag, 2005), 23.

10. One week after its publication, the editors admitted that this article was not written by Einstein but based on an interview he had given to a representative of the Jewish Correspondence Bureau in New York. They said Einstein had "approved" the text after making a number of "emendations."

2. YEARS OF CRISIS 1929–1939

1. Kiernan, *The Arabs,* 298.
2. Flapan, *Zionism and the Palestinians,* 68.
3. Ibid., 71.
4. Porath, *The Palestinian-Arab National Movement,* vol. 2, 4–5.

5. Kiernan, *The Arabs*, 193.

6. It has been called the Al Buraq Rebellion in some circles, but not by most historians (Mustafa Omar in Hurewitz, *The Struggle for Palestine*, 183).

7. Lockman points out that, despite its success, "in many parts of Palestine it was never total" (Lockman, *Comrades and Enemies*, 240–41). In at least one area, Haifa, Jewish workers were organized to take the jobs of striking Arab stevedores and longshoremen (ibid, 246).

8. Porath, *From Riots to Rebellion*, 238; also Lockman, *Comrades and Enemies*, 260.

9. "The British government, preoccupied with the Sudetenland crisis, did not feel it could heavily reinforce its garrison in Palestine as long as a European war threatened. . . . The agreement . . . at Munich allowed the British to dispatch large numbers of troops to crush the Arab rebellion" (Lockman, *Comrades and Enemies*, 260).

10. Hirst, *The Gun and the Olive Branch*, 209.

11. According to the *Encyclopedia Britannica*, 2007 edition, 329 Jews and 3,112 Arabs were killed during this rebellion.

12. Atiyah, *The Arabs*, 36.

13. Porath, *Palestinian-Arab National Movement*, vol. 2, 2. Prior to his appointment as attorney general, Bentwich had served for four years as legal secretary to the British Military Administration in Palestine (Wikipedia).

14. Clark, *Einstein*, 482, citing Bentwich, *My 77 Years*, 99.

15. Einstein to Bergmann, June 19, 1930.

16. Einstein had originally asked for an annual salary of three thousand dollars and then raised the question "Could I live on that?" The answer was clearly no, and Einstein's salary, arranged by his wife, Elsa, and Abraham Flexner, director of the Institute for Advanced Study, was set at sixteen thousand

dollars per year, to be continued after retirement. (Clark, *Einstein*, 544.)

17. Hoffmann, "Einstein and Zionism," in Shaviv and Rosen, *General Relativity and Gravitation*, 242.

18. An Editor's Note that appeared in *Falastin* with the letter stated that Einstein was "drawing a heavy draft on our credulity when he asks of us to take his ideal as that of the Zionist in Palestine. While believing to the full in his peaceful intentions and his beautiful ideal, we cannot judge the Zionist by Dr. Einstein" (Rowe and Schulmann, eds., *Einstein on Politics*, 182).

19. Possibly, Einstein felt the questioner was asking whether any personal threats had been made against him while in the United States. (The Einsteins had been in California for two months and then traveled across the country by train.) There had been several personal threats against Einstein from Nazis and pro-Nazis in Germany, threats that Einstein took quite seriously.

3. THE WAR YEARS 1939–1945

1. Lockman, *Comrades and Enemies*, 270. For a detailed discussion of this phenomenon, also see 266–321.

2. Shlaim, *The Iron Wall*, 23.

3. The new or more public Zionist position was adopted at a 1942 meeting at the Hotel Biltmore in New York.

4. Excerpt from Einstein's message to a dinner in his honor on June 5, 1944, at New York's Waldorf Astoria hotel.

5. Laqueur, *A History of Zionism*, 234.

6. Stachel, *Einstein from B to Z*, 71.

7. The *Princeton Herald* articles were published as part of a debate with Philip Hitti, head of the Department of Near Eastern Studies at Princeton. The first Kahler-Einstein piece was a response to the publication in the *Herald* of Dr.

Hitti's anti-Zionist testimony in February before the House Congressional Committee on Foreign Affairs, holding hearings on the future of Palestine. Dr. Hitti then wrote a response to Kahler and Einstein, published in the *Herald*, and they replied in turn.

Despite the byline, the Kahler-Einstein responses were written by Kahler (see Erich Kahler, *The Jews Among Nations* [New York: Frederick Unger, 1967], 123) and then cosigned by Einstein. Einstein clearly agreed with the sharp critique of the Arab rulers. In several of his letters, he criticized the Arab Muftis in much the same manner.

On the other hand, the first Kahler-Einstein piece makes two references to the goal of "Jewish Palestine," possibly advocating a Jewish state in Palestine, a position that Einstein did not support. Less than two years later, Einstein made this completely clear in his widely reported testimony before the Anglo-American Commission on Palestine: "The state idea is not according to my heart. I cannot understand why it is needed. It is connected with many difficulties and a narrow-mindedness. I believe it is bad."

The *Princeton Herald* articles are not reprinted in this book since (a) they were written by Kahler; and (b) much if not most of the lengthy articles are devoted to the historical argument over whose ancestors arrived in Palestine first and how long these Arab and Jewish ancestors occupied the territory. The full debate is available in the archives of *The Princeton Herald*. For the Kahler-Einstein pieces, also see Rowe and Schulmann, eds., *Einstein on Politics*, 224–33. Dr. Hitti's initial testimony is also available from the Government Printing Office, 1944, under the title "The Jewish National Home."

4. STRUGGLE OVER THE STATE 1945–1948

1. Einstein told the dinner guests:

   The peoples of the world were promised freedom from fear; but . . . fear among nations has increased enormously since the end of the war. The world was promised freedom from want; but vast areas of the world face starvation, while elsewhere people live in abundance. The nations of the world were promised liberty and justice; but even now we are witnessing the sad spectacle of armies . . . firing on peoples who demand political independence and social equality. . . .

   [Today the Jews,] one-fifth of the pre-war population, are again denied access to their haven in Palestine and left to hunger and cold and persisting hostility. . . . [A]nd the fact that so many are kept in the degrading conditions of concentration camps by the Allies gives sufficient evidence of the shamefulness and hopelessness of the situation.

2. Lockman, *Comrades and Enemies*, 322–23. Article is from the January 1945 issue of *al-Ittihad*.

3. Ibid., 332.

4. Ibid., 334.

5. Early May, 1948, Weizmann: "I strengthened our position with our friends in Washington [in] recognition of a Jewish state as soon as it is proclaimed" (Weizmann, *Trial and Error*, 477).

6. *New York Times*, March 11, 1948.

7. Earlier reports on Magnes's activity included:

   ARAB-JEWISH DEAL IN PALESTINE URGED
   Dr. Magnes Rebukes Extremists on Both Sides, Advocates

   UNION IN BI-NATIONAL STATE
   (June 14, 1942)

GROUP ADVOCATES JEWISH-ARAB STATE
(September 5, 1942)

And as late as 1947:

DR. MAGNES URGES ARAB-JEWISH STATE
(July 15, 1947)

8. Einstein's testimony was reported extensively in *The New York Times* (January 12, 1946), but never previously published in full.

9. Wise (draft statement) to Einstein, January 14, 1946; Einstein to Wise, January 14, 1946, cited by Sayen, *Einstein in America,* 235–36.

10. "Einstein believed that the major source of the problems of German Jewry was their loss of a sense of community. . . . Cultural Zionism, first espoused by Ahad Ha'am and Martin Buber, emphasized the cultural and spiritual renewal of the Jewish people. It saw itself in opposition to political Zionism, as espoused by Herzl, which focused on the establishment of a Jewish state": Stachel, *Einstein from B to Z,* 67–68. See also Laqueur, *A History of Zionism,* 162–69. For a more detailed history, see Stone, "The Other Zionism," part 2 of his March 1978 preface to *Underground to Palestine,* originally published in 1946.

11. Stone, "The Other Zionism," 7–8.

12. Laqueur, *A History of Zionism,* 375.

13. Einstein to I. Z. David, March 3, 1947. Also, "misled and criminal people": letter to Shepard Rifkin, April 10, 1948.

14. Einstein, *Ideas and Opinions,* 196.

15. Einstein interview by Bela Kornitzer in the *York (PA) Gazette and Daily,* September 20, 1948, courtesy of the York Country

Heritage Trust, with thanks to Joshua Stahlman. For more on Kornitzer, see Drew University (NJ) Special Collections.

16. Einstein's 1931 "Address on the Reconstruction of Palestine," *Ideas and Opinions*, 192–93.

17. Einstein to Zvi Lurie, January 5, 1955. Also see Stachel, *Einstein from B to Z*, 73. Einstein's entire letter to Lurie makes it clear that he disagrees with the pro-Western stance of the Zionist leaders: "Neutrality with regard to the international East-West antagonism [would] not only . . . enable us [the State of Israel] to make a modest contribution to alleviating the antagonism on a large scale, but we will also facilitate the achievement of good neighborly relations to the Arab nation and its governments."

18. Stachel, *Einstein from B to Z*, 70, citing Einstein, "Why Do They Hate the Jews?" *Colliers*, November 26, 1938. Also, Einstein, *Ideas and Opinions*, 195. When a woman at the 92nd Street YMHA was asked about arranging a discussion there about our book *Einstein on Race and Racism*, she quickly refused: "What has that got to do with Einstein's Jewishness," she declared. Perhaps had she known about Einstein's concept of Jewishness . . . Perhaps.

19. Clark, *Einstein*, 482.

5. THE FINAL YEARS 1948–1955

1. Walter Isaacson, in his bestselling biography of Einstein, writes, "He embraced the Zionist cause," and "Once he decided to abandon the postulate that all forms of nationalism were bad, he found it easy to embrace Zionism with greater enthusiasm" (Isaacson, *Einstein: His Life and Universe*, 282). And Neffe in *Einstein*, 311: "The idea of Judaism and a Jewish state captivated him [in 1923] for the rest of his life." See comments by Harrison Salisbury of *The New York Times* in the Epilogue to this book.

2. For seventeen years (1957–1974) editor in chief of Cairo's leading newspaper, *Al-Ahram*, Mohamad Hassanein Heikal began to appear on the fledgling Egyptian satellite station Dream in 2003, with transcripts of his programs widely disseminated in the press. Heikal quickly ran afoul of authorities by discussing critically the prospects of Gamal Mubarak succeeding his father as president, and was summarily banned from the Egyptian media. In response, Heikal signed a blockbuster deal to host a weekly, prime-time program on Al Jazeera, where his views immediately reached more Egyptians than on the domestic station (Lynch, *Voices of the New Arab Public*, 46).

"Egypt's greatest journalist—indeed, the Middle East's most famous scribe. . . ." (Robert Fisk, *The Independent*, April 9, 2007, "under the heading: Mohamed Hassanein Heikal: The wise man of the Middle East. From Khrushchev to Sadat, many world leaders have felt the venom of Heikal's acerbic commentary").

"An equally interesting phenomenon is the massive popularity of the television commentaries of Mohamed Hassanein, the doyen of doyens of political commentary in the Arab world, whose *Maa-Haikal* series (shown in the Thursday evening primetime slot on al-Jazeera) dissects the history—and present—of Arab politics. For decades, Mohamed Heikal enjoyed unrivalled popularity among Arab nationalists—a generation who now in almost all cases are in their sixth decade and upwards. Yet the programmes have proved vastly popular with younger Egyptians" (from column, December 7, 2006, by Tarek Osman, an Egyptian investment banker based in Bahrain who writes for *Business Today Egypt*, Egypt's largest English-language business magazine).

3. Farouk went into exile in Italy and Monaco, where he lived the rest of his life. In his later years, he weighed nearly 300

pounds (136 kilograms). He died in Rome on March 18, 1965, collapsing at the dinner table following a heavy meal.

4. Although the new Republic of Egypt was not formally declared until June 18, 1953, land redistribution began nearly right away. Under the king, fewer than 0.5 percent of the landowners had owned more than one-third of all cultivable land, while nearly three-fourths of the cultivators owned less than one *feddan* (about an acre) each. (Mansfield, *A History of the Middle East*, 244.)

5. Walter Lippmann was among Heikal's journalist contacts. ("I introduced him to Nasser.")

6. Officially, the Free Officers were led by General Mohammad Naguib, but the real organizer and leading force in the group was Col. Gamal Abdel Nasser, who would soon become Egypt's new president.

7. A sampling of Heikal's interviewees is included in his book *Revisiting History,* which has not been translated into English. These include Field Marshall Montgomery, Nehru, the shah of Iran, David Rockefeller, George Papandreou, and Einstein. A small part of the Einstein interview was published on the front page (bottom) of *Akhir Sa'ah* (*The Last Hour*) magazine, of which Heikal was then the editor.

8. "God gave me the stubbornness of a mule and a fairly keen scent": Einstein quoted in Whitrow, *Einstein, the Man and His Achievement*, 91.

9. Heikal, *Secret Channels,* 97. Heikal also told me that Nehru had told him that Bertrand Russell had asked him (Nehru) to ask Nasser if he would respond to Einstein's message. Heikal assumed that Einstein had asked Russell to speak to Nehru. Such behind-the-scenes conversations are difficult to confirm, but it is clear that whatever meetings took place, Nasser made no reply.

10. Beattie, *Egypt During the Nasser Years,* 114. Such anti-Arab

actions by Israel are described by numerous sources, even one
with as strong a pro-Israeli-government bias as Michael
Oren, who details (ibid., 353–54) an Israeli army (IDF) raid
into Gaza on January 26, 1953 (the pretext was increased
cross-border infiltration by Palestinians), killing five Arabs, as
well as the anti-Egyptian activities of IDF Special Unit 101,
commanded by Ariel Sharon. In October 1954, an Israeli raid
in Qibieh in the West Bank, led by Sharon, resulted in the
death of sixty-nine civilians.

11. Hofstadter, ed., *Egypt and Nasser,* vol. 1, 65.
12. Teveth, *Ben-Gurion's Spy,* 268.
13. See Hirst, *The Gun and the Olive Branch,* 290–96 (Israeli
agents in Egypt were "in clandestine contact with Tel Aviv")
as well as MidEastWeb Gateway and Wikipedia, to cite but
a few.
14. Israel vs. Nasser is the subject of numerous volumes. One
important element, in addition to the conflicts cited above:
Nasser fought with the Egyptian army in the 1948–49 war
against Israel. As staff officer of the Sixth Battalion Infantry,
he led Egyptian forces in the Battle of Irak-El-Mansheya in
which eighty-two Israeli soldiers were killed. (Heikal, *Secret
Channels,* 97.)
15. When the nonaligned nations held a summit conference
in Bandung, Indonesia, in 1955, they invited China's Chou
En-lai to participate. The United States, which had opposed
the nonaligned group of nations from its start, claiming it
was aiding the Soviet bloc, only intensified its opposition after the Bandung Conference. Israel's foreign policy was
clearly and unquestionably pro-Western. In the United Nations, Israel voted 100 percent consistently with the United
States—a policy criticized by Einstein, who "strongly supported the idea that Israel, like Nehru's India, adopt a neutral stance." (Sayen, *Einstein in America,* 240.)

EPILOGUE: MAKING A MYTH

1. Letter to Reuven Dafni, Einstein Archives, Hebrew University, archive #28-110.
2. Letter to Hans Mühsam, September 24, 1948.
3. Letter from Barbara Wolff to Mohammad Omar Farooq, July 15, 2006. Farooq, "Einstein, Zionism and Israel: Setting the Record Straight," http://globalwebpost.com/farooqm/writings/other/einstein.htm, updated July 2006.
4. Testimony before the Anglo-American Commission of Inquiry on Palestine, January 11, 1946.

FINAL NOTE

1. Harry J. Elam, *The Past As Present in the Drama of August Wilson* (Ann Arbor, MI: University of Michigan Press, 2004), xi.

APPENDIX: TEXTS ATTRIBUTED TO EINSTEIN

1. Author's interview with Barbara Wolff in Jerusalem, November 2005.
2. "It appears unlikely that Einstein ever sent the second draft to Nehru": Benny Morris, "Einstein's Other Story," *Guardian*, February 15, 2005.

EINSTEIN'S CORRESPONDENTS

1. Kantha, *An Einstein Dictionary*, 15.
2. Blumenfeld, cited by Clark, *Einstein*, 462.
3. Sayen, *Einstein in America*, 17.
4. Nathan quoted by Ruth and Bud Shultz, "Wasn't That a Time? A Century of Struggle. A Century of Repression." Human & Constitutional Rights Web site (http://www.hrcr.org), no date given.
5. Kantha, *Einstein Dictionary*, 232.
6. Einstein letter to York-Steiner, November 19, 1929. Archive #48-836.

ACKNOWLEDGMENTS

If ever a book resulted from a plethora of contributions and "the labors of other people"* above and beyond the efforts of the author listed on the cover, this is such a book. First, as I stated at the outset, the majority of this book is written by Einstein (and the work of more than thirty correspondents included in these pages). But even my small part relied greatly on the help and talents contributed enthusiastically by many friends and supporters, including the following.

Bob Apter and Dorothy Zellner, two old (longtime) friends and fellow travelers, whose assistance really made this book possible—not only by contributing their editing and research talents (and, in Bob's case, desk space) but also helping me with the dangerous undertaking of crossing the streets in Cairo (Bob) and still more dangerous crossing in Jerusalem and barriers and fences in the West Bank (Dorothy), even in the face of tear gas and arrests by the Israeli occupation army.

---

*"A hundred times every day I remind myself that my inner and outer lives are based on the labors of other people, living and dead, and that I must exert myself in order to give in the same measure as I have received and am still receiving" (Einstein, *The World As I See It*).

Mary Laub and her friend and assistant Janet Stannard, who provided a warm, well-lighted workplace, enhanced by their own warmth and light.

Barbara Wolff, whose skillful and meticulous work as archivist of the Einstein Archives at the Hebrew University of Jerusalem provided the basis for this study (and many another) and was matched only by her help, encouragement, and understanding as a friend.

A number of talented translators who helped bring to light this little-known Einstein, including Michael Schiffmann, Natalie Lipsett, Barbara Wolff, and my wonderful daughter Rebecka (with some help from her husband, Claes), as well as Raed and Majed Jarrar, who provided valuable translation from Arabic. Perhaps here a word of thanks might also go to Shelley Frisch, whose refusal to translate anything "that might be considered critical of Israel" ("Even Einstein?" "Yes, even Einstein") helped make it clear how frightening the subject of this book is—to some.

My agent, Frances Goldin, whose unflagging support—despite the fear of this book from many in the publishing business—made this possible and whose friendship and help made the work a pleasure.

My editor at St. Martin's, Daniela Rapp, whose patience and understanding and detailed suggestions went far beyond what this book's author deserved; and a number of most helpful librarians including AnnaLee Pauls at the Princeton University Library, Gila Ansell Brauner of the Jewish Agency in Jerusalem, and Dave Smith at the New York Public Library, who helped find workspace in their marvelous Allen Room.

Also, other friends who offered help with time and space and shoulders to lean on, including Cathy Boyd, Awatef Shiekh, Angela Soto, Carol Smith, Joe Esposito, Jacob Rosen, Josephine Gear, and Rodger Taylor (coauthor of *Einstein on Race and Racism*).

And many more good friends who helped to edit the manuscript, including Michael Denneny, whose editorial assistance (as with the two previous Einstein books) was beyond words; Ernie Herman, who contributed his invaluable professional-editor skills; and John Stachel, whose Einstein expertise needs no additional acclaim.

In addition, my dear friend Diane Alaimo, who lent hours of insightful copyediting, working tirelessly with my wife, Jocelyn—Jocelyn, who, more than anyone else, made this book possible, as with everything.

INDEX

King David Hotel bombing by, 153–54
Iron Wall, 302*n*37
Isaacson, Walter, 310*n*1
Israel
  attacks on, 191
  bombings by, 211–12
  declaration of independence by, 260
  Egypt and, 210–11
  Einstein on, 192–93, 206, 217, 223–24, 228
  Einstein's identification with, 202
  Haifa, 305*n*7
  Heikal on, 206
  Nasser and, 212, 313*n*14
  New York Times on, 192
  Ottoman Empire control of, 14
  presidency of, 1, 207–8
  State of, 191
  in UN, 313*n*15
  U.S. and, 210–11, 223, 313*n*15
  violence in, x, 191, 211–12
Israeli Defense Forces (IDF), 28, 193, 312*n*10
Israeli Philharmonic Orchestra, 219–20
Israeli Prize, 253
ITUC. *See* International Trade Union Confederation

Jabotinsky, Vladimir, 22–23
Jabotinsky, Zeev, 262
Al Jazeera, 195, 310*n*2
JCA. *See* Jewish Colonization Association
Der Jedenstaat (The Jewish State: An Attempt at a Modern Solution of the Jewish Question) (Herzl), 15
Jerome, Fred, 310*n*18

Jerusalem University, 42, 48
Jewish Agency for Palestine, 258–59, 260
Jewish Autonomous Region, 159
Jewish Citizens Committee, 147
Jewish Colonial Bank, 267
Jewish Colonization Association (JCA), 90, 92–93
Jewish Committee, 115
Jewish Congress, 123
Jewish Correspondence Bureau, 304*n*10
Jewish Culture Council, 146
Jewish Frontiers, 108, 257
Jewish Historical Society, 253
Jewish National Fund. *See* Keren Kajemeth
Jewish-Ottoman Colonization Association, 18
Jewish Technical Institute, 239
Jews. *See also* Judaism; Zionism
  Ashkenazi, 300*n*19
  assimilation of, 45
  community of, 50–51, 109, 121–22, 309*n*10
  definition of, 128–32
  deportation of, 9
  Eastern European, 7, 8–9, 31–33, 37–38, 45–46, 102, 122, 237–38, 300*n*19, 304*n*8
  Einstein's identification with, 198–99, 201–2
  immigration of, 7, 13, 19, 66, 99, 135, 148, 157, 161, 166–68, 169, 186, 190, 201, 218, 235–36, 247–48, 299*n*7, 301*n*22, 302*n*32, 304*n*8
  India on, 248–49, 250–51
  nationality of, 35, 36, 46–47, 51, 56–57, 76, 77, 82, 155

Union of South Africa, 249

United Hebrew Congregation of
Johannesburg, 262

United Jewish Appeal, 103, 109,
141–43

United Nations (UN), 166
Einstein on, 185, 186
India in, 249
Israel in, 313n15
Jewish representation at, 183
Mandate end by, 191
Palestine's independence by, xiii
U.S. in, 313n15

United Negro College Fund, 259–60

United States (U.S.)
anti-Semitism in, 45, 133–34, 187
Balfour Declaration support by, 28,
266
Egypt and, 210
Einstein in, 28–31, 39–40, 70,
198–99, 254–55, 303n2
Einstein on, 45, 133–34, 170–71,
184, 186–87, 223
fascism and, 263
Israel and, 210–11, 223, 313n15
Jews in, 13, 300n19
Middle East interests of, 161, 210
Palestine and, 170–72, 302n37
in UN, 313n15
Zionism in, 94–95, 257, 266

University of Berlin, 298n5

University of Manchester, 41

U.S. *See* United States

U.S. Zionist Convention, 140–41

Vaad Leumi, 256, 260

violence
Ben-Gurion and, 211–12
Einstein on, 69, 136, 148, 154,
183, 206, 214–15

in Hebron, 63, 236

in Israel, x, 191, 211–12

in Palestine, x, 62, 63–64, 65–67,
69, 70, 168–70, 206, 214–15,
236, 237, 240–41, 255, 267

in Safed, 63, 236

in West Bank, 312n10

Zionist, 135, 136, 148, 183, 206,
214–15

Wailing Wall, 64

Walker, Jimmy, 28

Wallace, Henry, 192

Warburg, Max, 90–92, 264–65

War Resistors International, 69

Weimar Republic, 258, 262, 299n6

Weizmann, Chaim, 1, 148, 199, 254,
308n5
on Arabs, 65, 79–81
on Balfour Declaration, 21–22,
80
Blumenfeld and, 11–12, 25
Brandeis rivalry with, 303n4
on Britain, 79
on Brodetsky, 82
death of, 207
Einstein and, 78, 79–83, 202,
204–5, 218, 303n6
on Magnes, 80, 81
Mendelsohn's work for, 261
peace talks with, 116–17, 118
presidency of, 30, 265

Die Welt, 254, 267

Werner, Albert, 217

West Bank, x, 312n10

Weyland, Paul, 300n13

"Why Do They Hate the Jews?"
(Einstein), 9–10, 124–34

William, Maurice, 102–3

Wilson, Woodrow, 27, 266